# The Prop Maker's
# Workshop Manual

# The Prop Maker's Workshop Manual

David H. Rigden

THE CROWOOD PRESS

First published in 2018 by
The Crowood Press Ltd
Ramsbury, Marlborough
Wiltshire SN8 2HR

**www.crowood.com**

**British Library Cataloguing-in-Publication Data**
A catalogue record for this book is available from the British Library.

ISBN 978 1 78500 503 9

Frontispiece: Scrooge's Door Knocker.

Typeset and designed by D & N Publishing, Baydon, Wiltshire

Printed and bound in India by Parksons Graphics

# CONTENTS

# INTRODUCTION

## 1,001 WAYS TO MAKE A PROP

There is an old saying: 'There are many ways to skin a cat'. This is a flat statement of fact, which can open a world of opportunities to prop makers and screams of complaint from cat lovers. Before you start to get worried – no cats have been harmed in the writing of this book – it is just an adage to highlight a point. What has this got to do with prop making? A pertinent question and well asked. In my thirty-plus years of making props professionally I have come to adapt this saying to '1,001 ways to make a prop'. As a prop maker, you should be flexible, adaptable, creative, and develop a wide knowledge of materials and techniques. Each prop can be made in many ways, the only limitations being the abilities, skills and knowledge of the individual prop maker. To use another metaphor, the more strings you have to your bow, the more options you have when you are designing and/or planning the making of a prop.

But why should there be '1001 ways'? A deliberate exaggeration, but one that I have used for many years when training students in the art of prop making for professional theatre. The problem I came up against in my early years of training students was getting them to comprehend that the materials and processes that we were using were not limited to the prop that we were making. For example, if we had made a teapot from card and papier mâché (or a gargoyle sculpted from scrimmed and textured polystyrene, or a tree from timber frames and poor man's fibreglass, for example), the assumption would be that every time you made a teapot it would be crafted from papier mâché rather than other any choice or combination of other materials that would fit the brief. The question to ask when tasked with making any prop is, 'what skills and resources are available to me to fit the budget and deadline that I have to make the prop within?'

Prop making is not an exact science; it is a largely creative process that is built on the foundations of trial and error – pretty much the story of human society in a nutshell. But that trial and error introduces us to another old saying: 'Necessity is the mother of invention'. Prop makers over the years have looked at a wide variety of materials to expand the possibilities of what can be achieved. These materials have been sourced and absorbed from industries all over the globe, from natural products like latex (natural rubber) to the latest thermoformable plastics and the possibilities of 3D printing. There are new materials popping up all the time that could have potential in the prop-making world, but whether you get to use them will come down to availability and cost. Some new products may be readily available in some countries but not others due to import restrictions, which could be because of patent issues or legality issues regarding transportation and/or different health and safety laws. Whatever the case, there will always be a way to achieve what you need to. It just requires knowledge and a little thought… Oh, and a fair bit of practice… I may mention this a few times throughout the book.

OPPOSITE: Bottom's heads from *A Midsummer Night's Dream*, from top to bottom: full head with articulated jaw with lower teeth and cable-operated bendable ears; slush mould latex casting with three-quarter face (rehearsal head); hand-moulded, stained and stitched leather head with steam punk goggles and mixed wool for the mane.

## WHO IS THIS BOOK FOR?

This book is aimed at anyone who wants an introduction to prop making, from basic skills through to intermediate-level advice, with the intention that once you have developed a proficiency of the materials and techniques within, you will be well equipped to achieve a multitude of tasks. Mastery of these techniques and processes comes through good old practice. The more you put into the work in terms of blood, sweat and tears, the more you will get out of it – which is the same with anything in life that is worth doing. Whether you are entering this from the perspective of a hobbyist or professional, the same principle applies. Through practice you will develop the hand-eye co-ordination required to make the work easier and quicker and thus become more proficient. You will also become more familiar with quantities and costs and the potential risks involved when choosing various materials and processes, which will help you to make the most appropriate choices for the job at hand.

## NO RECIPES

The title of the book, *The Prop Maker's Workshop Manual*, states the intention of the contents within. If you are expecting to open the book to find specific instructions on how to make a chicken, a Viking helmet or a fireside settle, you must suffer disappointment. This is not a recipe book for individual props. However, you will be presented with a multitude of choices and techniques that will enable you to make many hundreds of items. Within these pages, you will be presented with, and guided through, materials, processes and techniques that have been tried and tested over time to enable you to achieve pretty much any prop you might need to make. The text is accompanied by photographs and illustrations detailing the processes involved.

There are also pictures of various props that have been made over the years, some showing variations of the same prop that have been made using different methods and techniques. This is

the essence of prop making, and what I have been endeavouring over many years to teach would-be prop makers: there is no 'one size fits all' – each job is tailored to the specific requirements of the production. My own experience has been very much that of creating and constructing items for professional repertory theatre – that is, traditional prop making, with modest budgets and short deadlines, which have presented many opportunities to think outside of the box.

Whether you are a hobby prop maker wanting to learn more, a student prop maker or an ASM/prop maker looking to expand your repertoire or someone who is just curious about prop making, this book is for you. Most of the techniques and materials covered here can be used for a wide variety of interests, be it model railway enthusiasts, live action role playing (LARP), re-enactments, window dressing, carnivals, festivals or trade shows. This book is here to encourage anyone working in any props-related hobby or profession to make props to a higher standard through knowledge and practice, and to cater for a wide range of budgets.

## SUGGESTIONS ON WORKSHOP SPACE AND TOOLS

When starting out in prop making, or related ventures, it is not imperative to have a large, well-equipped workshop, as this can be very costly to achieve in one go. What you require will very much depend on what you are aiming to achieve, which might not be much if you are only making soft props, or, quite a lot if you are heading down the general prop-making route. Whatever your situation, you must have a warm, dry space to work in, with room to manoeuvre the materials and the items under construction. This 'workshop' could be a room, shed or industrial unit, depending upon your finances.

Assuming the generalized prop-making route, you will also need a good-sized, sturdy workbench, built to your waist height to avoid unnecessary bending and neck strain, with, ideally, a quick-release woodworking vice fitted and room for a metalworking vice (this can either be permanent or removable). Other workstations can be created around your space as required.

Buy tools and equipment as you need them. If you only have access to modestly priced (reasonable-quality) manual tools, hone your skills with those and upgrade to better-quality tools later, if necessary. Buying top-quality tools at reasonable prices can be achieved by using online auction sites, although they won't always have what you want when you need it. It is always better to spend a bit more on a reliable brand name of tool than to buy cheaper tools that have no provenance; this applies to both manual tools and power tools.

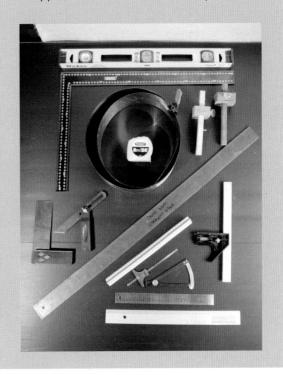

ABOVE RIGHT: These tools are specifically used to facilitate accurate measuring and marking, from depth gauges to a mortise gauge, tenon gauge to a scale rule, tape measure, squares and flexible straight edge.

OPPOSITE: Straw bales. Real bales can be used when suitably fireproofed but can be heavy and there may be issues with allergens. The ones here were made for a nativity tour to primary schools, and utilize a variety of processes and a certain amount of thinking outside the box.

RIGHT: A selection of useful power tools.

# 1

# AN OVERVIEW OF PROP MAKING

## WHAT IS A PROP AND WHAT IS PROP MAKING?

From a theatrical point of view, a prop is an item that is required for a production, normally to be interacted with by an actor or as a piece of set dressing that helps create the setting. This is of course a gross simplification, as within this description you can have costume props, actors' personal props, LX (lighting) props, SD (sound) props, set dressing props, construction props, SM (stage management) props, props department (finding, sourcing and making) and props construction department (making and modification). Thus you can see that the requirement for a prop can cross over departmental boundaries, with some props needing to be sourced (borrowed, bought or hired) and some requiring to be made. It shouldn't take too much logic to identify a potential 'make' from a 'find'. Finding a giant's cauldron for a Norse god can be challenging, and a suitable Tudor four-poster bed that isn't too heavy/expensive to use, hire or buy, will generally have to be made. If a theatre is lucky enough to have a props construction department, then the work will generally go to them; if not, then it may well be freelanced out. Timber props can be created by the set construction department (often

This sign was required for a touring production of Charles Dickens' *Hard Times*. Lightweight and extremely durable, the base material was 4mm plywood, the scrolled details were clay sculpts, plaster moulds and slush mould latex castings, glued to the plywood with Copydex. Once primed and painted, photocopied lettering was cut out and glued in place, then glazed.

referred to as construction or 'chippies'), but this will very much depend on their workload and individual skill sets.

## Example of Prop Types

**Personal props** Watches, pocket watches, watch chains, wallets, spectacles, gloves, bracelets and brooches, rings and so on. These are normally provided by the costume department, but may be sourced by stage management and may also in some circumstances be makes.

OPPOSITE: Two approaches to bird forms. The pigeon is made of a wire frame, coir fibres, calico and latex, with fur fabric Copydexed on, trimmed and painted; from start to finish, this took an hour to make. The chicken was one of seven to be made: a supermarket chicken was to used to create multiple plaster moulds, which were used to produce latex castings, clay head sculpt and plaster mould, steel rod core, fur fabric, trimmed and painted.

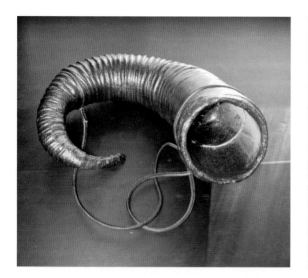

Cornucopia (horn of plenty) made for *A Christmas Carol*. The wire-frame construction was stuffed with newspaper then covered with Gypsona plaster bandage and a PVA/water mix. Quarter-inch (6mm) paper rope was used for detail with more plaster bandage and PVA/water mix moulded over this. Layers of gesso were applied and sanded, and base coats and top coats of paint produced the gold finish.

The King James bible was needed for a church set in *The Crucible*. The book boards were 6mm (¼in) plywood covered with calico. The spine was sectioned thick cardboard tube, the page shape and flow and inner spine were shaped card with thin polystyrene sheet dressed over. The page edges were enhance with Celluclay.

**LX/SD props/practicals** These are usually props that require some handling by the actor and must light up or make a noise. They may well be adapted by the department concerned or be made in collaboration with the props construction department or solely by the latter. This could include statues that have to illuminate from within, 'babies' that have to cry or speak and so on.

**Set dressing** This includes anything that is required to provide the look and detail of a set or scene, such as additional pieces of furniture, paintings, pictures, ornaments, dust and cobwebs, bottles, piles of books and paper. There should be nothing that is superfluous, just what is needed to create the correct feel and atmosphere. Set dressing is normally addressed by stage management under the watchful eye of the set designer.

**SM (stage management) props/prop makes** These are props that are sourced or made by the stage management department, normally the ASM's (assistant stage manager's). This role includes finding furniture, trunks and cases, glassware, china, set dressing, bicycles – basically anything a production requires that can be sourced. SM makes tend to be more in the region of 'running props' or consumables, such as paper props, letters and documents that get destroyed during the production; foodstuffs that get eaten; and improvised items, like a roughly made child's wooden sword or hobby horse. Generally, it comes down to the resources and skills available to the individuals in the department, who must consider any health and safety requirements. Where there is an ASM/prop maker and no resident prop maker, some of the more complicated props may be taken on by them.

**Costume props** These can take a variety of forms and can be part of the design of the costume (headdresses, masks, bizarre hats and so on), or can even be the costume itself such as a goose or a cow costume for panto. Some of these items may be made by the costume department, but it is also extremely likely that they will be made by the props production department, or in collaboration

Crowns made from different materials. From the rear: three crowns made from 10mm Plastazote, originally for *Alice Through the Looking Glass*; card and paper pulp construction with added details of wire and jewels; Cleopatra's crown, made of laminated leather pieces, gold braid and amber beads for cobra's eyes; two brass, copper and leather 'breakable crowns' for *King Lear*, using two fixing methods – joints and magnets.

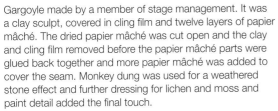

Gargoyle made by a member of stage management. It was a clay sculpt, covered in cling film and twelve layers of papier mâché. The dried papier mâché was cut open and the clay and cling film removed before the papier mâché parts were glued back together and more papier mâché was added to cover the seam. Monkey dung was used for a weathered stone effect and further dressing for lichen and moss and paint detail added the final touch.

between the two or freelanced out to a speciality prop/costume maker, again dependent on time, resources and skill sets.

We have seen that who ends up making a specific prop will be decided by the time, resources and skill sets available. In most cases this is more than likely to be the prop maker. This is not because the prop maker is necessarily the most gifted creatively, but simply because they are used to working with a wide range of materials and processes that are generally not used by the other departments and for which they are not equipped. If you aspire to be a master prop maker, then you need to become a jack of all trades. In absorbing different skill sets from different professions, you acquire the creative flexibility to construct and design amazing things, from the small to the large, because you can use a fusion of techniques and materials that complement each other. Yes, it takes time to acquire these skills and no, you won't be able to learn them all at once, but remember that you have a lifetime to learn and hone them, so take your time and enjoy the experience. You can never learn everything; there is always something new, something else to try, even if it is just reassessing what you already know.

## NO HARD AND FAST RULES

There are no hard and fast rules in how you approach making any prop, but there are certain considerations that may affect the way you look at what you need to do. Most of these will become apparent as you gain more experience with the techniques and materials, some of which will be mutually exclusive (although even here there are often ways around the problem). Designers often say that they want something to be made from a specific material or constructed in a certain way, which can be time-consuming and lead to unnecessary expense. What they usually mean is that they 'want it to look like this and do that'. At the same time the director might stipulate that 'it has to be as light as possible so that it can be picked up by one person, but it has to be climbed on by the cast, and it gets pushed over...' and so forth. This is where the '1,001 ways' of prop-making comes into play.

If you are asked to make an item, such as a barrel, an experienced prop maker should be able to come up with several suggestions off the cuff,

---

### AN EXAMPLE OF A CHALLENGING BRIEF FOR A PROP MAKE

Here is an example of a complicated prop requirement: for a Christmas production of *Treasure Island*, the director has asked for an apple barrel in which the actor playing Jim Hawkins must conceal himself to overhear a conversation about buried treasure.

The brief is:

- It must be big enough to climb into and hide in.
- The actor must be able to pick it up and move it easily, while in the barrel, to various locations around the stage, during the scene.
- It must have storage for six apples that can be thrown up and out of the barrel.
- It must have a bung hole for Jim to look through and listen at.
- It will also have a top added so that it becomes a tavern table/bar.
- It must look realistic.

How would you do it?

The picture of the finished barrel demonstrates one interpretation of this brief, but the crucial point to bear in mind is that is doesn't matter how you do it provided the finished item fulfils the brief, looks and 'feels' the way it should and survives the knocks and spills of the production. Ultimately, your decisions will be determined by your own abilities and the materials, equipment, budget and time available to you.

The finished *Treasure Island* barrel. There were quite a few steps required to get to this point.

including just getting hold of a real barrel. Obviously, there are other considerations here. Is it a modern or traditional barrel? How big is it? Does it remain where it is, or does it have to be moved; how quickly must it be moved and by whom? What sort of action is the barrel involved in? Are there any specific requirements, such as concealed access points or storage points? With a traditional barrel, weight is going to be the main consideration, as even the smaller ones, such as pins and firkins, could weigh as much as 20–30kg (44–66lb) without anything in them: not a problem if they are going to be rolled, but more of a issue if you have several them to strike in a blackout.

# COLLABORATION

Prop makers can often find themselves having to work in collaboration with other departments such as construction, scenic art, costume, lighting, sound and stage management. As has already been mentioned, the nature of prop making is versatile – it can cross all boundaries and has few defining boundaries of its own. Therefore it is not uncommon for people to try to wash their hands of certain things that aren't specifically props but don't fit squarely into another department's vision of what they are responsible for. 'That's not what we normally do, that must be a props make,' is a common phrase that can be heard in meetings and in discussions.

Communication is the key to success here, as well as knowing your own limitations. Do not allow yourself to be railroaded into something just because someone else doesn't want to or can't do it. Taking on a job that is beyond your capabilities, or is going to overload your budget and schedule, can end up being a lot worse than admitting that you can't, or don't have the time, to do it in the first place. Compromise is often the best solution, with each affected party taking on a piece or elements of the task that they are capable of handling. Again, effective communication and a proactive approach are vital in achieving a seamless result.

## The Role of the Director and Designer

The director and designer are the creative heart of the production, providing the intellectual and visual stimuli (that as an audience we hope to immerse ourselves in), working together to arrive at the requirements that they both wish to see in the production – but bear in mind it is the director who has the final say. It is then the job of each department to provide these 'requirements' within a specified time frame.

Preliminary meetings are held to ascertain the viability of what is being asked: the ideal is a prelim production meeting with the director, designer, production manager and all heads of department for a presentation of the design concept. After introductions, the director normally starts proceedings with their vision for the production and then hands over

Porter's trolley for a production of *Aladdin*. All the items were individually made and fitted to a 'pivot pole' secured to the trolley – giving the impression that everything might fall off.

to the designer, who explains how they have taken that vision and made it tangible via a model box. The model box is important, although at this early stage it is likely to be a 'white card presentation' (an unpainted version of the design), as this provides us with a 3D rendition of the space/theatre the production will be performed in, and how the set/sets fit into this space. At this meeting, there is also a presentation of the proposed costumes. After these have taken place, there is usually a Q&A session where the department heads get to show their appreciation and voice any concerns regarding workloads, practicality and potential costs. The intention is to be positive and proactive, suggesting potential alternatives to proposals that may be beyond feasibility.

It is unusual at this juncture to discuss more than the larger or very specific props makes and likely props involvement with other departments, as the director and designer probably won't have got down to that level of fine detail regarding props lists. It is tempting to think that once a script arrives, the stage directions for movement, furniture and specific props will be confirmed, but once in the hands of the director and designer everything changes to suit their interpretation of the production. Further model box meetings will provide greater detail as the concept gets refined, and ground plans and elevations, technical drawings and designs start to get distributed to the departments.

From a prop-making point of view, the designer may have a list of items that require making. It is not necessary for the designer to know how to execute the 'mechanics' of an idea, as this is the prop maker's job. At the very least, the prop maker should be able to advise the designer on the practicality of what is being asked for, given the constraints of budget and resources. A good prop maker should be able to provide alternative suggestions that arrive at the same end if they deem the original proposal impractical due to cost, logistics or even health and safety. This cooperation should make the designer's job easier and will hopefully result in the designs arriving all

the sooner. The important thing, from everyone's point of view, is to retain an open mind and not to dismiss any idea out of hand, as it may only require minor tweaking to make it work.

All careers develop their own 'secret languages' and the theatrical profession is no exception to this. As you gain experience you will pick this language up, but it is important that if you don't understand something, you ask to have it explained. After all, we are all working toward the same end and to do so we need to understand the method of getting there. Information is key.

# DESIGNS AND WORKING DRAWINGS

## Design

A design is a pictorial representation of what a designer is envisaging. It is essentially an illustration, preferably in colour, or with colour references, with written details regarding any specifications such as texture, operation and indications as to size and dimensions. Alongside the design, you may be provided with pictorial references gleaned from a variety of sources such as books, magazines, catalogues, the internet and so on, all intended to help you realize the vision of the director and designer.

## Working Drawing

A working drawing is more of a technical representation done to scale (1:25, 1:10, 1:5, for example) using a scale rule, drawing board, set squares, radius aids and so on, so that detailed measurements can be taken from it, and it normally contains different elevations representing views from the front, side and top. The intention is that you work from this drawing directly to build an accurate full-scale version of the object. It is now increasingly likely that these working drawings will

Fig. 1 Jacob Marley chain design.

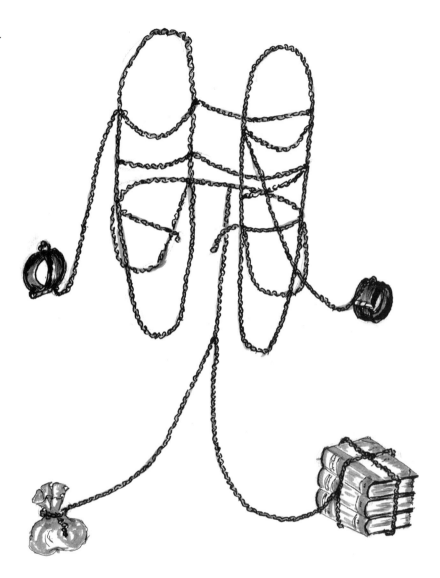

be created on a computer using a CAD (computer-aided design) program and either printed or sent as CAD files electronically.

## Scribble

A scribble is a designer's attempt to impart their vision to the person making the object, while at the same time trying to avoid providing a more valid representation of what they are asking for, usually because they don't have the time. It is not unusual with this form of representation for the final image

to bear no relevance to the measurements that are ascribed to it, resulting in the common question: 'Do you want me to go by the measurements or by the sketch? If the former it won't look like the latter and, if the latter, what is the maximum dimension that you would like it scaled to?' On the plus side, with one solid measurement to work from, it is often possible to extrapolate all the other required measurements proportionally from a rough sketch, and you could get started on it sooner than if you were to wait for a proper design. On the minus side, it does mean that you are doing the designer's job for them.

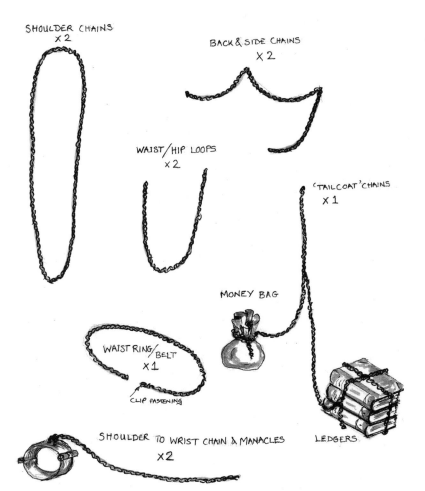

SHOULDER CHAINS
x 2

BACK & SIDE CHAINS
x 2

WAIST/HIP LOOPS
x 2

'TAILCOAT' CHAINS
x 1

MONEY BAG

WAIST RING/BELT
x 1

CLIP FASTENING

SHOULDER TO WRIST CHAIN & MANACLES
x 2

LEDGERS

Fig. 2 Jacob Marley chain design detail.

## What Constitutes a Good Design?

A good design is an accurate illustration of an idea that the director and designer have in mind, which:

- Is accurate in its depiction of what they require as a finished piece – albeit in two dimensions
- In most cases, provides an indication of what it should look like from different angles – front, top and side, rather like a working drawing, if not illustrated as an isometric, three-quarter profile or 3D representation
- Includes an accurate colour reference, preferably intrinsic to the design itself, though a clearly explained legend detailing colour specifics will often suffice

- Provides the necessary key dimensions. From this point of view, it is important that the illustration of what is looked for is at least roughly in proportion with the dimensions that are given, otherwise we end up with the problem described above, with having to compromise on look or dimensions. Specific size requirements should be stated here – for example where the finished object needs to fit through a doorway or into a box
- Is a clear illustration of a decent size; in the case of small items, actual size or larger than life is good
- If for a larger item, is drawn to an appropriate (if approximate) scale, such as 1:25, 1:20, 1:10 or 1:5, depending on what is needed to create

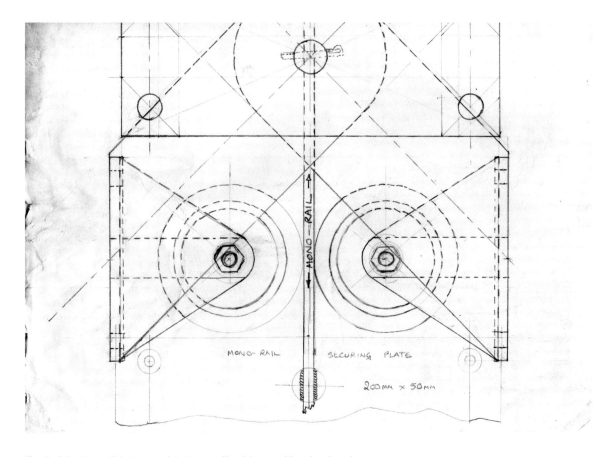

Fig. 3a *Merchant of Venice* gondola 'monorail' guide – working drawing plan.

a clear and precise image that is convenient to work from; perhaps with exploded detail sections to clarify any specifics

It is important to double-check the dimensions of designs/working drawings, as it is very tempting for a designer looking at a scale rule to decide that it looks perfect, without using a tape measure to check the actual measurement. It is not at all unusual, where this simple precaution has been bypassed, for the prop in question to become much larger or smaller that intended, which can result in a lot of wasted time and money, with the item having to be remade. Experienced recipients of designs should be able to see a life-size image in their mind's eye from a scale drawing, and pre-empt measurement anomalies. This ability comes with practice of constantly translating drawings to full scale as part of the job. Coupled with an understanding of the materials and processes, it can afford a better grasp of reality and the laws of physics when it comes to scaling up these designs, which is important when it comes to the finished build and how it can be executed… That said, there is nothing quite like the challenge of trying to achieve the impossible!

## What Constitutes a Bad Design?

Bad designs come in many different shapes and sizes but, simply put, are a result of the designer having omitted to consider or ignored the points illustrated above. Rough scribbles are unacceptable as a finished 'design', whether on a piece of paper, tracing paper or the back of an envelope!

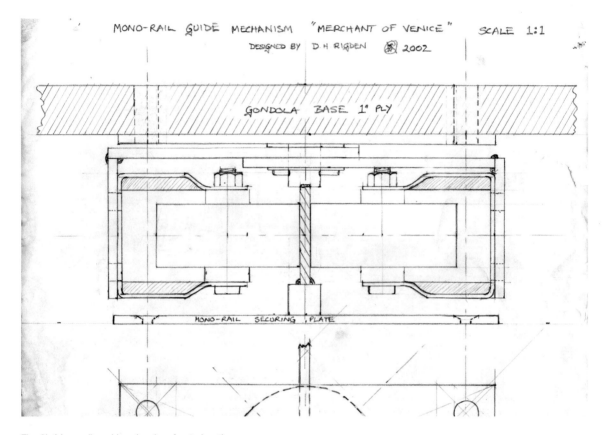

MONO-RAIL GUIDE MECHANISM "MERCHANT OF VENICE" SCALE 1:1
DESIGNED BY D.H RIGDEN 2002

GONDOLA BASE 1" PLY

MONO-RAIL SECURING PLATE

Fig. 3b Monorail working drawing, front elevation.

A scribble can have its place as part of a preliminary discussion, thrashing out ideas on paper or a whiteboard, but this should always lead on to a finished design. After all, it may not be you making it, but another team member, so the design must contain all the relevant information so the 'build' can happen without having to go through the entire discussion process again. It is vital that you get accurate and clear designs, with sufficient information, if you are to realize the director's and designer's vision.

Having said this, there are times when designs are not required from a designer: these are when:

- You have undertaken to design the prop personally
- It is an everyday item or object and you have references and specifications, which have been agreed upon, to work from

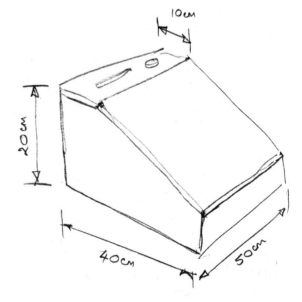

Fig. 4 Writing desk – sketch/scribble.

## WHEN ARE MODELS OF PROPS EXPECTED?

Usually a model of a prop is only provided for larger items that need to be represented in the model box and demonstrate any specific functions required. This is a bonus for the prop maker as it provides a fully three-dimensional aspect that can be used to enhance the designs and working drawings.

There are times when the prop maker may find it necessary to create a model themselves from the designs provided by the designer, to illustrate the mechanics of how it will actually work, using a scale representation of the proposed construction process. Items acquired from model, hobby and craft shops that simulate scale versions of the materials being used can help with this.

## INTERPRETING THE DESIGN

### Design Precaution

As a precaution, always make sure that the designs you are presented with have been cleared by the director prior to starting work on them. In my early career, there were a few occasions when I got caught out by not doing this, and, due to the director and designer not sharing quite the same vision, this resulted in the props in question having to be made again from scratch. Likewise, beware of designers who only provide you with a 'verbal sketch' and say, 'I'll leave it up to you how to do it', then a few days later come back and say, 'that's not quite how I envisaged it'. This is the point at which an actual design, sanctioned by the director, becomes essential.

A similar thing can of course happen with a verbal description from the director for a prop they have in mind, which can result in many revisits and comments from them of, 'that's not quite how I see it in my head'. It is always better to get them to provide some imagery to give you a clearer idea of what they are after, preferably working alongside the designer – who, after all, is paid to work with ephemeral concepts from the deepest regions of the director's subconscious.

In most cases a prop maker is working from two-dimensional representations of what a designer requires, so a certain amount of interpretation of those images will be necessary. This is why it is so important that you are provided with sufficient information, so that there is as little deviation as possible between what is required by the director and designer for the production and the way that the prop maker interprets the designs.

The designer and the director should be encouraged to become frequent visitors to any department that is making things for them, as this way you can keep in regular contact and may be able to pre-empt any wasted time and effort. If there is any potential problem or a query regarding information provided by the designer, it can usually be resolved by a simple discussion with them or the director. Conversely, if the designer or director have any qualms about a prop, be it function, dimensions or weight, they can discuss it now rather than waiting until it has been built. Pertinent information will hopefully be coming out of rehearsals via the DSM (deputy stage manager), although, with the modern reliance on emails and texts, you may not actually see anyone in person from one week to the next.

The DSM is an important link between the rehearsal room and the production departments and, in my early years in professional theatre as a DSM/prop maker, I found it invaluable to make the rounds of the departments to discuss the latest rehearsal notes, enquire as to any concerns and find out how things were progressing in general. Not only did this demonstrate an appreciation for what the departments were doing, it also meant that I could pre-empt any potential snags and sudden changes to requirements because I was already aware of what was happening within each department, and the potential ramifications of an off-the-cuff change requested in rehearsals. Although modern technology provides many conveniences and can be a valuable time-saving tool, it is at its most effective when enhanced by face-to-face interaction.

## Designer's Influence

A designer can certainly state a preference for the materials they would like something to be made from. However, at the end of the day, what they are after is the 'look' of a thing, and if there are cheaper and quicker ways of achieving that look, those are more likely to be the methods that will be chosen. Often the requirements of the prop will dictate a specific choice of construction and materials and those requirements may make a designer's preferences inappropriate. Remember, this is an industry that sells illusions and that must be balanced against the practicality of achieving the desired ends. The prop maker's expertise and experience are more likely to affect the construction process and the choice of materials than the designer's. It is the former's skill that will create the desired look and function and make the illusion believable, producing what the director and designer have envisaged.

# RESEARCH AND LEARNING

Never underrate the importance of research and the simple pleasure of just learning something new. It can be very tempting to rush into a project with only some basic designs and a bit of reference but, as prop makers, we need to broaden our knowledge to help us function more efficiently as the creative builders of a multitude of different objects from the broad spectrum of the universe and beyond. This may sound over the top, but advances in technology have already brought us fascinating glimpses into our solar system, molecular and genetic structure, and the discovery of new and wondrous creatures in the ocean depths. Expanding your information base is something that will stand you in good stead throughout your career because you will always have a potential starting point. You will never know everything but, the more research you do, the more you will learn.

This electric chair was made as an 'impact' prop: the chair and the actress placed in it were the centre of attention, and thus it needed to look correct. It was crafted with traditional carpentry techniques from ash, which provides a wonderful grain and responds well to stains and glaze-paint effects. The restraints were made from stained, vegetable-tanned leather.

A selection of skulls. Even for something as simple as a skull there can be many choices and design options. Here we have wire frames, polyurethane resin and slush mould latex.

**RECOMMENDED RESEARCH AREAS FOR PROP MAKING**

- Different periods in history
- Costume
- Theatre
- Woodworking
- Metalworking (including engineering and blacksmithing)
- Leatherworking
- Mask making
- Upholstery
- Crafts
- Model making
- Calligraphy
- Sculpture
- Natural history
- And, yes, prop making

There is a very useful saying from a chap called Aristotle: 'If you intend to hit the target, first you need a target to aim at!' Research is what makes that target bigger and clearer and thus easier to hit.

In our modern world, information has become so easy to access that we take it for granted. With a little organization, you can find some very useful material out there, whether it be pictures, articles or videos, that can make your journey into enlightenment more fruitful. And don't forget the value of good, old-fashioned reference books, magazines and periodicals, which can also provide invaluable information and illustrations.

Research should not be limited to what you are making but should also include the tools and materials that you might use to build things with, and may well involve investing in a training course or two to broaden your skill set.

## BUDGETING

### The Five Considerations of the Prop Maker

The overriding thing that affects what we can do as prop makers is budget. With sufficient budget, you can overcome most issues. Here is a simple equation:

$$\text{Budget} = \text{Space} + \text{Resources} + \text{Materials} + \text{Manpower} + \text{Time}$$

Therefore:

Greater budget = Greater efficiency and potential

If you have sufficient budget, you can:

- Hire appropriate workshop space and facilities
- Hire/buy additional specialist tools and equipment
- Afford a broader range of more appropriate materials
- Hire skilled workers to reduce a heavy workload

All the above buy you more time, because they increase efficiency, reducing the time it takes to do things in the first place. When you take on other skilled workers you have literally doubled, trebled or quadrupled the amount of work hours available to you.

The reality, however, is that you must often make do with small budgets while working in inadequate spaces, with little in the way of resources and materials... on your own. This does not mean that you can't have job satisfaction alongside any frustrations there might be; it can be challenging and fun.

It doesn't matter whether you are working as a professional prop maker or an amateur or hobby prop maker – you will still have to work within the limits of what you can afford, and this is called 'budgeting'. Here is a little-known secret: you can get by on basic maths (arithmetic) and the world will not implode because of it. Most people learn sufficient maths from their time at school to be able to make do on a day-to-day basis, providing tricky equations don't sneak up on them unannounced. All you need is a reasonable amount of time, a pencil and paper to scribble with, and a calculator.

The tricky bit of budgeting is working out the quantity of any individual material that you require.

As you become more experienced with the materials and their monetary value, you become more adept at working out what is going to be the most suitable and cost-effective way to build any type of prop.

## Working out Quantities

### TIMBER SHEET

These are straightforward to work out as timber sheets are normally used for covering an area or cladding something, and in this case (stage floors or flattage) it is simply a question of obtaining the sheet size (length × width) and working out how many sheets you require to cover or clad a specified area. The only other variable, besides the quality of the product and its suitability for the job at hand (is it purely decorative

Making items out of timber and sheet materials is simply a question of looking at images of what you are trying to make and breaking it down into a flat pack. This is a piano made to house an electronic keyboard as well as to provide storage for various props.

or does it have to be structural), is the thickness of the material.

A good timber merchant will also offer a cutting service, at a price, so that you can have sheets cut to specific sizes. It is also possible to order non-standard sheet sizes in certain materials.

When using sheet materials for building three-dimensional structures, such as a box, a mine cart or a piano, it simply comes down to how many of the component pieces can you fit onto the chosen sheet material. With a regular cube shape that has equal dimensions on all sides, you take the measurement from one side and see whether you can fit six of those onto a sheet (if it is an open-topped box with no lid, you only need to fit five onto a sheet!). With the mine cart the same thing would apply, although the ends of the cart might not be square but rhomboid, depending on the type of mine cart. With a piano, there are a few more things to account for, not least what type of piano it might be, but it can be 'deconstructed' in the same way by measuring the dimensions of sides, top, base, back and front and keyboard area, and seeing if these will fit onto a single sheet or more. It then simply comes down to choosing the appropriate thickness of the sheet material that you are using, based upon the requirements and the type of fixings you are going to use.

Round and cylindrical objects can be created by cutting discs or rings, dependent on size and weight. A simple trick for costing these is to treat each disc as a square and work out how many of these you can fit onto a sheet size. You can also draw to scale a sheet size and then draw on the required shapes. Bear in mind, when cutting rings, that the discarded inner material may be of a size that could make smaller rings or discs.

## POLYSTYRENE/STYROFOAM

In professional theatre, we buy polystyrene in the same sheet sizes as we do timber sheet materials, the only difference being density and thickness. You can select from different densities and thicknesses to suit your budget. Polystyrene comes in thicknesses from 25mm (1in) to 600mm (24in) and is normally priced by the inch thickness, although it will be sold in millimetres. Therefore, if you were paying £10* for a sheet that was an inch thick, you would be paying twenty-four times that for a sheet that was 2ft thick: £240.

Sculpting in polystyrene, on the face of it, can look dauntingly expensive, but the actual cost is proportionate to what you are trying to achieve. It is not necessary to buy in an 8ft × 4ft block that is 2ft thick to sculpt a standard-sized pumpkin. It may be that the manufacturer has an offcut that will be ideal for what you need. Alternatively, you can purchase a full 8ft × 4ft sheet that is only 1in or 2in thick and will be plenty big enough to make your pumpkin by cutting multiple shapes from it that can be glued together in layers, forming a rough pumpkin shape, and refined further from there. If you were making an entire pumpkin patch, then the full-thickness block would become appropriate, if it were to be fully used, as each pumpkin

Polystyrene offcuts. Notice the larger cell structure in the SD (standard density) polystyrene, centre and top left, compared to the EHD (extra hard density), bottom and top right.

would have the same cost as an individual pumpkin cut and layered from a thinner sheet.

Let us assume that we are making a large pumpkin that is 16in (roughly 41cm) in diameter and 10in (roughly 25cm) high. A sheet of polystyrene 1in (25mm) thick will provide us with eighteen cut squares at 16in × 16in × 1in or discs at 16in diameter × 1in that can be glued on top of each other. Each piece of polystyrene is an inch thick (25mm), so that ten glued on top of each other will

### JUST AN EXAMPLE

* The price of £10 is purely used for illustration purposes. The actual price of polystyrene fluctuates due to world markets, supply and demand and other factors. The density of polystyrene varies depending on the volume of virgin beads being used to make up the block sizes... but more on that in Chapter 5.

come to a height of 10in with eight spare pieces, or just under half the sheet remaining.

The cost of the polystyrene pumpkin is either that of the sheet (£10) or the actual polystyrene used (if the offcut/remaining polystyrene is going to be used for another prop, and therefore costed against that) – £5.56 (rounded up).

Assuming we need an entire pumpkin patch of the above pumpkins, it is easy enough to work out our quantity of polystyrene because we know that we can get eighteen pumpkin diameters from one full sheet size (8ft × 4ft). Therefore, if we were to

buy the sheet in at a thickness of 10in (the height of our pumpkin), we could make eighteen pumpkins from one 10in-thick sheet.

The cost of the polystyrene sheet would be £100, but each polystyrene pumpkin would cost £5.56. Even if only sixteen pumpkins were required, they would still only cost £10 each (including the price of the offcut). If nineteen or twenty pumpkins were required, then thinner sheets could be bought in as well to make up the extra numbers, and layered together as for a single pumpkin. If only nine pumpkins were

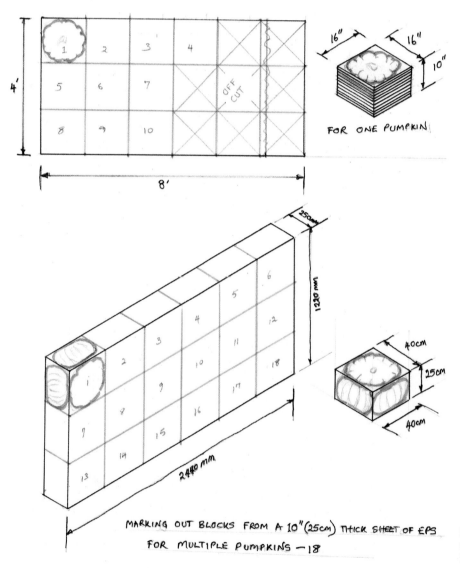

MARKING OUT BLOCKS FROM A 10"(25cm) THICK SHEET OF EPS FOR MULTIPLE PUMPKINS — 18

Fig. 5 Pumpkin marking-out for polystyrene – layers and blocks.

required, then a 5in-thick (13mm) sheet could be bought in that would provide two blocks per pumpkin to make up the full-sized legume costing £50 for the sheet and £5.56 for each polystyrene pumpkin.

It is worth remembering that this part of the costing is purely based on the cost of the polystyrene for the sculpt and does not include the cost of whatever you use to cover the polystyrene with, glue for sticking it together, or paints and finishes.

The key point to take away is that different thicknesses of polystyrene sheet can be layered up for more challenging projects.

## CLAY, LIQUIDS AND POWDERS

From clays and plasters to adhesives and paints, expanding foams to resins to our trusty friend water (whether hot or cold) that we use to create fluid products from powders prior to them turning into solids, these make up a large variety of the products that we might use as prop makers. The simplest way to cost for these is visualization. This is a very handy ability to acquire, as these products vary in how they are sold. Some are sold by the litre or millilitre, gallon, pint or fluid ounces, whereas others are sold in kilos and grams or pounds and ounces. The defining feature of any of these is the size and shape of container that they

This is a fresh 25kg bag of grey clay that has been marked out from the whole volume down to a sixteenth part to enable us to get a better sense of how much it would cost to use a given amount. This could also be done in decimal increments.

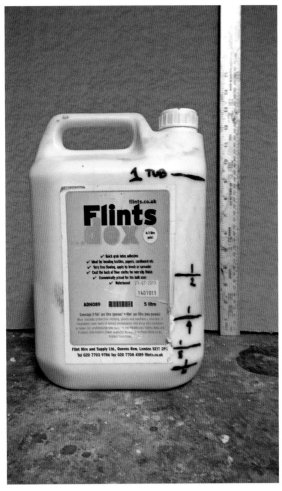

A tub of Flints…dex divided into increments from a whole down to a sixteenth volume.

come in. Not all containers will look the same, but there will be a consistency for product types. We only need concern ourselves with the container that our consumable is stored in – one vessel at a time! Obviously, you could weigh out the required amount, or measure it out by volume, but that requires extra time and is not always practicable, especially if you do not have the item in stock. My tip is to visualize the container that the product is in and consider how much of that, or how many of them, are going to be required for the job at hand. If it is straight multiples, all you do is count the number of containers and multiply the cost for one by the number of containers required.

For example, if you are going to require eight 1-litre pots of paint at £23/pot that would be:

$$8 \times 23 = £184$$

If, however, you are painting a smaller object you can simply look at the paint pot and estimate how much of that pot you are likely to use. Then 'visually' divide that pot/container into equal proportions to ascertain proportionately how much of the volume you will be using. The division could be in halves, quarters, eighths or sixteenths, or in decimal increments such as tenths, twentieths and so on. You could even do it by finger widths or measure it with a ruler… it doesn't really matter, as the principle is the same – once we have the visualized measure we simply divide the cost by the amount of overall divisions and multiply it by what we are going to use.

For example, if we are going to use a quarter of the pot of paint at £23 a pot, we can simply divide the cost by four to provide my costing for paint used:

$$23 \div 4 = £5.75$$

If we find that the visual measure is going to be three-tenths then we can work out the cost in two stages:

£23.00 ÷ 10 = £2.30
£2.30 × 3 = £6.90 for ³⁄₁₀ of the volume

This process can be applied to a bag of plaster, a tub of glue, latex, containers of silicone and

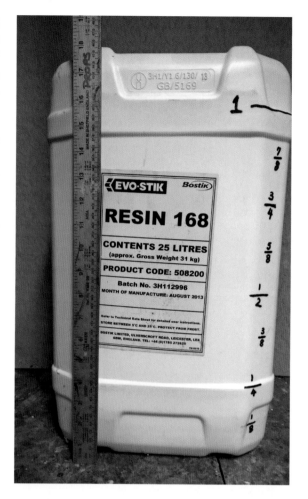

Evo-Stik Resin 168 PVA divided into eighth increments.

catalyst, polyester resins – almost anything that comes in containers. The more experience you gain, the easier it is to know what your requirements will be. The process of assessing the materials required is based upon logic and its friend guesstimation (the ability to judge by eye and rationalization the volumes and quantities required for any job), both of which develop with experience. Maths is still involved, but nothing that we can't resolve with a calculator or a scrap of paper and a pencil.

There are some products, such as expanding foams, that can throw a bit of a curve ball because, to visualize the volume required, you need to know the expansion rate of the product, which can also be affected by ambient temperature and the temperature of the product. Once you are aware of these variables, you can use your visualization technique as before.

Here is an example of how to cost expanded polyurethane foam:

1. You want to fill a latex casting with a two-part (Part A and Part B) flexible expanding polyurethane foam.
2. The foam is a simple 1:1 mix, equal parts by volume of each product.
3. The void you wish to fill in the latex casting is equal to the volume of one of the two tins that the foam comes in.
4. If the expansion rate of the foam is thirty times the combined volume of the two tins, and if the tins each contained 1ltr volume of product, that would equate to a 60ltr expansion in ideal conditions:

$$(1ltr + 1ltr) \times 2 = 60ltr$$

---

**CONTAINERS**

Not all containers are filled to the brim when you buy them. This is particularly true of heavy substances like silicone rubbers, which are sold by the kilo rather than the litre. You will often find that they are sold in a generic-sized container: 5kg (11lb) of silicone, for example, will arrive in a 5ltr container and the container will only be two-thirds full. There are two reasons for this:

- Silicone rubbers tend to be sold in kits as a total weight: the silicone and the catalyst together making the whole weight, with the catalyst supplied in a separate container
- The product's weight is greater than that of the container's 'equal' volume – so 5kg of the substance does not take up 5ltr of volume

With some liquids, you will find that weight and volume are not too different – for example, 1ltr of water does weigh 1kg – but it should not be taken for granted that all products are like this. Referring to the product data sheets, and experience through usage, should help.

---

5. This is more than the 1ltr volume that is required to fill the latex casting – by 59ltr!
6. By scaling back, we can find the optimal base volume for our expansion to 1ltr. In this case we want a sixtieth of the base volume (33g), dividing it by two (16.5g), to get out two equal parts for our 1ltr expansion.
7. Having found out how much product is required to create the correct expansion, the costing can be calculated by dividing the overall cost of the two parts by the volume of the combined, unexpanded product. When mixing the products, you would divide the total volume by two to provide the correct volumes of Part A and Part B. But, for costing purposes, the two parts, A and B, are sold together as equal parts so your visual pricing of the overall volume used can be done by using one container against the total purchase price of parts A and B.

## The 10 Per Cent Rule

When budgeting, it is always prudent to utilize a safety precaution called the 10 per cent rule. This simply means that when you have worked out all the costs involved (not forgetting consumables such as screws, nails and adhesives), you add a 10 per cent margin to allow for unforeseen eventualities – like changes in requirements due to events in rehearsals; the customer deciding they want a different finish to that previously stated; fluctuation in product prices; your usual supplier being out of stock and the prices at the alternative supplier being higher and so on. This is a sensible and reasonable up-front precaution that is intended to prevent further unaccounted-for expenditure down the line.

## Tax

A lot of industry suppliers will give their prices exclusive of tax. In the UK this is known as VAT (value added taxation). Make sure you are aware of this when purchasing, because you have to pay the VAT and it will add an extra lump of money to your outgoings. Currently, VAT in Britain is charged at 20 per cent. Some company's prices are inclusive of VAT. In either case, you may be able to claim the VAT back against costs when registered as self-employed (if you have a large enough turnover).

## ENVIRONMENTAL CONSIDERATIONS

It would be wonderful to think that everything we make as prop makers will be preserved for posterity and that thousands of years into the future archaeologists will be coming across our work and holding it up as a wonder of twenty-first-century creativity. Not wishing to burst any bubbles, but the likelihood is that at some point what we have made will be taking up space and potentially harming the environment. Therefore, it is important that we consider the types of things that we are using and endeavour to use as many environmentally friendly products as we can. Certain products break down naturally with little or no harmful effects, others could still be around causing problems for generations to come. What with time constraints and work pressures, it is not always possible to avoid using products that we might choose not to under ideal circumstances. By becoming aware of the potential environmental hazards, we can at least adopt a less cavalier attitude to what we use and the waste we create.

## HEALTH AND SAFETY COMMON SENSE

Theatre has been slower on the uptake with health and safety legislation (H&S) than a lot of other industries, but the issue is now getting full attention.

Health and safety is there for everyone and plays a key role, but it is everyone's responsibility to make it work – and to do so, we need to apply and develop common sense.

Throughout this book you need to consider what tasks are being undertaken and what the potential risks are. There are certain products, known as PPE (personal protective equipment), that it is good practice to have in your workshop, which include:

- Eye protection
- Latex and vinyl disposable gloves
- Work gloves and heatproof gloves
- Barrier hand cream/foam
- Properly rated dust and fume masks/respirators – either disposable or reusable

Also make sure you are appropriately dressed in decent-quality work clothes or overalls and work shoes or boots appropriate to the work you are undertaking. All clothing should be cleaned regularly to preserve skin health.

There are four key components to good health and safety practice:

- Observe
- Evaluate
- Be aware
- Act appropriately

If you place an object right on the edge of a bench, it will get knocked off (perhaps not the first time you do it or the second, but at some point it will), maybe causing injury, contamination, and lost time cleaning up, or the loss of an expensive tool. If you are using a sharp knife, actively be aware of what you are doing, and how you are cutting, and where the rest of you is so that you don't accidently reconfigure yourself. When handling products, be aware of the potential hazards and use appropriate PPE.

Dusts, such as plasters, can be an irritant to the skin, eyes and lungs. Handle them with respect, being aware of the problems they can cause: use extraction; wear an appropriately rated dust/fume mask; wear eye protection and apply barrier cream or barrier hand foam to exposed skin.

Liquid products can be corrosive, highly flammable and have fumes that can affect awareness and even prove a risk to life; these can potentially cause problems through inhalation, absorption through the skin or ingestion due to the bad practice of having food and drink within the workshop areas. Some products may appear innocuous but with repeated use without proprietary protection can cause ongoing medical problems such as asthma, emphysema, skin irritations and occupational dermatitis. The key is not to take anything for granted, get into the habit of employing 'good practice', work methodically and develop your creativity by using common sense.

## COSHH

Associated with H&S is COSHH, or the Control of Substances Hazardous to Health regulations. Put simply, if you can avoid using a product that has proven health risks in favour of using something that has less risk or, ideally, no risk, then go for the lower-risk option. The critical point to note is that it is the severity of the associated risk that is important, rather than the number of potential risks. For example, you might have the choice between using two products. Product 1 has only one risk factor – it could kill you if used without the proper equipment, but you cannot guarantee this equipment will be available in all the circumstances in which you might want to use it. Product 2 has three risk factors – it can cause slight reddening of the skin with mild irritation, make the eyes itchy and watery, and has an unpleasant aroma that could cause a sensation of mild nausea, but no long-term effects. Assuming both products were suited to performing the same task, it should be a no-brainer that product 2 should be used in preference to product 1, as the risk of death due to an oversight is much more severe that the mild discomfort that you may experience due to forgetting use the appropriate PPE with product 2.

There will be occasions where it is simply not practicable to replace a high-risk hazardous substance, because of cost factors or just because there is no other suitable product available. However, this can be balanced out through the correct and stringently applied practices in the use of the product, as well as reducing the potential risks elsewhere by eliminating products that have other viable, user-friendly alternatives.

The products and techniques used in this book have had the COSHH principles applied to them, which does not mean to say that they are without risk, but just that the risk is deemed to be manageable for a moderately well-equipped workshop. Some of the products dealt with may not be appropriate for workshops with limited resources.

All products should come with product and health and safety data sheets, informing you of the risks and precautions. If the product you are using hasn't come with these, you should be able to acquire the information from your product supplier or download it from their website or that of the product manufacturer.

## H&S, COSHH and You!

It has been mentioned before, but it is of such merit that it should be mentioned again: H&S applies to everyone and it is everyone's responsibility.

Whether you are an employed aspiring working professional or a hobby prop maker, the only difference is that the legal aspects of the Health & Safety at Work Act does not apply to private individuals, which includes sole traders/freelancers and hobbyists. It is good practice, however, for all of us to take on the merits of H&S in the interest of common sense and our own prolonged good health. It is worth bearing in mind that, even as a hobbyist or freelancer, should your actions cause injury to another because you ignored H&S principles you would still be liable to prosecution due to negligence via the civil or criminal courts. Adopt best practice, and eliminate risk.

# 2
# PAPER PROPS

Cinderella's pumpkin was made from papier mâché layered over the top of a real pumpkin, which was removed once the papier mâché was dry by carefully cutting the papier mâché into two halves and pulling them off the original form. Gesso and paint and the original dried pumpkin stalk finished the overall effect. It still survives over ten years later.

Prop making has changed over the years as more materials have been added into the mix of what we can use. Some of those materials have come down in price as they come into more general usage, whilst others still maintain a high price tag due to production costs or their more 'high-tech' nature. Although it is tempting to use these new materials, it is also worth remembering that they are often created to take the place of more traditional techniques that are, overall, more environmentally friendly and cost effective. The main downside is that the 'traditional' materials and techniques may take longer and have extended

OPPOSITE: Wolf's head, papier mâché from a clay sculpt.

drying times, although the finished result will still tick all the boxes. That is not to say that we can ignore the more advanced materials and processes; we simply need to learn when and where each method of production is most appropriate to the requirements of the job at hand. It is worth mentioning at this point that the more traditional techniques can demand a higher standard of concentration and craftsmanship, but if you master these techniques, it prepares you better for those more high-tech aspirations.

## CREATING PERIOD PAPERS

There is nothing that can dispel the illusion of the period of a production quite as easily as someone walking onto the stage with the wrong type of paper. Imagine a production of *Macbeth* set in Scotland during the Dark Ages, a time and place where mass-produced paper just does not exist, and onto the stage comes a messenger with a crisp white sheet of A4 printer paper. It does not matter how convincing the writing on that paper is or what seals may or may not have been attached. The glaring whiteness of the paper and the clean-cut edges and precise dimensions are going to be a point of anachronism within the play that William Shakespeare did not intend to be there and will act as a distraction for the audience.

The available budget can be a key factor in the selection of paper for productions, especially where the paper prop in question becomes a 'running prop', something that must be replaced for each show because it is screwed up or torn to pieces. As a result, it is not uncommon for stage management teams to resort to photocopier

A3 photocopier paper that has been distressed by tearing the edges of the page, tea stained multiple times, through immersion and the use of a brush and stronger applications of tea, as well as very light and sparse flecking with paint and glaze. The overall effect is intended to create the look of a time-worn parchment or old chamois leather.

The paper being used here is thin enough to see the details of each of the covered telegrams. These were photocopied onto 45gsm typewriter paper, which, being so thin, has an off-white appearance. Made for *The Cherry Orchard*, each telegram is written in Russian.

paper for running props, due to its relatively low cost and easy accessibility. Fortunately, there are a few simple measures that we can employ to make that humble and ubiquitous photocopier paper less obvious. Three things are immediately obvious when you hold up a standard piece of photocopier/printer paper:

- Its regular shape and sharp edges and corners
- Its sound
- Its colour/shade/texture or lack thereof

Any one of these three things can interfere with the illusion that we are trying to create, but the following techniques, when applied correctly, can fool the senses into believing that even standard photocopier paper is something that it is not. And if you can achieve that with photocopier papers, just imagine what you can do with better-quality papers.

The first two points can be dealt with quite simply and effectively.

## Changing the Shape of the Page

Modern papers, as has been mentioned, are made using modern industrial processes and, therefore, have precise dimensions and cleanly cut edges. Admittedly, when medieval monks were using parchment and vellum they would accurately cut the skins to a specific size ready for binding into the books that they were making. However, where the 'paper' is being used as individual sheets we can indulge in a little poetic licence and distil the essence of period without necessarily being 100 per cent precise, while creating the illusion that we are. This is something that we can usually get away with in theatre because of the physical distance from the audience. In film and television, close-up shots often require the real thing, while in re-enactment the demands are for total authenticity. Ultimately, we are affected by supply and budget: most theatres would be unable to afford the cost of real parchment and vellum, as they are craftsman-made items (and thus very pricey), and the chances of blagging it for a credit in the programme are slim. Film and television usually have larger budgets and carry more weight with the offer of credits.

It is fortunate for us that most theatregoers have never held actual parchment or vellum, only their modern, mass-processed equivalents, which bear very little resemblance to the real thing. Along with changing the colour, we can employ the simple expedient of resizing the paper we are using and creating different effects at the edges as we do so.

## USING A RULER/STRAIGHT EDGE

This can be used in two ways:

*The Straight Tear for a Regular, Softened Edge*
**Materials**
• Paper

**Equipment**
• A sturdy ruler or straight edge that is preferably longer than the longest edge of the paper that you need to modify (a straight edge is effectively a ruler without markings that acts as a guide for you to mark or cut against)

**Process**
1. Place the paper onto a flat surface and the ruler against one of the edges, allowing about 5mm to show beyond the edge of the ruler.
2. Push down firmly on the ruler with one hand while taking hold of the exposed edge at the top

corner in the other and gently tear the paper toward you while peeling it against the ruler's edge in a continuous tearing motion.
3. Repeat this process on the other three sides.

When you have completed your controlled tear, you will see that you have softened the edges, making them look less processed but still regular.

*The Jagged Tear for an Irregular, Natural Edge*
If we execute this process using controlled pinching tears with the finger and thumb, you will see that the effect has become somewhat feathered and irregular, which is an effect seen on handmade rag and pulp papers that have not had the edges trimmed. This detail, especially when used on better-quality papers such as artist's watercolour paper, produces superb results for 'official' documents, such as edicts, that are large and brash (with illuminated writing and wax seals) and held prominently for the other characters and audience to see their importance.

*Alternatives to the Ruler/Straight-Edge Approach*
You can get a similar result without a ruler by folding over the paper's edge and making a sharp crease along the folded edge with your thumbnail or other appropriate tool, such as a ruler or pen top, two or three times. Unfold the paper, refold it in the opposite direction and crease again. Repeat this process, back and forth, a few times. Place the creased line so that it is tight against a sharp table edge, with the excess paper overhanging the edge, and, taking hold of the top corner of the excess, gently but firmly tear down against the table edge until the excess is removed. Repeat the entire process for each of the other three sides.

It is also possible to free-form tear along the creased edges. Hold the paper up and start the tear at the top crease line; and then, with your fore-fingers and thumbs, at opposite sides of the paper, pull away in opposite directions against the tear line, working your way down the page. Alternatively, with the paper placed on a flat surface, use one hand to press the page down firmly and the thumb and forefinger of the other hand to pull away from the

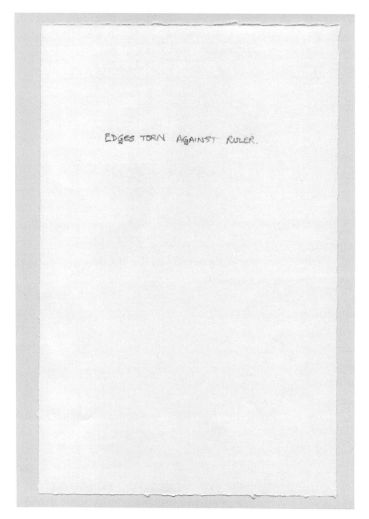

EDGES TORN AGAINST RULER.

Resized paper torn against the edge of a ruler. For the top and bottom paper edges it is good practice to fold and crease the edge to be torn a minimum of three times each way to aid tearing, as you are working against the grain of the paper. As seen here, without creasing the effect is a more irregular tear.

crease line while keeping contact with the table with the first knuckle of the forefinger and the outside edge of the thumb as you work your way down the crease line. The tearing process just takes a little practice and confidence to perfect – and a very sharp crease line – but none of us are strangers to tearing paper; we are just exploring several ways of exploiting the effect that the tearing makes.

## Changing the Colour of the Paper – Tea Staining

Tea staining is an effective and traditional theatre technique that allows for a simple change in the colour or tone of the paper being used. It can be used to simply take away the brightness of the paper, or to provide an ageing effect. It is also very cost-effective. Over the years, some people have tried using coffee in place of tea, but this is not recommended as it not only leaves the paper smelling like coffee, but can also make the paper sticky and costs more.

The following method is particularly useful when you are having to produce copious amounts of modified paper.

### Materials
- White paper
- Hot water
- Cold water

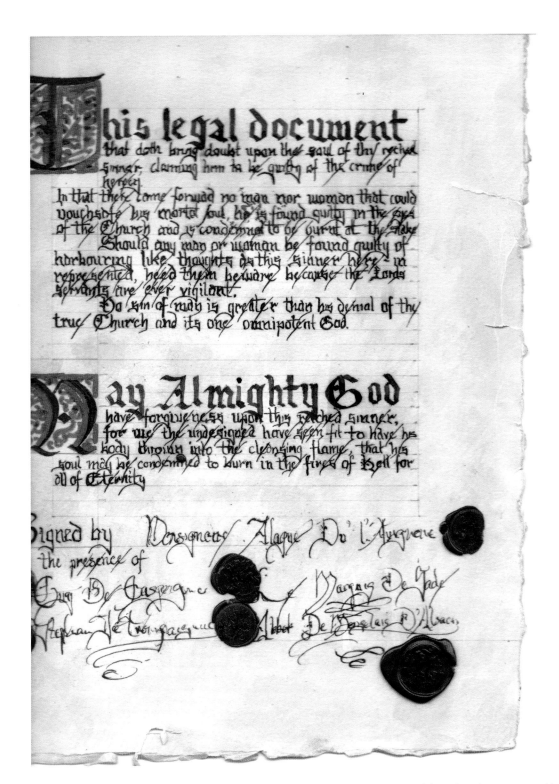

# This legal document

that doth bring doubt upon the soul of this wicked
sinner, claiming him to be guilty of the crime of
heresy.

In that there came forward no man nor woman that could
vouchsafe his mortal soul, he is found guilty in the eyes
of the Church and is condemned to be burnt at the stake.

Should any man or woman be found guilty of
harbouring like thoughts as this sinner here in
represented, heed them beware because the Lords
servants are ever vigilant.

No sin of man is greater than his denial of the
true Church and its one omnipotent God.

# May Almighty God

have forgiveness upon this wretched sinner,
for we the undersigned have seen fit to have his
body thrown into the cleansing flame, that his
soul may be condemned to burn in the fires of Hell for
all of Eternity

Signed by Monsigneur Alague Do' l'Avgnene
the presence of
Guy De Casengne                    Marquis de Jade
Stephen De Tonpage,nu    Abbot De Nongleis d'Alsace.

Edge detail of the Heresy Document. It can be seen here how the extra thickness and texture of the watercolour paper provides added effect to the torn edges.

*Creasing and pinch tearing paper compared to creasing and pinch tearing against a ruler. Either can work effectively – which you choose depends on the effect you wish to create.*

- Tea bags or loose tea (regular tea, nothing fancy; but if you use a cheap tea expect to have to use more of it). Remember, we are going for strength of colour not flavour or aroma

**Tools**
- Kettle or urn to provide freshly boiled water (tea requires freshly boiled water to properly infuse)
- Large teapot/jug (minimum 1ltr capacity) for the hot water
- Tea infuser (or a square of butter muslin tied into a pouch around the loose tea if you have no teabags)

- Jug (at least 1ltr capacity) for the cold water
- Large rectangular bowl or deep tray to pour the tea into – ideally bigger than the largest size of paper you will be using
- Smaller bowl, pot or old mug (250–500ml capacity) for the darkest brew of tea
- Two 12mm (½in) or 25mm (1in) general-purpose paintbrushes
- Offcuts of sponge/foam rubber (optional, but useful)
- An area to lay out or hang up the tea-stained paper to dry – if possible, a line strung across an area of your workspace with old towels below to catch the drips, or some sort of drying rack or airing cupboard

Paper creased and torn all round. By folding and firmly creasing the edges, it is possible to get a softened but clean edge when the edge is gently torn away along the line.

CREASED & TORN ALL ROUND

## Process

1. Place four or five teabags, or spoons of loose tea (in an infuser or muslin pouch), into the teapot/jug. Boil the kettle/urn and poor the freshly boiled water over the tea and allow to brew for at least three minutes – the longer the brew, the stronger the colour.

2. Pour approximately a quarter to a third of the brewed tea into the large bowl/deep tray and then add warm water to this (a mix of the boiled water and cold water but it could be warm water from your water supply). The aim is twofold: to reduce the temperature to a comfortable level so that it won't burn your fingers; and to dilute the colour of the tea to a light stain to provide a background colour for the next stage. You will require a sufficient volume of this diluted tea mix to be able to submerge the paper (one sheet at a time) as you draw it through the mix in the bowl.

3. Take your first sheet of paper by the bottom short edge and, with the bowl in the same orientation, slip it beneath the surface of the liquid using one hand to feed and the other in the tea mix to keep it submerged. Once fully immersed, take the top short edge to draw it out from the opposite side of the bowl. Allow the excess liquid to drip back into the bowl and then set aside the stained paper to dry. The staining will tend to dry darker than it at first appears, but if you want it darker or lighter, simply add more of the dark tea

The *Cherry Orchard* telegrams, demonstrating the effect of immersion tea staining on printer paper, standard and crumpled.

brew or more warm water to get the colour you require. Once the paper is dry, you can always run it through the mix again – each run will add a little more colour to the page.

4. Once you have the brew that you are happy with, run all the paper that needs staining and set it aside to dry. Do not place the pages on top of each other to dry because they will stick together, and tear when you attempt to separate them! If you are placing the pages on a flat surface, such as a bench or table, cover that surface with poly-thene, and be sure that you have allowed as much water to drip back into the bowl as possible be-fore carefully laying out the pages. If you are simply toning down the brightness of the paper, the only other step required may be to press the paper flat once fully dry, by stacking it and placing a board

and heavy weight on top and leaving to settle for at least a few hours. An alternative is to iron the paper flat with a moderately hot iron and a piece of calico or a tea towel placed over the paper as you smooth it out.

5. To 'mottle' the pages, pour the dark tea mix into the smaller bowl or old mug.

6. Taking one of the paintbrushes – a 12mm (½in) brush works well for this – dip it into the dark tea mix and dab in an irregular pattern all over the top surface of the page. What we are trying to simulate is the look of a parchment or vellum (traditional animal-skin 'papers'), which preceded the inven-tion of the printing press, and do not have the uniformity of colour supplied by mass-produced modern papers. A useful point to bear in mind here is the adage, 'less is more': in other words, it is easier to add more to what you have done, should it be required, than to take away that which you didn't need.

7. Apply the desired effect to the first side of all the pages that you are treating, working systemati-cally. Once you have completed the last of these, you can return to the first page and turn it over and continue down the line with the second sides of each page, applying the same process.

8. Allow all the pages to dry fully and assess and modify where necessary. Once dry, you can fin-ish with the text of your choice. It is possible to put these pages through a printer or photocopier, but advisable to perform this action via the manual feed option.

## VARIATIONS

- For a more blended effect, try applying the darker stain before the lighter stain has dried – which means that you will be applying both effects to the page before putting each page aside to dry
- Add another shade of tea into the mix so that you have a light, a mid and a dark option to play with
- Instead of brushes, try using offcuts of sponge or foam rubber to apply the tea and create the effects. When applying product with a sponge

① FEED PAPER THROUGH THE LIGHT TEA-MIX

REMOVE & ALLOW
EXCESS TEA TO
DRIP BACK IN.
– ALLOW TO DRY

② WITH A POT OF THE DARKER
TEA & A BRUSH, WORK YOUR
WAY

ACCROSS THE PAGE
IN AN IRREGULAR
FASHION.

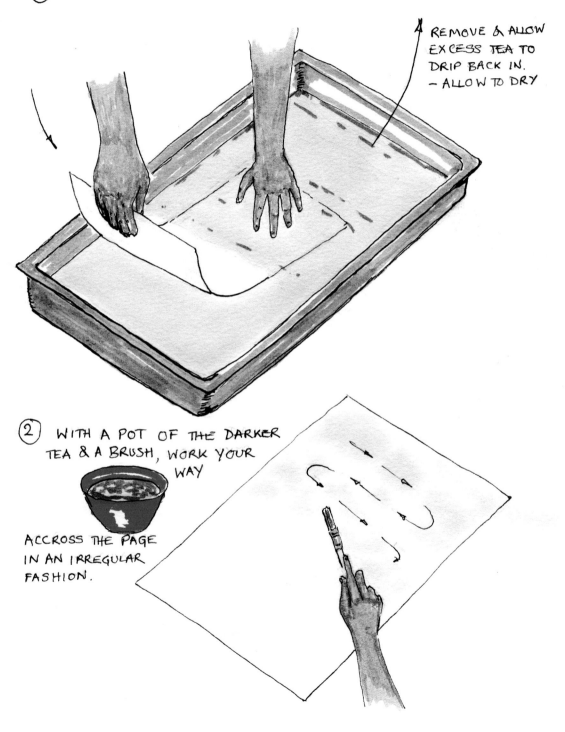

Fig. 6 Tea staining – bowl immersion process.

Tea stain immersion on watercolour paper, smooth and crumpled. This is a relatively dark stain and the nature of the paper means that it will register well. Note how the exposed fibres of the torn edges have taken up more of the stain.

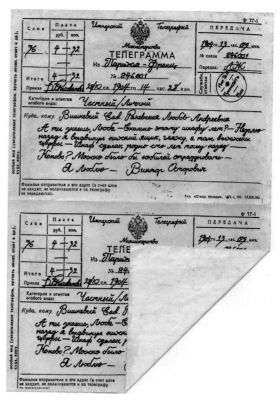

The *Cherry Orchard* telegram with the initial wash applied with a paintbrush – useful when a large bowl is unavailable or impractical. Very good results can be produced with this process, although it can take a little longer. This process will only stain one side at a time. Over-wetting the paper will cause it to fall apart.

or foam, always pluck away at any sharp edges on the sponge/foam that you are using with your fingers, to stop those sharp edges transferring to the surface that you are working on – unless that is the effect you are after!

## Paint Washes

A paint wash is, simply put, a small quantity of paint and a larger volume of water mixed together, which, when applied to a surface, gives a much paler, translucent version of the undiluted paint. Paint washes are an advance upon tea staining, although they can be used in addition to the tea staining process as well as on their own as a background effect.

## Materials
- White paper
- Cold water
- Yellow ochre and raw sienna acrylic or scenic acrylic/water-soluble paints

## Equipment
- Two small bowls (approximately 500ml capacity) to hold the water and paint wash
- Two 12mm (½in) or 25mm (1in) paintbrushes
- Tongue depressors/stirring sticks (a minimum of two)

## Process
1. Into one bowl place ¼–½ level teaspoon of yellow ochre paint and into the other a ¼–½ level

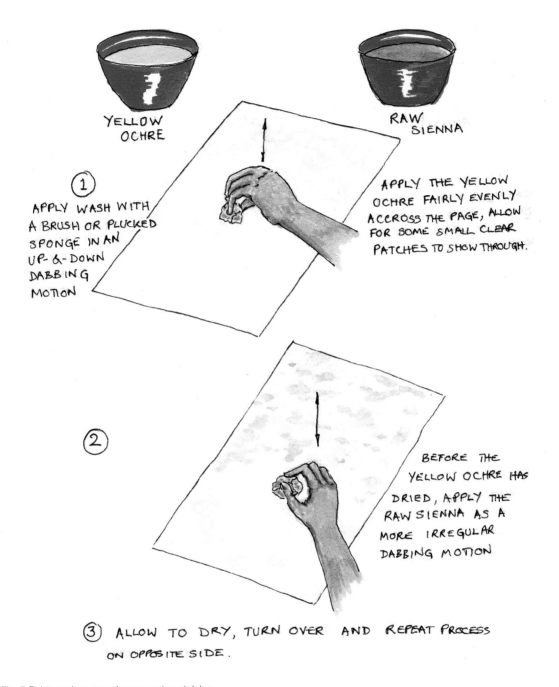

YELLOW OCHRE

RAW SIENNA

① APPLY WASH WITH A BRUSH OR PLUCKED SPONGE IN AN UP- & -DOWN DABBING MOTION

APPLY THE YELLOW OCHRE FAIRLY EVENLY ACCROSS THE PAGE, ALLOW FOR SOME SMALL CLEAR PATCHES TO SHOW THROUGH.

② BEFORE THE YELLOW OCHRE HAS DRIED, APPLY THE RAW SIENNA AS A MORE IRREGULAR DABBING MOTION

③ ALLOW TO DRY, TURN OVER AND REPEAT PROCESS ON OPPOSITE SIDE.

Fig. 7 Paint washes, an advance on tea staining.

teaspoon of raw sienna paint. The actual volume of paint will depend on the strength/richness of colour, but this should be a good quantity to start with.
2. Add 300ml of cold water to get the required dilution of water to paint. Mix well.

3. Test your colour on some spare paper. Allow to dry. If the colour is too faint, add some more paint, mix well and test again; repeat until you have the effect that you want. If the colour is too strong, pour out some of the mix and add more cold water

to dilute it further; repeat this until you have the colour you are after.

4. As in step 6 of the tea-staining technique above, apply the paint with the paintbrushes, starting with the yellow ochre as your base colour but allowing flecks of the original paper colour to show through.

5. Apply the raw sienna sparingly and randomly over the page for contrast and still remembering to allow the odd flecks of the original paper to show through. You are not trying to soak the page – less is more!

6. Set aside to dry, and then repeat on the other side.

If you want to, this can also be used as a 'drag through the bowl' technique.

## Paint and Glaze Effects

Paint and glaze effects can help your prop more accurately mimic the finished effect of a parchment or vellum, and this is enhanced by sponge application rather than brushes, since we are dealing with undiluted paint. We need to apply the paint in microns of thickness rather than slapping it on, and a sponge/foam rubber application enables us to do this. For preference, I like to use a fire-retardant (FR) glaze such as Mylands Emulsion Glaze FR Matt. Choosing a matt glaze over a gloss glaze means the effect won't to be too shiny.

The sponge cube is a very versatile painting tool. It can be used for a range of heavy or light

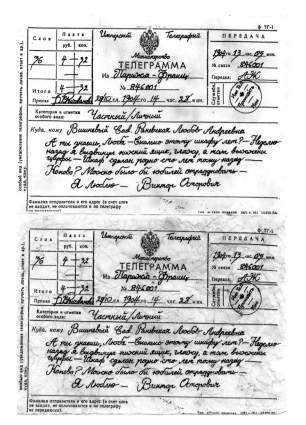

The *Cherry Orchard* telegrams, on standard printer/copier paper, have undergone a paint wash effect with yellow ochre as a base wash and raw sienna for the mottling detail. Notice how the crumpled effect allows for greater pick-up of the wash effect.

The *Cherry Orchard* telegrams on standard printer/copier paper. The glaze and paint effect work differently. The glaze prevents the paint from soaking into the paper, meaning that the colour is suspended in the glaze on the surface of the paper, so application requires more finesse.

applications on many different surfaces and can be plucked and cut to create a variety of effects. It has six surfaces and eight corners, which can each supply different colours to the work you are undertaking. It can also be used to blend and tone these colours with each other, or simply to blend and fade a single colour by using drier, cleaner areas of the sponge. And yes, sponges can generally be washed clean after use – some products may prevent this happening but, being cost-effective, they can be thrown away without breaking the bank.

## Materials
- Paper of your choice
- Matt emulsion glaze
- Yellow ochre and raw sienna acrylic or scenic acrylic/water-soluble paints (because a glaze is being used here, which will fix the paint, watercolour paint could be used)

## Equipment
- Two small bowls (approximately 500ml capacity) to hold the matt glaze and paint mix
- Offcuts of sponge or foam rubber (roughly 25–50mm/1–2in cubes), plucked so that there are no square edges and any flat surface is pitted and irregular
- Tongue depressors/stirring sticks (minimum of two)
- Barrier hand cream or foam
- Disposable latex or vinyl gloves

## Process
The technique is very similar to that of the paint washes, but rather than using a watery substance you will be using a translucent paint, which is thicker, and that also has the advantage that it will dry quicker. Remember the 'less is more' adage.

1. With the stirring sticks, measure roughly ¼–½ a level teaspoon of the yellow ochre and raw sienna paints into separate bowls.
2. Add approximately 300ml of the matt glaze to each bowl. Quantities of paint and glaze can be reduced or increased to accommodate the volume of paper that you are treating. The suggested volumes should cover between ten and twenty pages on both sides, depending on the effect you are trying to achieve.
3. Taking one of the sponges, dip it lightly into the yellow ochre mix and then gently drag the sponge against the edge of the bowl as you take it out to return any excess mix to the bowl. Only a modest amount of paint mix is required, as a little goes a long way.
4. Lightly dab the sponge with the yellow ochre mix over the front page of the paper. Mottle the page with this mix in an irregular pattern allowing for untreated areas of the page to show through. Varying the pressure with the sponge allows for a better sense of realism and texture. You should be aiming for a suggestion of colour change without obvious blocks of colour.
5. Repeat steps 3 and 4 with the raw sienna mix, but much more sparingly: the idea is simply to add more depth and texture.

Look at your hand, front and back, and you will see that it is not all one colour. If you really observe the detail you will notice mottling and shading, and the different tones and textures that go into making your perceived skin colour as well as the fact that that 'colour' has depth to it. This is the same effect that we are attempting to apply to the vellum and parchment effects (which are after all just skin effects… admittedly, dry, treated skin effects, but the principle remains the same).

6. Once dry, repeat steps 3, 4 and 5 on the second side of the pages you are treating. If you can, try to avoid making the second side too obviously different from the first side, as the colouration of one side would naturally continue through to the reverse side.
7. Once the paper is fully dry, you can apply whatever text, illuminations or seals that are required.

Of course, if you were doing a project that had a specific colour theme, you would simply swap the yellow ochre and raw sienna for the colours that will provide the effect that you require. Be it monochrome, sepia, reds or blues, prop making is about exploring and creating options.

## Shellac

Shellac is a natural product, the secretion of the female lac bug found in India and Thailand. It has been used for over 3,000 years for a wide variety of jobs, but most of us will be aware of it because of its use in French polishing (a specific type of colour application and varnishing on fine furniture). It was also used as the forerunner to vinyl records, as an insulator in electrical products, and in theatre for prop making and scenic art for a good few hundred years.

Shellac can be purchased in dry form, as flakes or buttons for you to mix yourself, or in liquid form, pre-mixed and ready to go. The mixing solution is ethanol (alcohol) or methylated spirit (de-natured alcohol – that is, ethanol with additives to deter people from drinking it), into which the shellac flakes/buttons are added to be dissolved, and gradually mixed to an even consistency. Liquid shellac produces strong fumes and is very flammable. Therefore, keep pre-mixed shellac away from naked flames and ignition sources and use in well-ventilated areas or wear a fume mask when using for extended periods of time.

There are a variety of shellac products that we can choose from. Product names may vary slightly depending upon manufacturer and supplier. What we require is a transparent polish or white hard varnish and a couple of colours, such as lemon, which will make a pale yellow/gold colour (the equivalent of our yellow ochre), and brown (which is the equivalent, for this process, of the raw sienna paint used above).

### Materials
- Shellac transparent polish
- Shellac lemon
- Shellac amber or brown

- Paper (the better the quality, the more realistic the result) or appropriate fabrics (see below)
- Methylated spirit (meths) or ethanol

### Equipment
- A minimum of three containers (depending on the number of colours required; it is possible to forego the brown shellac), and one extra for cleaning the brushes with meths/ethanol
- 12mm (½in) general purpose brushes or foam rubber offcuts
- Barrier creams/foams
- Protective gloves (latex or vinyl)
- Appropriate fume mask (where levels of extraction and ventilation are insufficient)
- Suitable eye protection to guard against splashes
- Polythene sheeting to protect the worktop from spillage

### Method
As with the paint and glaze effect, the aim is to use the base coat, in this case the transparent polish, to randomly and lightly progress over the paper that you are working on, leaving untreated areas of the paper to show through. Where the transparent polish contacts the paper it makes it somewhat translucent, which is the effect that we are after. The untreated paper showing through becomes the equivalent of fat deposits within the parchment or vellum. You can, of course, apply the transparent polish to the whole piece of paper, sparingly, and then apply your colour effects, the lemon followed by the brown either before or after the base layer has dried, depending upon the effect that you are after. It is very easy to apply too much of the colour and ruin the effect – a light touch is best practice, allowing for further build-up if necessary.

To vary the effect, you can allow the piece to dry completely and then execute a second application of colour, to produce accents that add depth to the work. In this instance, the colour will not bleed into the base coats and it is therefore especially important not to be heavy-handed.

Bramwell, Curragh
& Bell.
Solicitors at Law,
Lincoln's Inn.
London.

Dear Mr. Rivers,

        I write regarding the matter of Miss Jane Eyre: She's a young orphan she was educated at an orphan asylum and left to be a governess to a ward of a certain Mr. Rochester. Mr. Rochester professed to offer honourable marriage to Miss Eyre and, at the very altar, she discovered he had a wife yet alive, though a lunatic. Miss Eyre left Thornfield Hall the following night. The country was scoured far and wide, but no vestige of information could be gathered of her. This was nearly a year ago. A short time ago a lady named Miss Fairfax asked me to resume the search and place advertisement in the newspaper to which you have now responded. If you have any information as to the whereabouts of Miss Eyre I would be extremely interested to know of it.

        Yours Sincerely .

        Isaac, Bramwell

This letter, originally created for a production of *Jane Eyre*, was photocopied onto watercolour paper and reworked to create an older-looking letter. The parchment effect was done with shellac button polish and shellac amber applied with a brush.

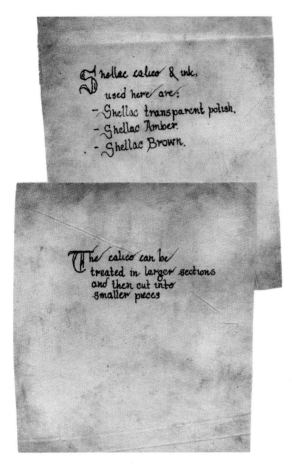

Shellac calico & ink.
used here are:
– Shellac transparent polish.
– Shellac Amber.
– Shellac Brown.

The calico can be
treated in larger sections
and then cut into
smaller pieces

Calico, shellac and ink. Using calico as a base for creating documents provides added durability. The base coat of button polish stiffens the calico without overtly changing the colour of the base material. The application of coloured shellacs, usually amber and a brown, provides tonal range and a parchment-like effect.

It will very much depend on the thickness of the paper or fabric being used, but on lighter papers you may find that you will not have to apply the effect to the other side of the page, unlike with the tea and paint processes.

When using fabric as our 'paper', it is necessary to paint the entire surface of the piece with the transparent polish to stiffen it, as any untreated areas will react very differently to the treated areas when inks are applied to them, causing bleeding of the ink and snagging of the writing implement. You can, at this point, allow the transparent polish to dry fully before applying the other shellacs,

but sparingly applying the lemon, and, even more sparingly and randomly, the brown shellac before the previous coat has dried, creates a more blended, natural effect. Again, highlights can be applied with the coloured shellacs once the fabric has dried.

## Alternatives to Paper

There may be occasions where a more robust paper is required, and this is where we can turn to fabric. Fabric on its own is not going to create the look and feel that we require and, in most cases, is going to be too floppy. Consequently, we can use a variety of products to stiffen the fabric and make it more conducive to write or print on. From this point of view, the selection of the fabric is imperative, as it is necessary to use entirely natural products such as muslin, calico and canvas, all of which come in varying thicknesses.

Muslin, calico and canvas are all cotton fabrics, so will absorb the various products that we wish to use with them.

**Muslin** can be used to make a lighter product, but it will need to be of a tighter weave, such as butter muslin, for the processes to work properly.

**Calico** is an excellent choice for robust documents as it comes in a choice of light, medium or heavy, which allows us to vary the effect more easily.

**Canvas** can produce a very sturdy result due to its heavier nature, and again comes in a variety of thicknesses. Be aware, though, that some of the lighter-duty canvases can have a rougher look to them, which may or may not suit what you are trying to do.

As a rule, it is recommended that you use either a medium or heavy calico, as this offers a good tightness of weave without being too costly, providing good durability and affordability. It does, however, depend on the result that you are after.

If you are unfamiliar with buying fabric, it is generally sold by the linear metre, and price from bolt to bolt, of the same fabric from the same supplier, will vary depending on the width of the fabric. For example, you may see a medium calico at a width of 1.2m at a certain price and then what looks to be the same product next to it at half as much again. Upon closer examination, you realize that the new bolt is almost twice as wide but at a lower cost, meaning a potential saving, or not having to join it together, depending on your requirements.

## Documents Made Using Latex

For a production of *The Way of the World*, a restoration comedy, I was faced with the challenge of creating documents that would be used vigorously, screwed up, thrown about and risk being destroyed in every performance. With thirty-two performances consuming fourteen documents a show, a total of 448 documents were required, all hand written, most with wax seals, some with ribbon ties... you can probably appreciate the challenge. The resources available were limited but we had a stock of slush latex left over from a previous show, so I commenced with prototyping.

The effect was very successful, probably helped by the fact it looked different to modern paper despite not being 'correct'. It looked right and took a lot of punishment without obvious signs of wear and tear. The sealing wax took to it beautifully, and the breaking open of the sealed documents was done with very small tabs of hook and fluff Velcro.

### Materials
- Natural fabric suited to the job at hand, such as canvas, calico or muslin or old sheets etc
- AL 360 slush mould latex (this is a pre-vulcanized latex that dries to a creamy white colour, and is intended for semi-rigid, hollow, rubber castings. There will be more on latex in Chapters 4 and 5)

Optional extras:

- Dipping latex
- Yellow ochre acrylic paint
- Raw sienna acrylic paint
- White acrylic paint

### Avoid Brushes

Although it is possible to use brushes with latex when taking special precautions (such as working washing-up liquid or soap release into the bristles), it is more than likely that the brushes will get ruined and therefore it is best not to. Use offcuts of foam rubber instead to create a more controlled effect with a much more even application without the risk of brush stokes marring the effect; furthermore, using something that is a waste product from previous work saves money!

### Equipment
- Mixing bowls (one to hold the slush mould latex and large enough to hold sufficient latex for the task at hand, although you can always refill a smaller bowl)
- 5cm, 7.5cm or 10cm (2in, 3in or 4in) rough-torn squares of foam rubber, preferably of a 5cm (2in) thickness, unplucked for this technique
- Tongue depressors
- Fabric scissors or other suitably sharp scissors (for dry work)
- A wipe-clean work surface and/or polythene to spread over and securely tape down to the work surface
- Appropriate PPE, including vinyl gloves
- Workshop 'washing lines', preferably three or four finger-widths apart, to hang the drying pieces of latexed fabric up and out of the way
- Paint palette; you do not need to buy one, you can make your own out of a sealed/varnished piece of plywood 6mm (¼in) thick, or even the lid of an old biscuit tin or ice-cream tub – it just needs to be something that you can put paint onto to be able to blend it

### Method
1. Cut away the selvedge from the fabric that you will be using (the loom-bound edges of the fabric that run down either side of the linear length).

Some of the original latex process documents from *The Way of The World*.

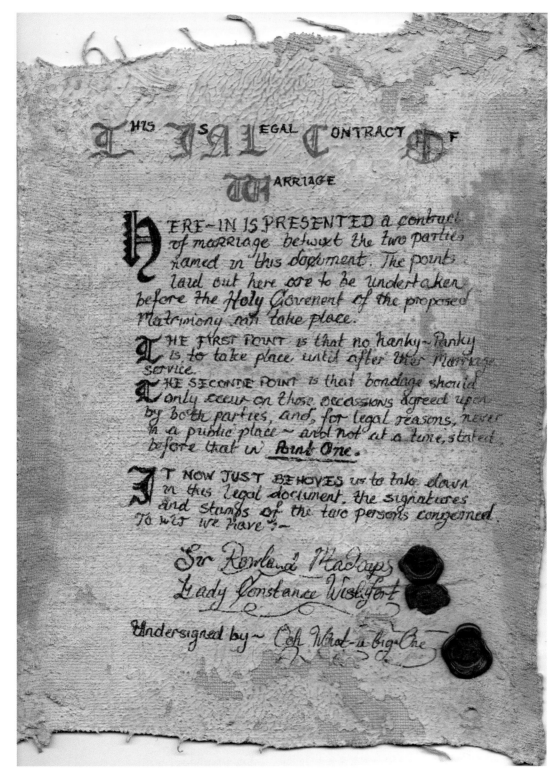

# THIS LEGAL CONTRACT OF MARRIAGE

**HERE-IN IS PRESENTED** a contract of marriage betwixt the two parties named in this document. The points laid out here are to be undertaken before the Holy Covenent of the proposed Matrimony can take place.

**THE FIRST POINT** is that no hanky-Panky is to take place until after the Marriage service.

**THE SECONDE POINT** is that bondage should only occur on those occassions agreed upon by both parties, and, for legal reasons, never in a public place ~ and not at a time, stated before that in <u>Point One</u>.

**IT NOW JUST BEHOVES** us to take down in this legal document, the signatures and stamps of the two persons concerned. To wit we have :-

*Sir Rowland Machaps*

*Lady Constance Wishfort*

Undersigned by ~ *Ooh What-a-big-One*

This certificate of marriage, written up for a production of *The Way of the World*, is thirty years old. It is showing signs of aging, but considering we normally require a prop like this to survive a month of performances, it is not doing too badly. This was made using slush mould latex and canvas, and due to quantity and time constraints, the writing was executed with black and red biro. The sealing wax is genuine and was applied in a traditional manner.

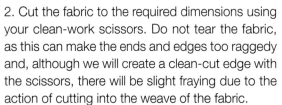

Canvas that has had slush mould latex sponged on to it. This produces a more regular effect than immersion and uses less product, with minimal wastage.

The sponged latex application process applied to calico. Latex documents can either be written onto as soon as they are dry, or can have a paint, glaze and dipping latex finish added to them.

2. Cut the fabric to the required dimensions using your clean-work scissors. Do not tear the fabric, as this can make the ends and edges too raggedy and, although we will create a clean-cut edge with the scissors, there will be slight fraying due to the action of cutting into the weave of the fabric.

3. Lay the fabric out onto the polythene-covered surface. Do not worry about any creases in the fabric from where it has been folded, as these will be smoothed out in the application of the latex. You can, of course, iron out any creases prior to application but make sure your fabric has come back to room temperature before applying the latex or the excess heat can will cause the latex to set more quickly, which could result in bobbling and an uneven texture on the sponges and fabric.

4. Pour the slush mould latex into a clean bowl. Dip a flat surface of the sponge you have chosen to use into the latex and evenly sponge the latex

onto the first side of your fabric, starting at one end and working systematically to the other, making sure not to leave any patches. The amount of latex you apply will be determined by the fabric you are using, but there should be no splurges or puddles left behind, just an even application of latex.

5. Repeat this process with any other pieces of fabric that you are working on, or as many as you can fit onto your work surface at any one time.

6. Once the latex-treated fabric is dry to the touch, peel it gently off the surface. Make sure it doesn't fold onto itself or make contact with any other treated pieces because at this stage it has adhesive properties and could stick! If necessary, you can wipe/rub away any dried latex on the worktop from the previous application prior to turning the fabric over and repeating on the second side. You

① APPLY SLUSH MOULD LATEX TO THE FABRIC.

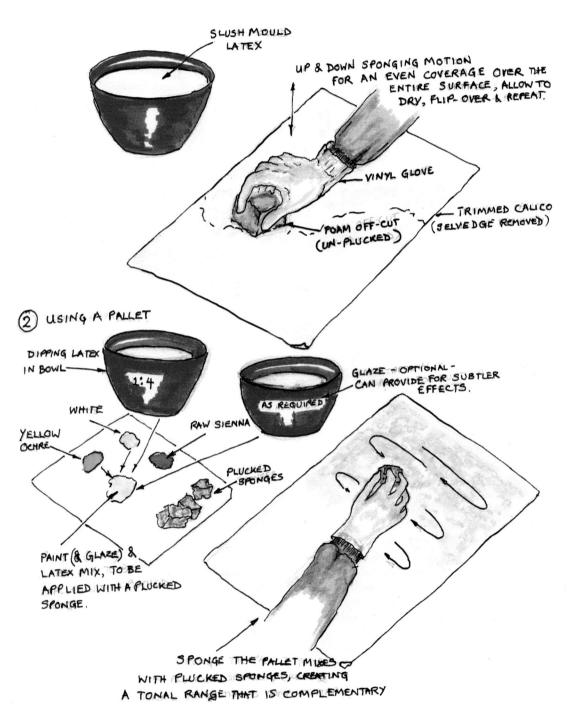

SLUSH MOULD LATEX

UP & DOWN SPONGING MOTION FOR AN EVEN COVERAGE OVER THE ENTIRE SURFACE, ALLOW TO DRY, FLIP-OVER & REPEAT.

VINYL GLOVE

FOAM OFF-CUT (UN-PLUCKED)

TRIMMED CALICO (SELVEDGE REMOVED)

② USING A PALLET

DIPPING LATEX IN BOWL

1:4

GLAZE - OPTIONAL - CAN PROVIDE FOR SUBTLER EFFECTS.

AS REQUIRED

WHITE

YELLOW OCHRE

RAW SIENNA

PLUCKED SPONGES

PAINT (& GLAZE) & LATEX MIX, TO BE APPLIED WITH A PLUCKED SPONGE.

SPONGE THE PALLET MIXES WITH PLUCKED SPONGES, CREATING A TONAL RANGE THAT IS COMPLEMENTARY

Fig. 8 The evolved latex process for documents.

may observe, depending again on the thickness of the fabric used, that some of the latex has bled through. Do not let this concern you, simply repeat the application process, paying close attention to a consistent and systematic approach.

If you do have more fabric than you can fit onto your worktop at any one time, at this point you could simply hang the already latex-treated first sides up on your workshop washing line (untreated sides onto the line), clean away any dried latex from the worktop and repeat the process until all the first sides are done, and then apply the same process to all the second sides.

7. Again, once it's dry to the touch, the latex-treated fabric can be gently peeled and hung up out of the way on your workshop washing line with the drier first side in contact with the line. These can be left here until you are ready for them; in

Calico, slush mould latex, paint, glaze and dipping latex. The effect here is subtle, but, as with standard paint and glaze effects, can be made to suit your own objectives. Dipping latex is used to make sure the paint and glaze stick to the slush mould latex, otherwise it will peel away.

good ambient conditions, they should be ready to use in an hour or two.

You may find at this point that the latex and fabric effect provide you with just what you are after, especially with certain types of fabric used. On the other hand, you may decide that you want a little extra something to pep things up. If so, this optional set of instructions is for you.

8. Pour some dipping latex into a bowl and then place some yellow ochre, raw sienna and white scenic paints onto your pallet.

9. Using a small cube of foam, take small samples of the yellow ochre and white paint and blend them until you have the colour that you want. The idea is to create a complementary mottled effect that works with the natural creamy colour of the slush mould latex.

10. It is essential at this point that the latex is added to the paint or the colour will wear off. We are using dipping latex as it dries translucent and therefore will not adversely affect the colour that we have created when mixing. Lightly dip your paint sponge into the dipping latex and collect sufficient to make up a quarter to a third of the volume of paint that you have, a 1:4 or a 1:3 ratio of latex to paint. The objective is to create a latex paint. Mixing the latex into the paint makes it flexible, preventing it from cracking. This technique has the added advantage of enabling the paint to bond to the latex. It is actually the latex in the paint that is bonding to the latex surface it is applied to. If you do not add latex to the paint, then the paint would crack and come away or peel off depending on the type of paint you are using. The paint you use should always be water soluble. Latex bonds to latex superbly, which is why we use vinyl gloves when using latex, unless you want flipper hands!

11. Apply the newly created latex paint to the surface of your latex-treated fabric using the same approach as for paint and glaze… and yes, if you want to use glaze and apply dipping latex into the glaze mixes on the palette, you can. Basically, keep experimenting and see what works.

A piece of untreated calico alongside the latex document with added latex and paint techniques.

Latex documents are extremely durable and will take a world of punishment. Natural latex is also naturally heat-resistant to very high temperatures, so it does not require any extra fireproofing. The 'latex paper' does have some rather un-paper-like qualities though. If you screw it up into a ball, it will spring back out, unharmed when released. With thinner fabrics, it can be quite floppy, and it obviously feels different to real paper. It does, however, have a weight to it that allows it to be thrown around in more flamboyant ways than you could with other types of paper, and although I wouldn't recommend it as the go-to method for all your reproduction documents, it does have a valid place within the repertoire for certain types of productions.

Examples of where this technique can be effectively applied are where directors and designers ask for documents that are out of the norm – for example super-long, fast-unravelling scrolls, tug-of-war letters, large volumes of letters/scrolls/illuminated documents that are receiving rough treatment – and it would be impractical to have as running props. This technique has been used in restoration comedies, panto, Shakespeare plays and touring TIE (Theatre in Education) productions. If in doubt, provide a sample/samples (using different thicknesses of fabric) document for the director and designer to look at, and take it from there. You can write on slush mould latex documents with real ink and ink pens, due to the fact that this particular type of latex is not fully watertight because of the way it has been manufactured and the bulking process that makes it a semi-rigid product.

## Documents Made Using PVA, Paint and Fabric

This is basically an extension of the above technique that is useful when a stiffer, more realistic paper effect is required. Natural fabrics are recommended and, often, a medium calico will suffice. The finished article has good sound qualities, good visual qualities and will take an excellent crease. It can be written on without too many problems with a variety of inks and writing implements. Wax seals can also be applied, as well as any ribbons and other dressings that are required. In scroll form, it will take on a slightly springy nature like the real paper it is replicating. Unlike the latex 'paper', it will retain any creases from having been screwed up and roughly treated, but if it has not been treated too severely it can be smoothed out and used again. It should not tear with typical use, although it is possible for it to be torn if that effect is desired, depending upon the thickness of the fabric used and the strength of the actor.

### Materials
- Medium-weight calico
- A decent-quality general-purpose PVA/wood glue such as Evo-Stik Resin 168 (it is tempting to buy cheap PVA to keep the cost down, but it is quite likely that it will lack the viscosity of the better-quality products, creating more mess and less bond)

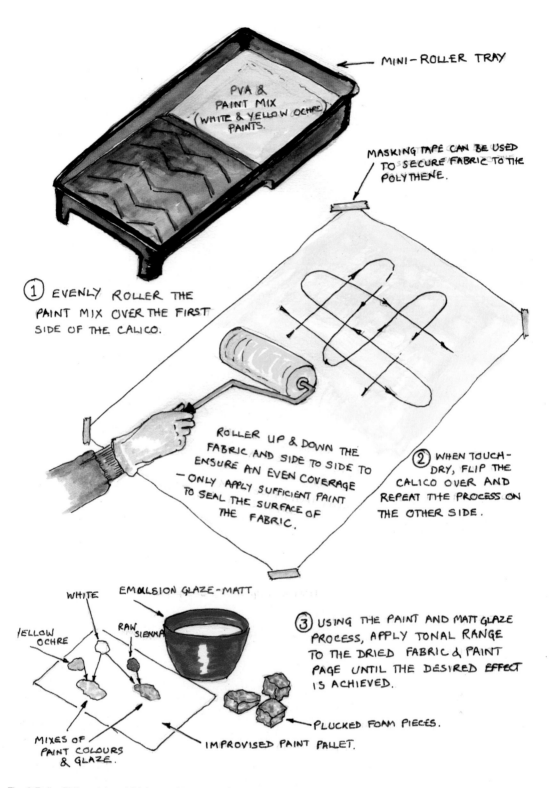

MINI-ROLLER TRAY

PVA &
PAINT MIX
(WHITE & YELLOW OCHRE)
PAINTS.

MASKING TAPE CAN BE USED
TO SECURE FABRIC TO THE
POLYTHENE.

① EVENLY ROLLER THE
PAINT MIX OVER THE FIRST
SIDE OF THE CALICO.

ROLLER UP & DOWN THE
FABRIC AND SIDE TO SIDE TO
ENSURE AN EVEN COVERAGE
— ONLY APPLY SUFFICIENT PAINT
TO SEAL THE SURFACE OF
THE FABRIC.

② WHEN TOUCH-
DRY, FLIP THE
CALICO OVER AND
REPEAT THE PROCESS ON
THE OTHER SIDE.

EMULSION GLAZE-MATT

WHITE

YELLOW
OCHRE

RAW SIENNA

③ USING THE PAINT AND MATT GLAZE
PROCESS, APPLY TONAL RANGE
TO THE DRIED FABRIC & PAINT
PAGE UNTIL THE DESIRED EFFECT
IS ACHIEVED.

PLUCKED FOAM PIECES.

MIXES OF
PAINT COLOURS
& GLAZE.

IMPROVISED PAINT PALLET.

Fig. 9 Roller PVA, paint and fabric used to create documents.

These 1950s-style *Macbeth* maps of Scotland circa 1630 were made for a dystopian approach to the play. They were originally mounted onto stained wood map boards that had castors affixed to them. Flagged map pins were also made to be inserted into them, and painted card 'army' designators were adhered with black tack (stronger version of Blu-tack).

PVA and paint roller effect with detail of the reverse side when not painted. Applying paint to both surfaces is necessary for documents where both sides are seen and/or written on, unless a specific effect is being sought.

- White emulsion or scenic acrylic paint
- Yellow ochre scenic acrylic paint
- Raw sienna scenic acrylic paint
- Matt emulsion glaze

## Equipment
- Mini roller tray
- Mini foam rollers
- Squares of offcut foam rubber, plucked and unplucked
- Paint mixing bowls
- Paint palette
- Tongue depressors/mixing sticks
- PPE – barrier creams, disposable gloves (latex or vinyl)
- Polythene to cover the work surfaces

## Method
You can either perform this technique with a piece of foam rubber about 10cm (4in) square and applying the PVA/paint mix in the same fashion as for the latex document process, which is ideal for a small volume turnout, or use a mini roller tray and mini roller. The roller application will get the job done quicker but the clean-up afterwards takes longer. However, the roller technique is ideal when you have many documents to deal with or large surface areas. You can also prepare a long cut of fabric with this process that can be cut into the required page sizes after it has fully dried (although drying will probably have to be done on the bench to avoid ruining the effect).

1. Put a quantity of white paint into a paint mixing bowl. The combined volume of paints that you

This is an exaggerated shellac effect on standard printer paper. The amber shellac has been applied before the button polish had dried, allowing for more tonal range.

are using should be about a quarter of the overall volume that you intend to make up.

2. Add a small quantity of yellow ochre paint, and mix. The amount of yellow ochre that you put in depends on how dark you want this base colour to be, but start off small because you can always add more if you need it.

3. Having achieved the desired colour mix for the base colour, you can now add in the PVA. The ratio of PVA to paint should be about 3:1, so if you had made up 250ml of paint, you would add approximately 750ml of PVA. Thoroughly mix together. The reason for mixing the paint colours first and then adding the PVA is to make sure that the colour that we require is correct. If we were to add the individual paint colours into the PVA, the actual

This good-quality writing paper was originally a pastel yellow in colour; it has been lightly crumpled and tea stained through immersion, followed by additional tea washing with a paintbrush.

The paint and glaze effect has been created as an alternative to shellac where workshop conditions are unsuited to the latter process and COSHH may be more of an issue. This is standard printer paper that has been crumpled. The folded-back corner at bottom left shows the necessity of applying the process to both sides of the paper.

colour mix would be obscured by the white colouration of the PVA and we wouldn't know what the true colour was until the PVA had dried, when it becomes translucent.

4. Pour a quantity of the paint mix into the mini roller tray. Prepare the mini roller by running it into the paint and then making an even coating over the roller by rolling it onto the bed of the tray, at the same time removing any excess paint.

5. Systematically, roller the paint onto the fabric surface, working from one end to the other using a forward and backward motion and making sure that you do not leave any bare areas. Depending upon the size of the piece of fabric that you are covering, it may be necessary to re-prime the roller several times. Top up the roller tray reservoir as necessary.

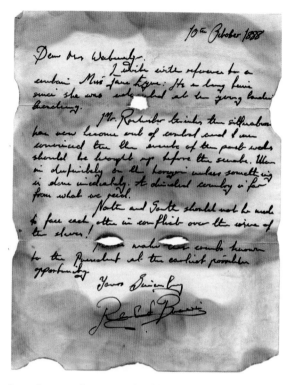

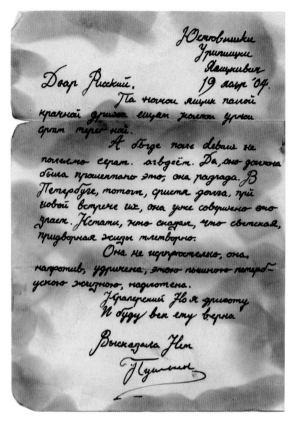

A candle, properly supported and kept away from other combustibles, can make a very effective way of quickly aging paper. The page is held above and away from the flame to collect the soot that comes off it. This example was for Agatha Christie's *Spider's Web*.

BOTTOM RIGHT: This envelope and 'rare canary-coloured stamp' are a crucial part of *Spider's Web* so had to be carefully made. The usual tea-staining effects can be employed to tone down the white of the envelope. A pale photocopy was made of an original stamp, colour washed by hand and affixed to the envelope when dry. The franking marks were made using a card template, a radius aid and a 0.5mm Rotring pen.

This is the candle and soot technique, again for *Spider's Web*, on a Russian-style letter. Less scorching has been employed here – just the natural colour of the paper and the soot from the candle produce the effect.

6. Allow the first side to dry, either by leaving it on the bench (depending on how much more you must do) or hanging it up on your workshop washing line with the wet side up.

7. When the first side is dry, repeat the process on the other side and, again, allow to dry.

8. With both sides dry, you can now apply any additional finish to the paper, one side at a time and allowing to dry, by employing the same top coat applications used with the paint and glaze effects or using any left-over base colour mix to blend as you see fit with the colours that you have

More examples of franked envelopes using a bit of research and card templates, a radius aid and a 0.5mm Rotring pen. These were made up for a production of *Under Milk Wood*, using genuine stamps from 1956.

Other than the paint and texture finish, this jug is entirely made of paper products and was one of two made for a production of *Macbeth* in 1990 and is still going strong. The design for this prop immediately suggested a papier mâché balloon construction with added cardboard and paper rope elements. The finish is a light monkey dung to suggest a crank clay effect and the dressing is hessian.

put onto your palette. Just always remember that less is more!

9. While your paper effect is drying, take the opportunity to clear away. Any larger quantity of unused base mix can be placed into a sealable container, clearly labelled and stored away for the next time you need to use it.

# PAPIER MÂCHÉ

It is a commonly held opinion that papier mâché is a technique that is best forgotten once you have left primary school, as it is 'a very simple mediocre process that is only useful for creating piggy banks out of old newspapers, balloons and egg cartons'. Most people are unaware that this is an ancient craft process that has been used for hundreds of years – not necessarily to make piggy banks but for items that range from finely decorated boxes, candlesticks and picture frames to furniture. It has been used for bowls and tableware, masks and armour decoration, and it is still being used today in ways that are a far cry from pre-school and primary school education although, in essence, it is the same product.

It is worth considering, as we become more aware of the effect that we are having upon our environment and the need to recycle, that papier mâché was one of the earliest forms of recycling of a man-made product – manufactured paper. The original paper was time-consuming to produce and expensive to buy and, human ingenuity being what it is, another purpose was sought for it once the original purpose had been served – hence, papier mâché (literally 'chewed paper').

Two paper pulp products: Celluclay and DAS Papier Mâché.

## Papier Mâché Pulp

There are two types of papier mâché – layered and pulp – and they can be used independently of each other or in concert. Basically, it depends upon the effect that you require and the amount of detail you want in the project that you are undertaking. Both processes use paper and glue as their basis but papier mâché pulp has other ingredients added to make it into a clay-like substance and give it more body. This enables the papier mâché pulp to be used as a stand-alone product, like an air-drying clay, but it is best used in moulds, over forms or as a build-up of detail on wood, card or papier mâché sculpts.

It is possible to make your own papier mâché pulp, but it is a time-consuming and laborious process when there are readily available products on the market that can suit a variety of budgets and purposes. Some of these are ready-to-use products while others are dry particulate products that simply require the addition of water to make them useable. Some of the dry products have plaster of Paris (or the like) added to bulk them out and make them set quicker, which has its advantages

and disadvantages. If you were to buy a non-plaster-added papier mâché pulp like Celluclay (grey-toned) or Celluclay II (bleached white), you can add in the plaster product yourself when you are after a faster set or leave it out if you want a longer working time – or you can stock the assorted products for different tasks.

All these commercial products will come with their own usage instructions: read them, follow them and then explore other ways of using them. It can be more economical to use the dry products, because stored correctly they can last indefinitely and they are there when you need them – you simply make up the quantity you need as required. Although the dry products are costlier at initial purchase because you are having to buy a larger quantity in one go, in the longer term you get more bang for your buck. Ultimately it will come down to whether it is of use having a stock item that can be called upon as you need it or the convenience of using a pre-made product for the job and budget that you are undertaking. There is no right or wrong approach here as the individual product and personal preference will come into play.

## The Layered Approach

Layered paper is a simpler product to analyse as it is just layers of paper systematically bonded together with glue. However, there are many different papers and many different 'glues' or binding media that can be used. It is possible, for example, to use polyester resins and epoxy resins with papers, providing the paper is completely dry and you follow the health & safety and COSHH advice for the products. However, using these products will increase the cost – in the case of epoxy resins, substantially so.

## Moulded Paper

There is actually a third way of using papier mâché: moulded paper. This process simply involves taking sheets of newspaper, soaking them in water and then mashing them together into the shape or form that you have in mind (perhaps you wanted to create a bird, animal or fish form that you are going to papier mâché over). This can be a very cost-effective and quick way of creating a form that can be used with various products once it is dry but

Jugs made from balloons and a spice dish made from thin card and papier mâché.

is particularly suited to papier mâché work because of its complementary nature, both layered and pulp.

The trick is to wet the sheets thoroughly and then screw and mash them into each other with your hands while squeezing out the maximum amount of water possible, making sure that you pay attention to the shape and form that you are creating. Although you can use glue mediums instead of water, it does end up being a messier process that dries harder but is less easy to manipulate once dry. Do not over-complicate things by attempting to make an entire form in one go. If your form has a body, head, arms and legs, for example, make each separately while paying attention to the proportions of the whole form.

A more advanced version can be achieved with the moulded paper process by mashing it around a pre-prepared armature made from single-strand galvanized wire.

It is also possible to mash the paper into moulds that have relatively simple shapes. Custom-made plaster (use shellac and wax to seal the plaster once dry) or silicone moulds can be used for this, but also household moulds used for cakes and jellies. The important thing to bear in mind is that we need to remove as much water as possible when mashing the wet lumps of paper together. Once this has been done, the form can be gently teased from the mould, tweaking it as necessary, and then set aside to dry in a warm environment, or a suitable oven or dryer (important: no naked flames).

Once dry, the moulded paper can be trimmed and shaped and fitted together ready for the next stage in its evolution into a fully fledged prop.

## The Glue

We can use traditional options like a flour and water mix for the glue, or a wheat-based wallpaper paste (preferably without the fungicide added), but more commonly these days we rely upon a quality PVA/wood glue, the white stuff that dries clear. The reason for using PVA is that it is easy to prepare and apply and provides a very strong finished result. It will dry relatively quickly in a warm, non-damp environment.

## The Paper

The paper that is used for papier mâché very much comes down to the effect that you want, but if it absorbs the glue (avoid glossy papers) it should work. The cheapest paper, and the most commonly used, is recycled newspaper, but craft papers can be used and even tissue paper for specific effects such as texturing. Thicker, absorbent papers/thin card are more prone to creasing and rucking and are best used for structure (the card construction processes are covered in the next section).

## Applying Layered Paper (Laminating)

### Materials
- Newspapers
- Yellow Pages/coloured newsprint/phone directories
- PVA glue
- Water
- Red and blue water-based paint (optional)

### Equipment
- A clear work area with enough space to undertake the task at hand, and then some
- General-purpose paintbrushes (the size of the brush depends on the task to be undertaken. For example, a 12–25mm (½–1in) brush is suitable for jobs between the size of a large grapefruit and a good-sized Halloween pumpkin)
- Pots or containers to mix the glue and water (one if using different-coloured papers, two if using paint to colour the glue)
- Barrier hand cream or foam
- Latex or vinyl gloves
- Clean polythene to cover your workbench
- Craft knife/scalpel for trimming once dry
- 100 grit sandpaper/abrasive paper

The following will be required if you are applying papier mâché over an existing object that needs to be removed once the papier mâché is dry:

- White petroleum jelly/Vaseline or soft soap release agent, or a spray furniture polish or wax polish to act as a release agent
- Bowl of water, at room temperature, to wet the paper to provide a second release and glue barrier, and/or cling film

### Method

1. Prepare the PVA. A decent-quality wood adhesive can be diluted by as much as a 1:1 equal parts PVA to water, with clean, cool water (hot water will cause it to separate). If you dilute it any more than this, it will lose its adhesive properties. Remember that the higher the water content, the more fluid the product becomes – meaning more run-off – and the longer it will take to dry. With a PVA such as Evo-Stik's Resin 168, with a good viscosity, a dilution of no more than 3:1 ratio of glue to water is best. It is possible to use the glue neat, but with the higher viscosity things can become very tacky very quickly, giving you a shorter working time, which is something that should be avoided in the first six layers or so.

If using paint to colour the PVA, do this now. Make the PVA and water mix in one pot and then pour half of it into a second pot. At this point you can add your two water-based paint colours (for example blue and red), one into each pot. You only need to add sufficient paint to provide a colour tint, which for 500ml of glue and water mix would be between a half and one level teaspoon of paint, depending on the strength of colour that the paint provides.

2. Tear your paper into strips, making equal quantities of each of the two colours of paper if you have them. The width of these strips, as mentioned previously, will be determined by the size and shape of the object that you are applying your papier mâché to. This could vary from 12mm-wide (½in) strips for smaller objects, up to 15cm-wide (6in) strips for a larger pieces.

## USEFUL TIPS FOR LAYERING PAPIER MÂCHÉ

- It is very easy to lose track of which layer you are currently on when undertaking layered papier mâché work, particularly when working on larger three-dimensional projects that are very symmetrical. For this reason, it is advisable to use at least two different colours of paper; starting with one colour and moving on to the next when you have completed a layer with the first. In addition, you can also

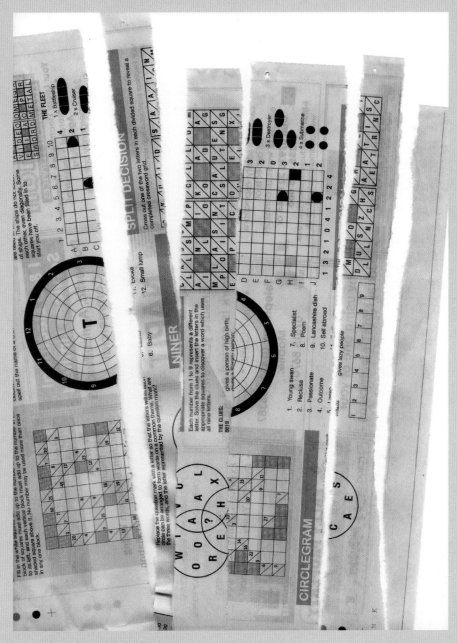

A straight tear along the grain of the paper.

*continued overleaf*

### USEFUL TIPS FOR LAYERING PAPIER MÂCHÉ *continued*

make a record of each layer as you complete it, either with a pen and paper or a marker pen onto the polythene worksheet, or with a small piece of the coloured paper you are currently using.

• Tear, do not cut the paper. With layered papier mâché work, we are attempting to create a blended, uniform whole. By tearing the paper, the fibres of the paper become exposed in a feathered effect

A tear against the grain of the paper.

that makes it indiscernible from the paper beneath it when wetted down correctly with the glue. A cut edge does not blend very well, particularly when using thicker papers.

- Paper has a grain. To test the grain of the paper you are using, take hold of a sheet of it between the thumb and forefinger of each hand about 25mm (1in) from an edge, and tear a continuous strip from

Varied sizes and shapes of paper for papier mâché work.

*continued overleaf*

## USEFUL TIPS FOR LAYERING PAPIER MÂCHÉ *continued*

top to bottom of that edge whilst still holding the paper at the top between the thumb and forefinger of each hand. If the paper comes away in a relatively straight line, you have found the grain, and this is the edge you will tear down to prepare all your pieces of paper. If, however, the paper tears erratically, tearing across the page and back, you are tearing against the grain. Turn the page through 90 degrees and start again, and you should find that the paper will tear to better effect.

- A paintbrush has three main components: the head or bristles; the ferrule, the metal collar that holds the bristles in place and attaches them to the handle; and the handle. This may seem rather obvious but, the point to be made is that each of the components of the brush can be made to serve an additional purpose when applying paper and glue to your papier mâché project.

- Because you are working with gloved hands, you can use your fingers, while still holding onto the brush, to smooth down areas of paper as well as applying the paper to the workpiece with them. It is best practice to keep one hand as glue-free as possible to manipulate the dry paper and the object being covered.

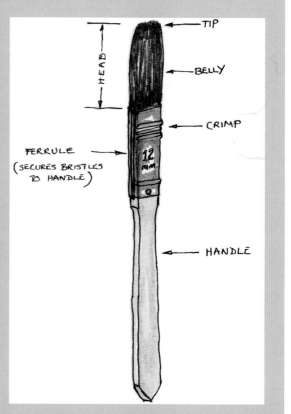

Fig. 10 Anatomy of a paintbrush, an all-round tool for papier mâché.

The paper strips can at this point be torn across the length into squares or rectangles that may be better suited to the shape of the item to be covered. A mix of strips, rectangles and squares will tend to suit most applications. It is of course possible to create custom shapes for awkward areas with a bit of judicious tearing. Remember, do not use scissors or knives until the papier mâché is dry. If the object you are covering is an intrinsic part of the structure, and does not require removal following the drying process, move on to step 5.

3. If you are applying papier mâché over an object that is to be removed intact afterwards (such as a vase, lamp base or marrow), at this point you should apply a layer of white petroleum jelly (useful for most sealed, hard objects) or soft soap release (suitable for plaster and other porous surfaces), furniture polish (suitable for varnished wooden objects), or even cling film (where a more general shape is to be covered – particularly useful on fruit and veg), to aid in removing the dried papier mâché and prevent it from sticking to your form or mould.

4. Apply a layer of wetted paper (this could be newspaper or tissue paper, if preferred) over the release agent-coated object by taking pieces of dry paper in your fingers and running them through the water. Drag the wetted paper against the edge of the water bowl or between your fingers to remove any excess water and then apply to your object. Make sure you overlap each piece of paper sufficiently, to prevent gapping. One layer of wetted paper all over is sufficient.

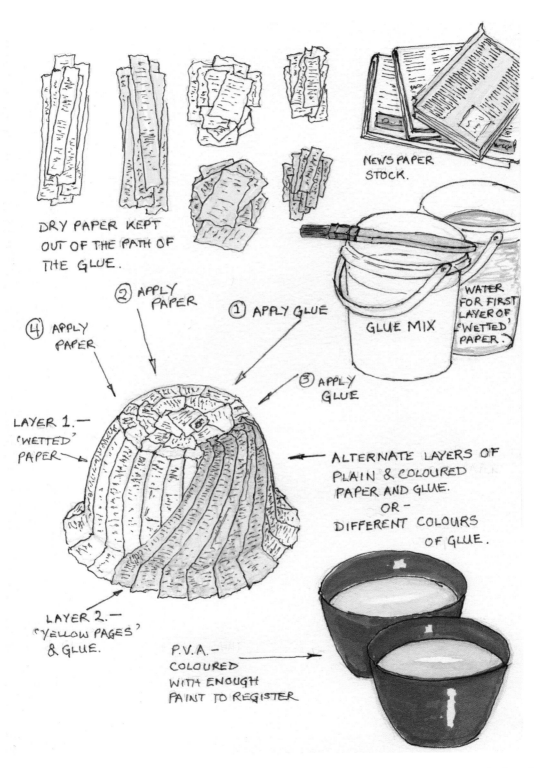

DRY PAPER KEPT OUT OF THE PATH OF THE GLUE.

NEWS PAPER STOCK.

② APPLY PAPER

④ APPLY PAPER

① APPLY GLUE

③ APPLY GLUE

GLUE MIX

WATER FOR FIRST LAYER OF 'WETTED' PAPER.

LAYER 1. — 'WETTED' PAPER

ALTERNATE LAYERS OF PLAIN & COLOURED PAPER AND GLUE.
OR -
DIFFERENT COLOURS OF GLUE.

LAYER 2. — 'YELLOW PAGES' & GLUE.

P.V.A. - COLOURED WITH ENOUGH PAINT TO REGISTER

Fig. 11 Papier mâché work layout, wetted paper layer and layered papier mâché process with coloured paper and coloured paint application alternatives.

Round dice with a gesso and paint finish. Twelve layers of papier mâché were applied over each die. When dry, the papier mâché was sanded to remove irregularities and painted with six layers of gesso, sanding between layers when dry.

5. With your brush, apply a layer of glue to part of the surface area to be covered, then place a piece of coloured paper (a different colour from that used for the wetted paper layer, if used) onto this area and 'wet down' with more glue. Repeat this process with further pieces of the same coloured paper, making sure to provide a good overlap to avoid gapping, until the entire surface of the object is covered. Make a record of the layer. A good overlap is between a quarter and a third of the width or length of the paper – whichever applies.

6. Repeat step 5 with your second colour immediately upon finishing the first layer, and when your second layer is complete, record it. Most of the hobby papier mâché books suggest allowing the paper to dry between layers, but many years of experience have shown that applying all layers in one sitting produces a smoother, more durable result. It is a time-consuming process, but taking regular breaks and listening to the radio or an audiobook can help to alleviate the tedium.

Keep repeating this process until you have completed twelve full layers. Remember to work the paper down well using your brush 'multi-tool' and your fingers to work down the edges and any creases, and make sure that each layer is fully laminated to the previous ones without air pockets.

7. Leave to dry in a warm environment. If your workshop has good drying conditions (it is warm with no excess humidity), drying should occur overnight and can be sped up by raising your object from the bench top by placing something beneath it to increase air flow. Another option would be to hang it up if you have somewhere to do this and the object is not too large, heavy or cumbersome. Increasing the room temperature will also help, or you could use a purpose-built drier or airing cupboard or an industrial oven if you have one. Be aware that excess glue may drip off if you have

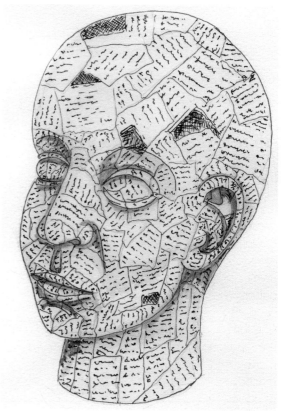

Fig. 12a Puppet head, modelled on a form.

Fig. 12b Selecting a cutting line for removing papier mâché.

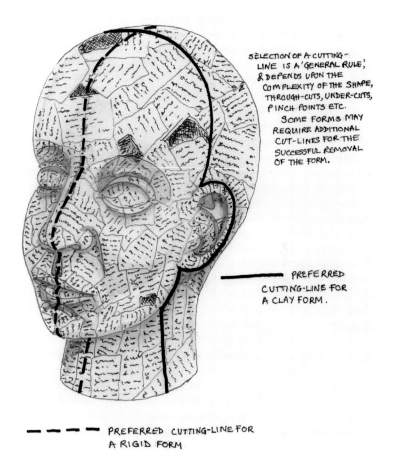

SELECTION OF A CUTTING-LINE IS A 'GENERAL RULE', & DEPENDS UPON THE COMPLEXITY OF THE SHAPE, THROUGH-CUTS, UNDER-CUTS, PINCH POINTS ETC.
SOME FORMS MAY REQUIRE ADDITIONAL CUT-LINES FOR THE SUCCESSFUL REMOVAL OF THE FORM.

—— PREFERRED CUTTING-LINE FOR A CLAY FORM.

— — — PREFERRED CUTTING-LINE FOR A RIGID FORM

been overly enthusiastic in its application. Do not place your object in or over a heat source if you have applied your papier mâché over a balloon or other sealed object, as the expanding air within the form could lead to disastrous and even dangerous repercussions.

8. Once dry, it is good practice to give it a once-over to look for any defects or thin areas. Trim away any unsightly wrinkles and loose bits of paper and give it a sanding down with 100 grit sand/abrasive paper.

9. If form removal is required, mark a line around the optimal release point with a pencil or fine marker pen that will show up against the papier mâché. Carefully follow that line with a craft knife or scalpel, trying not to damage the original form. Keep the cut line as precise as possible, as this will make it easier to join the pieces back together

afterwards. Tongue depressors, tapered to a wedge at the ends, can be used to facilitate easier removal of the two halves of the papier mâché structure by inserting them into the cut line and under one half of the piece to be removed. By jiggling them about, you can usually release the suction between form and casting. Repeat this process on the second half, which is normally easier because you do not have the other half to work around, and therefore have a more direct access to get between the form and the casting.

Once removed from the form, you may find that the casting will need a bit of tweaking to get the two halves to realign accurately, but this is not normally a major problem. Whatever you do, do not put the pieces aside without realigning them, as the two halves are likely to do their own thing as they continue to dry, making joining them back

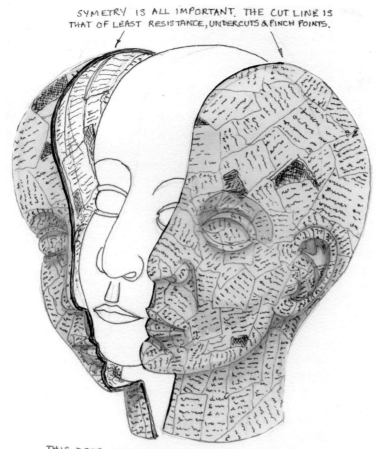

SYMETRY IS ALL IMPORTANT. THE CUT LINE IS THAT OF LEAST RESISTANCE, UNDERCUTS & PINCH POINTS.

Fig. 12c. Removing papier mâché from a solid form.

THIS DOES, OF COURSE, MEAN THAT YOUR GLUE & PATCH LINE RUNS RIGHT THROUGH THE DOMINANT FEATURES. HOWEVER, CAREFUL WORKING CAN MINIMIZE ANY OBVIOUS LINE.

together later more difficult. Best practice is to glue them together as soon as you can after removal and realignment. This is done with neat PVA adhesive and masking tape. Once the rejoining has dried, you can remove the masking tape, trim away any excess glue or untidy pieces of paper and apply more papier mâché over the join, working it down well. One or two layers are normally sufficient. Allow to dry and give the whole piece a light sanding with 100 grit sand/abrasive paper to provide a key for any subsequent techniques.

10. Papier mâché is rarely used as the finished product: it is a part of the structural process that is a means to an end. There is a wide variety of techniques that can be used to get us to that end, and these will be covered in detail in later sections, but here are a few options.

## Finishes

### Papier Mâché Pulp

Papier mâché pulp is a very useful product that can be used to apply greater detail and enhance aesthetics that would have been impractical simply using the layered paper approach. The pulp can also be used to set in other pieces of appliqué decoration, such as 'gems', eyes, metals and

Fig. 12d Removing papier mâché from a clay form.

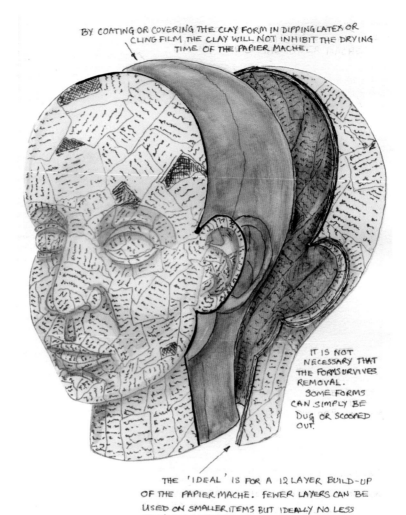

BY COATING OR COVERING THE CLAY FORM IN DIPPING LATEX OR CLING FILM THE CLAY WILL NOT INHIBIT THE DRYING TIME OF THE PAPIER MACHE.

IT IS NOT NECESSARY THAT THE FORM SURVIVES REMOVAL. SOME FORMS CAN SIMPLY BE DUG OR SCOOPED OUT.

THE 'IDEAL' IS FOR A 12 LAYER BUILD-UP OF THE PAPIER MACHE. FEWER LAYERS CAN BE USED ON SMALLER ITEMS BUT IDEALLY NO LESS THAN SIX LAYERS.

other inserts. Once dry, the pulp can be sanded to a fine finish ready for the next stage. Be aware that the thicker the application of the pulp, the longer it will take to dry and the more obvious any shrinkage will be. It is often better to do any thicker build-up in a series of lighter layers.

## GESSO

Gesso is a traditional medium that has been used by craftsmen and fine artists for hundreds of years. It involves a glue medium and ground chalk and is used as a fine sealed finish in preparation for painting and gilding. It is applied in even layers with a brush and allowed to dry after each layer;

then it is sanded to remove any irregularities, the process being repeated until the required build-up has been achieved. Fine artists and scenic artists use it for canvasses, wooden surfaces and walls to seal them and create a nicer surface to paint on. It is also used over papier mâché and carved wooden objects such as sconces, candelabra, chandeliers and sculpted figures, where it can be applied to build up extra detail and provide a very fine surface, masking the grain of the wood, before painting and/or gilding. It can also be carved into, to add the finest of details.

Nowadays there are many commercial brands of gesso on the market, most of them acrylic.

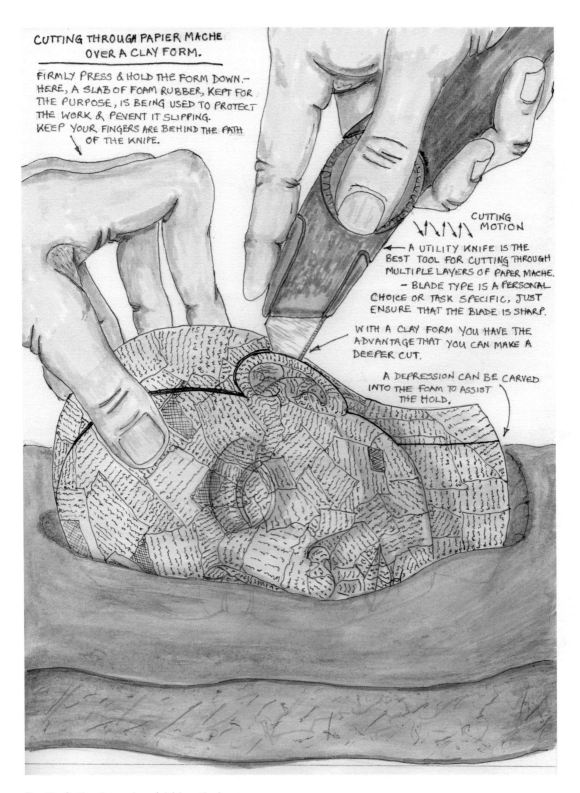

CUTTING THROUGH PAPIER MACHE
OVER A CLAY FORM.

FIRMLY PRESS & HOLD THE FORM DOWN.-
HERE, A SLAB OF FOAM RUBBER, KEPT FOR
THE PURPOSE, IS BEING USED TO PROTECT
THE WORK & PEVENT IT SLIPPING.
KEEP YOUR FINGERS ARE BEHIND THE PATH
OF THE KNIFE.

CUTTING
MOTION

- A UTILITY KNIFE IS THE
BEST TOOL FOR CUTTING THROUGH
MULTIPLE LAYERS OF PAPER MACHE.
- BLADE TYPE IS A PERSONAL
CHOICE OR TASK SPECIFIC, JUST
ENSURE THAT THE BLADE IS SHARP.

WITH A CLAY FORM YOU HAVE THE
ADVANTAGE THAT YOU CAN MAKE A
DEEPER CUT.

A DEPRESSION CAN BE CARVED
INTO THE FOAM TO ASSIST
THE HOLD.

Fig. 12e Cutting the papier mâché from the form.

Celastic Comedy and Tragedy masks, enhanced with Celluclay papier mâché pulp. The gold details were added in Cerne Relief outliner from Pebeo.

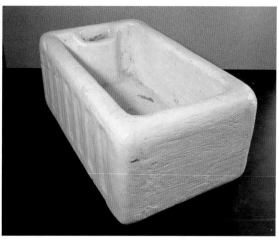

A Belfast-style sink made of scrimmed polystyrene with multiple layers of gesso, sanded and glazed.

Papier mâché pulp build-up with Celluclay on a scrimmed polystyrene base. It can be shaped and formed easily. When dry, it can be sanded, carved and drilled.

Ultimately it will come down to budget and application as to whether you use these or create your own from traditional recipes or improvise an alternative. It is not uncommon for cheap white emulsion to be used for priming canvasses, for example.

## MONKEY DUNG

Monkey dung is so called because of its texture and the fact that the most common colours used with it are the earthy pigments. Made up from paint, PVA and sawdust, it is an almost indestructible medium that can provide a variety of textured finishes from very smooth to very rough – all depending on how much you sieve the sawdust. It's great for producing tree bark and stone effects but can also be used for 'icing' prop cakes, such is its versatility. Other mediums can also be used to bind the sawdust to reduce its aggressive nature when used as a very coarse medium.

## FILLITE

Fillite was developed as an inexpensive bulking agent and filler for polyester resin castings, and in theatre has made its way into other products to create stone and cast-iron effects. It has the advantage of being lightweight but does not absorb the binding medium in the same way that sawdust, for example, does. Its pale-grey base colour can influence lighter colours that are mixed with it, but over-painting will generally remedy this minor inconvenience.

ABOVE LEFT AND RIGHT: Monkey dung texturing on cakes and topiary. Both the base icing and the detailed piping are achieved by using mixes of monkey dung. The texture on the topiary is given a coarser texture to give the impression of small leaves.

ABOVE LEFT: Paper rope is a valuable accessory for papier mâché, and is great for making rims, bases and handles for pots and jugs, cast iron detail and the like. It glues almost instantly when used with latex adhesive onto any other porous surface – especially other paper rope.

ABOVE RIGHT: A very simple papier mâché bowl moulded over an existing form and enhanced with paper rope.

Simeon the newspaper puppet. The designer was very keen that real newspaper was used, so this is newspaper glued onto calico. The hands are wire, paper rope and papier mâché with dowel control rods; the head a 'slush mould' latex casting, reinforced with glass fibres and coated with newspaper pieces; the ears paper rope; the hair sculpted from newspaper and Rosco FlexBond.

PSA62:10 ... TRUST NOT IN OPPRESSION, AND BECOME NOT VAIN IN ROBBERY: IF RICHES INCREASE, SET NOT YOUR HEART UPON THEM.

THE LORD SHALL FIGHT FOR YOU

SATISFIED AS WITH MARROW AND FATNESS; AND MY MOUTH SHALL PRAISE THEE WITH JOYFUL LIPS:

PSA63:6 WHEN I REMEMBER THEE UPON MY BED, AND MEDITATE ON THEE IN THE NIGHT WATCHES.

PSA63:7 BECAUSE THOU HAST BEEN MY HELP, THEREFORE IN THE SHADOW OF THY WINGS WILL I REJOICE.

PSA63:8 MY SOUL FOLLOWETH HARD AFTER THEE: THY RIGHT HAND UPHOLDETH ME.

PSA63:9 BUT THOSE THAT SEEK MY SOUL, TO DESTROY IT, SHALL GO INTO THE LOWER PARTS OF THE EARTH.

PSA64:10 ... GLAD IN THE LORD, AND SHALL TRUST IN HIM; AND ALL THE UPRIGHT IN HEART SHALL GLORY.

PSA65:1 PRAISE WAITETH FOR THEE, O GOD, IN SION: AND UNTO THEE SHALL THE VOW BE PERFORMED.

PSA65:2 O THOU THAT HEAREST PRAYER, UNTO THEE SHALL ALL FLESH COME.

PSA65:3 INIQUITIES PREVAIL AGAINST ME: AS FOR OUR TRANSGRESSIONS, THOU SHALT PURGE THEM AWAY.

PSA65:4 BLESSED IS THE MAN WHOM THOU CHOOSEST, AND CAUSEST TO APPROACH UNTO THEE, THAT HE MAY DWELL IN THY COURTS: WE SHALL BE SATISFIED WITH THE GOODNESS OF THY HOUSE, EVEN OF THY HOLY TEMPLE.

PSA65:5 BY TERRIBLE THINGS IN RIGHTEOUSNESS WILT THOU ANSWER US, O GOD

# 3
# CARD CONSTRUCTION

Card is not only an excellent medium for small- to medium-scale projects on a tight budget, but also lends itself to situations where more conventional materials, such as timber and steel, could prove to be too heavy or lack flexibility for the demands of the design. Of course, it is always possible to combine aspects of wood and steel construction for reinforcement, with card construction processes when using it for larger projects. When using card, there is always going to be a concern with regard to fire and combustibility. Thankfully there are a variety of fire-retardant products that can either be painted or sprayed on to significantly reduce the risk.

Card can be used to produce a variety of structures from the refined to the quirky. Projects using card construction processes are generally very durable and cost-effective. The processes can be used in conjunction with a wide variety of dressing materials, from papier mâché to poor man's fibreglass and GRP. It can also be used in concert with polystyrene and expanding foams. Once again, the limit is your imagination and creativity.

Astrolabe detail on Merlin's staff made for *The Knight before Christmas*, which was constructed around a steel 'pin' that had been inserted into the top of the ramin dowel cane. Laminated card rings were made up from modelling card with Araldite and then glued to the pin and each other with more Araldite – quick, inexpensive and effective.

OPPOSITE: King James set-dressing bible for *The Crucible*. As well as using a partial cardboard tube for the spine of the book, card has also been used to shape the page binding of the open book and the curve of the pages as they flow out from the spine to the boards (covers) of the book.

## CONSTRUCTION METHODS

### Card Choice

As with papier mâché, there are many different types and thicknesses of material that can be used. Your choice of materials will come down to what is most suitable for the project that you are undertaking – for example, if you were making a delicate snuffbox, it would probably not suit the task if you were to use a thick-walled corrugated cardboard. Conversely, if you were making a pot-bellied stove, thin craft card would be unlikely to be suitable unless it were for a doll's house. Avoid waxed and glossy cards as these will not absorb the glue.

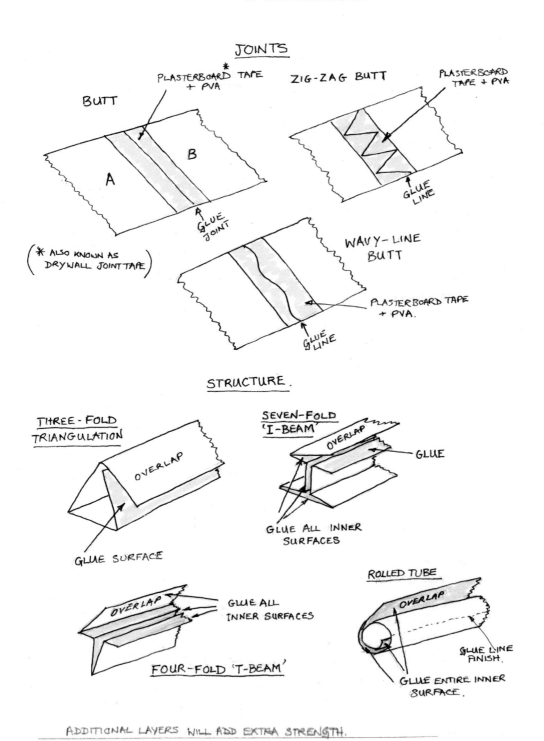

## JOINTS

**BUTT**

PLASTERBOARD TAPE * + PVA

A

B

A

GLUE JOINT

( * ALSO KNOWN AS DRYWALL JOINT TAPE )

**ZIG-ZAG BUTT**

PLASTERBOARD TAPE + PVA

GLUE LINE

**WAVY-LINE BUTT**

PLASTERBOARD TAPE + PVA.

GLUE LINE

## STRUCTURE.

**THREE-FOLD TRIANGULATION**

OVERLAP

GLUE SURFACE

**SEVEN-FOLD 'I-BEAM'**

OVERLAP

GLUE

GLUE ALL INNER SURFACES

OVERLAP

GLUE ALL INNER SURFACES

**FOUR-FOLD 'T-BEAM'**

**ROLLED TUBE**

OVERLAP

GLUE LINE FINISH.

GLUE ENTIRE INNER SURFACE.

ADDITIONAL LAYERS WILL ADD EXTRA STRENGTH.

Fig. 13 Card construction – joints and structure.

## THINGS TO CONSIDER WHEN CONSTRUCTING WITH CARD

**Structure** When using card construction, we need to think in terms of structural support, as screws and bolts are going to be of limited use to us here and could even compromise the integrity of the structure that they are trying to support. If you attempt to stand a piece of card on end and let go, it will fall over. If you take that same piece of card and fold it in half, then open it out to a 90-degree angle and stand it on end again, it should support itself and become free-standing.

If you take that same folded piece of card and place it face down on the table with the creased spine upward and the two outer edges touching the table-top, and then push down on the spine with one finger, the spine will move down, and the edges will spread outwards. To prevent this happening, take some Sellotape or masking tape and tape across the open gap between the two free edges three or four times up the length of the card. When you try pushing down on the spine of the card now, you will find that the card will be prevented from spreading and, depending on how thick your card is, only flex where there is no tape preventing it from doing so. We are using 'triangulation' and angles here to provide structure in the simplest of ways. These are only two of many structural techniques that can be used to make our card structures durable. Others include circular tubes, triangular reinforced tubes, tube-reinforced triangles, honeycomb structures, triangulated squares, I beams and T beams.

**Adhesives and glue application** There is a bewildering array of adhesives that we could use for card construction, and for prop making in general, but some are more suitable than others. There are paper glues, either the twist-out stick variety, such as Pritt Stick and Gloy, or liquid types (although most of these are PVA-based); PVA wood glues, like Resin 168; hot- and cool-melt glues; fast-set glues like superglue; polystyrene cements manufactured by Revell and Humbrol; epoxy glue systems, such as those manufactured by Araldite; natural rubber (latex) adhesives such as Copydex or Flints…dex; synthetic rubber contact and impact adhesives, such as those manufactured by Evo-Stik; and polyurethane contact adhesives such as those produced by Bostik, to give examples of but a few. This list demonstrates that there are diverse types of adhesive that are used for hobby, DIY and construction, some of which are ready to go, and some require either mixing or additional pieces of equipment to use. So, what do you use? Keep it simple. We want a strong, affordable, reliable, rigid adhesive that provides a good working time and a reasonable drying time. Answer: wood glue/PVA – of a decent quality.

## CARD BRIDGE TASK

Build a bridge span that will support at least 1kg (2lb) of weight when it is placed to span between two robust supports (such as paint tins, upside-down buckets or stools). Your construction materials are PVA glue and thin A4 craft card (which is about twice the thickness of standard printer paper). Use as few pieces of card as you can to achieve the support of the maximum weight possible using just glue and card: it should not be necessary to cut the card – just fold, roll and laminate. The 'road surface' should be unimpeded to allow a free flow of 'traffic', and the bridge width should not exceed 10cm (4in). There should be no more than 5cm (2in) of each end of the road surface resting on the supports when you test the weight limit. And, finally, there should be no structure coming from the underside of the bridge to the floor.

You can of course plan this challenge out, research bridge construction, get an engineering degree… But this is simply a task to demonstrate the suitability of the product and the processes that can be employed. By the way, it doesn't require anything architecturally fancy, but feel free to 'dress' it. On completion, you should find that it will hold far more than 1kg, with correct application of technique and if it is permitted to dry fully.

As a rule, card construction is used as a relatively inexpensive, lightweight structural process to acquire shape and form, over which we will then apply additional products like papier mâché, texture mediums, scrims, expanding foams, resin processes and so on to refine that form prior to any finishing techniques. Below are the basic tools that you will need.

## Materials
- PVA glue (neat)
- Cardboard appropriate to the job in hand (this can be a variety of cards for various aspects of the same job)
- Plasterboard reinforcing joint tape (paper variety), or strips of thin card 5cm (2in) wide
- Roll of 25mm (1in) masking tape

## Equipment
- 12mm (½in) and 25mm (1in) brushes
- Pot to put the glue in or a bottle of PVA that can be refilled when empty
- Latex or vinyl gloves
- Polythene to protect work area
- Utility knife for cutting the card and/or general work scissors
- Cutting board to protect your work surface
- Straight edge to assist with straight cuts when using the utility knife

## Lamination

Lamination, as mentioned with layered papier mâché, is a process whereby you increase strength by binding layers of glue and (in this case) card together until you have achieved either the desired thickness or durability or both. If you have tried out the bridge task and used lamination for your road surface, you will observe that not only does the process increase thickness, but also reduces the flexibility with each layer that is applied and permitted to dry. Lamination is not limited to flat surfaces either, as can be seen if you look at moulded pieces of furniture and construction

**WASTE NOT, WANT NOT**

Try not to be wasteful. A 500ml bottle of PVA bought from a supplier can be refilled again and again from your bulk stock – and it is advisable to have at least 5ltr of PVA in stock as it is the most commonly used adhesive. A 500ml bottle is a very convenient size to hold and is well suited for running a line of glue down the edges of your workpieces in a controlled manner prior to bonding together.

**STRAIGHT EDGES AND RULERS**

There is a difference between a straight edge and a ruler. It is true that some rulers will have straight edge attachments, and that some are made entirely from materials that make them suitable for being used as a straight edge (such as steel rules). However, rulers made from wood, plastic or aluminium (unless with specific attachments/reinforcement) are not suitable for running blades or metal scribers against as they will soon become anything but straight. An actual straight edge does not have any markings as it is simply a tool for being able to mark or cut a reliable straight line between two points, or a series of points that have previously been made by a measuring device – a ruler.

Straight edges can be made from a variety of materials, but ones used for cutting or inscribing along the edge are usually made from steel, sprung steel or anodized aluminium. The very simple purpose of a straight edge is to prevent damage occurring to your precision measuring device (your ruler) by having a tool that is suited to the job. Straight edges are generally longer than rulers, ranging in length from 30cm (1ft) up to 5m (16ft). A 5m straight edge made from sprung steel can be rolled up to about 30cm in diameter, pegged to itself and hung up out of the way for future use.

processes for roof beams. As soon as you combine curves and corners with your lamination, the strength aspect increases exponentially. This is the principle behind plywood (bendy ply aside). In the case of plywood, the laminated layers are

This prop was a modification of a flatbed Action Man/GI Joe lorry that was converted into a 1:18 scale replica of the set piece for the play *Madame Macadam's Travelling Theatre Company*. The conversion involved careful removal of all items save for the chassis cab and wheels. The rear of the truck and above-cab platform were constructed from laminated layers of thin corrugated card, recycled from a prior delivery, and bonded together with PVA. A paint effect was then applied to match that of the actual set piece. In this case, it was a lot quicker to modify than to make from scratch – the time taken to make this prop was approximately 2–3 hours.

applied with the grain of each layered piece being laid at 90 degrees to the previous layer, creating a cross-ply effect that is resistant to flexion. The effect of grain is not something that we need overly concern ourselves with when working with cardboard. However, it could be employed to strategic effect when working with corrugated cardboard for larger constructions where greater rigidity may be required.

## Butt and Overlap Joints

Two pieces of card can be joined together in a variety of ways, depending on what we are attempting to achieve. The two simplest methods are the butt and overlap joints, which can be used together when laminating, or independently when working on the form of an object.

### Butt Joint

To make a butt joint, make sure the two edges to be joined are straight. Apply your PVA to one edge, align it with the other piece of card and push them together – this is called butting. The joint can be held together with masking tape prior to applying an 25mm-wide (1in) layer of glue to either side of the join and then running a strip of plasterboard reinforcing joint tape over the glued joint and smoothing it down. If you want to avoid the risk of the card creasing as you move it, overlap the card by a reasonable amount – 12–100mm (½–4in), depending on how big your pieces of card are – and mark a zigzag cut line along the length of the joint, with the pieces still overlapped, and cut along the line. What you should have when you separate the two pieces of card, apart from some jagged offcuts, is two edges that look like regular, fanged monster teeth that interlock perfectly.

Glue the zigzagged edge and then apply glue and plasterboard tape to the join. This makes the joint less likely to fold when dry because you have increased its surface area, extending it either side of

Turkish delight box made to a specific design for a production of *The Lion, the Witch and the Wardrobe*. Modelling card was flexed over a rounded table edge to form the smooth curves for the sides of the lid and box. These were butt jointed and then had a second layer of card laminated on, off-set so that the butt joints on each layer were at opposite sides to each other.

The Turkish delight box illuminated. Being an enchanted box of Turkish delight, it required internal lighting, which was a simple matter of a small but bright battery-operated light source reflecting off the gilded interior onto the actor's face.

the original line. A similar effect can be achieved with a regular wavy line, for those with a monster phobia, but either will do the trick.

### OVERLAP JOINT

To make an overlap (or lap) joint, simply apply glue to a strip 12–100mm wide (½–4in) along one edge of the pieces of card to be joined together, and then lay the other piece on top to the required overlap and press together. Apply a suitable amount of weight until the join has dried. Glue and plasterboard tape can be used to apply additional strength to the join.

As mentioned above, a variation of these two joining methods can be used together when laminating if you apply the 'brick-laying' approach where your bottom layer of bricks (or in our case, card) is half overlapped, either side of each join, by the bricks (card) in the next layer up. This will create a very ridged lamination, as the butting and overlapping reduce risk of buckling.

## Corners and Triangulation

There are several ways we can create corners or triangular supports. On thinner cards, we can use a straight edge to help us create a crisp fold to make a simple corner, or three equally spaced creases that will allow for an overlap to create a triangular section.

For thicker and tougher cards, it will be necessary, once again using a straight edge, to score a line with a work knife (Stanley or the like) at the point to be folded, to no more than half the depth of the card. Turn the card over and, using the straight edge along the reverse side to the scored line, bend the card against the straight edge to the desired angle, forming a neat crease.

The same process can be used for triangulation, but make sure that you perform all scoring activity on the same side before turning the card over and creasing. It is very easy to get carried away and score and fold as you go, but this can lead to you forgetting to turn the card back and scoring the wrong side… which can be a little frustrating!

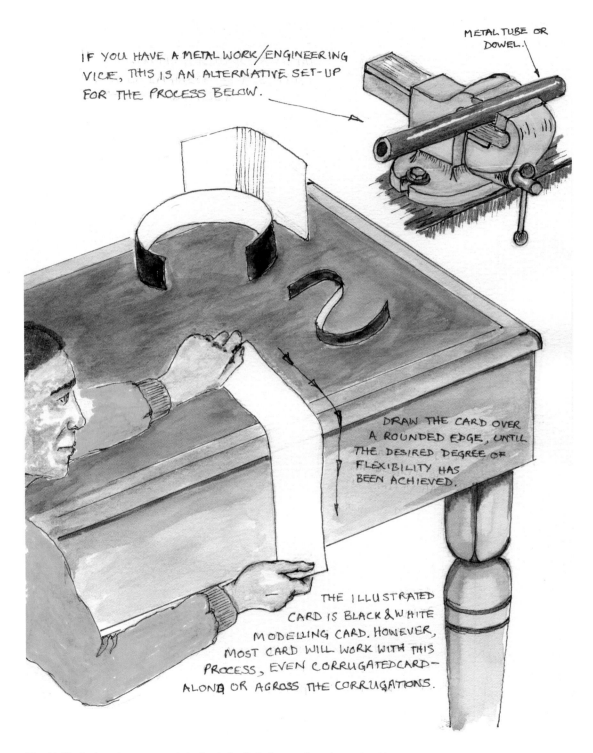

IF YOU HAVE A METAL WORK/ENGINEERING VICE, THIS IS AN ALTERNATIVE SET-UP FOR THE PROCESS BELOW.

METAL TUBE OR DOWEL.

DRAW THE CARD OVER A ROUNDED EDGE, UNTIL THE DESIRED DEGREE OF FLEXIBILITY HAS BEEN ACHIEVED.

THE ILLUSTRATED CARD IS BLACK & WHITE MODELLING CARD. HOWEVER, MOST CARD WILL WORK WITH THIS PROCESS, EVEN CORRUGATED CARD — ALONG OR AGROSS THE CORRUGATIONS.

Fig. 14 'Flexing' card over a rounded edge to facilitate the creation of even curves.

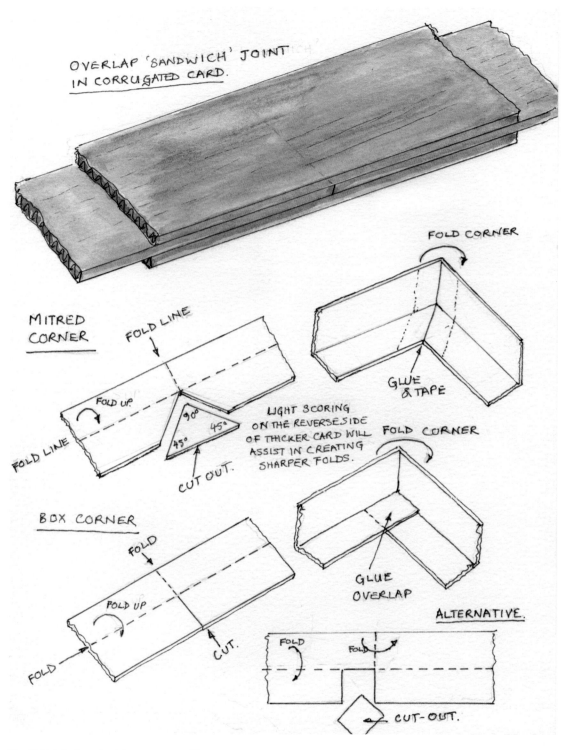

OVERLAP 'SANDWICH' JOINT IN CORRUGATED CARD.

FOLD CORNER

MITRED CORNER

FOLD LINE

FOLD UP.

FOLD LINE

90°

45° 45°

CUT OUT.

GLUE & TAPE

LIGHT SCORING ON THE REVERSE SIDE OF THICKER CARD WILL ASSIST IN CREATING SHARPER FOLDS.

FOLD CORNER

BOX CORNER

FOLD

FOLD UP

FOLD

CUT.

GLUE OVERLAP

ALTERNATIVE.

FOLD  FOLD

CUT-OUT.

Fig. 15 Detail of overlap joins, corners and box corners.

## T and I Beams and Tubes

There are many shapes and reinforcements that we can create to add strength to our structures, and they can be very simply made by cutting, folding or rolling card into the required shapes and applying PVA to glue them into shape, reinforced with plasterboard tape/thin card strips. We need not get too carried away with intricately scaffolded constructions that could take many hours to build. Part of our card construction arsenal is the sheets of card and boxes that we have available to us. For example, to build a rock structure or an enclosed altar can be achieved relatively simply with either sheet materials or boxes. If either has to be sat or stood upon, then we could add a minimal timber sub-structure, either throughout the object or at strategic points, depending on production requirements.

The point is that we can use similar construction techniques for card as for sheet materials like plywood, chipboard and MDF. The difference is that it is a lot easier to cut, shape and fix cardboard and, furthermore, we can bend it and fold it, glue it, tape it and clamp it. We can create or use pre-existing box structures. We can use existing cardboard tubes of assorted sizes to assist with shape and form, either in lengths or small sections, cut straight or at angles. We can use butt joints, lap joints, and edge half-lap joints (*see* below) to join across the card sheets (the same principle is used to separate and protect glass bottles in cardboard boxes) to create inter-connected forms. We can cut and shape the card over pre-existing or custom forms, tapping it into shape, knowing that the lamination process will make it all the stronger.

## Free Form Card Construction

This takes a little practice and a certain amount of pre-planning by sketching out how you will convert the design into card shapes. It's easiest to use a series of discs, profiles, ribs and strainers for the sub-structure.

## Task – Make a Rugby Ball

The task is to make a rugby ball or American football shape with card construction principles using a standard modelling card or other card 1–2mm thick. There are several ways in which you can go about this. The method given below is for two ball profiles and fourteen half discs. You could also opt for one full ball profile and seven half-lapped discs to make up the main shape, with two half-ball profiles that are half-lapped into the discs, to either side and at 90 degrees to the original full ball profile.

1. Accurately mark and cut two lengthwise ball profiles with centre lines running from tip to tip and from the mid-point of those lines to the outer edges, forming a right-angled cross on each profile. You will edge half-lap joint these later. (To help you visualize this, hold your hands up in front of you, fingers pointing toward each other, palms toward you. Make a gap between your middle fingers on each hand. Turn your right hand towards yourself through 90 degrees until the palm of that hand is facing the

This crown was made free form from a design sketch for a production that required an antler crown as an incidental item. Although there were several routes that could have been taken to achieve the end required, with a low budget and a short time frame, card construction was chosen, with a dressing of papier mâché pulp.

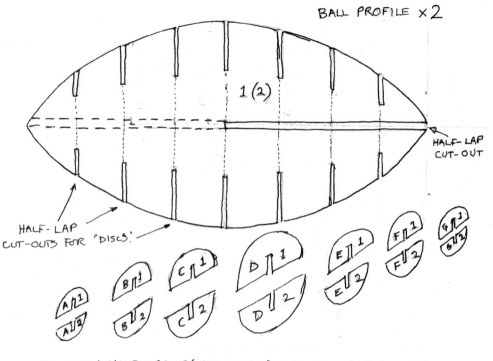

BALL PROFILE × 2

1 (2)

HALF- LAP
CUT-OUT

HALF- LAP
CUT-OUTS FOR 'DISCS'.

FOURTEEN HALF-CIRCLES (NOT TO SCALE), WITH HALF-LAP CUT-OUTS.

ALTERNATE CONSTRUCTION METHOD

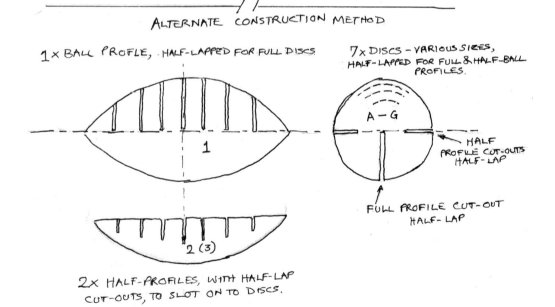

1 × BALL PROFILE, HALF-LAPPED FOR FULL DISCS.

7 × DISCS - VARIOUS SIZES,
HALF-LAPPED FOR FULL & HALF-BALL
PROFILES.

1

A - G

HALF
PROFILE CUT-OUTS
HALF- LAP

2 (3)

FULL PROFILE CUT-OUT
HALF- LAP

2× HALF-PROFILES, WITH HALF-LAP
CUT-OUTS, TO SLOT ON TO DISCS.

Fig. 16 American football mark-out.

floor. Move your hands toward each other into the gaps that you made between your fingers, until they are prevented from moving any further. Notice that your fingers are now positioned over the back and palms of each hand. This is the principle that you will be employing with your edge half-lap joints).

2. Using your ball-shaped profiles, you will now mark out the position of the supporting ribs. Divide the overall length into seven equal sections. An effortless way of doing this is to take a strip of paper that is the length of your ball profile and fold it in half so that it is now half as long and form a nice sharp crease. Fold the folded paper in half again and sharply crease and then repeat the process once more. Unfold your strip of paper and you will see seven evenly spaced creases. You can now use this improvised custom ruler as is or transcribe the divisions onto a piece of stiff card to make it more durable. This ruler can now be used to make the incremental markings onto your ball-shaped pieces of card along the centre line, working from the mid-point of this line out to either end. Once done, mark perpendicular lines from the centre line to the outer edges of the profile.

3. Measure from the centre line to the outer edge of the ball profile along each of the seven lines that you have marked in; these measurements are the radii of the discs that you will mark and cut to form the ribs that will provide the round profile when the construction is looked at end on. To avoid confusion, allocate and mark a number or letter to each of the lines that you have measured as well as the measurement taken for the radius of each disc. This gives you something to refer to later.

4. Using a compass adjusted to the radius of each of your discs, mark each of them out on the same thickness of card as the ball profile. Through the centre point indicated by the point of your compass, draw a straight line, using a ruler or straight edge, to the opposite edges of your circle. Mark another line at 90 degrees to the first, again going through the centre point, using a set square. On the first line that you have marked from edge to edge, mark a point either side of the centre mark, exactly half-way between it and the outer edge.

5. Place the point of the compass on one of the newly marked points and the pencil/pen point on the other mark, and inscribe an arc that passes out and beyond the second, perpendicular, centre line. Swap the compass around so that tip and pencil/pen point are on the opposite marks and repeat the process to inscribe a second arc, creating two crossover points in each hemisphere of the circle.

6. Place your ruler/straight edge so that it runs through the points at which the two arcs meet. Draw a line through these arcs from the outer edge of the circle to the opposite edge, which will pass though the centre point of the first line at 90 degrees to it. As you mark each disc, and before cutting them out, apply the relevant reference mark and measurement to it…twice (along each side of the centre line).

7. Either side of the centre line, mark another line that is half the thickness of the card you are using for the ball profile.

8. Cut out each disc as precisely as possible, with a tool/tools suited to the thickness of the card that you are cutting.

9. Cut along the card thickness lines that you added on each side of the centre line. You should be left with two distinct halves, and a thin strip that represents the thickness of the ball profile card – this can be put to one side or discarded.

10. To mark the edge lap joints, select one of the ball profile pieces and measure down each divide line from the outer edge to a point that is halfway between the outer edge and the centre line, minus half the thickness of the ball profile card. Either side of each of the divide lines, from the outer edge of the ball profile to the previously marked point on the lines, mark parallel lines that are half the card thickness away from the divide line. Repeat on the opposite side of the ball profile. There is no need to repeat this on the second ball profile.

11. Taking all the half circles, measure up the centre divide line from the flat edge to a point that is halfway between the flat edge and the outer edge, making no allowance for the thickness of the ball profile card as you have already accounted for this. Either side of each of the lines, from the flat

## PAPER ROPE

There is a very useful product called paper rope, which is exactly what it says: a rope made from a pale-grey tissue paper that is compressed together along its length and bound externally with a cotton mesh sheath. Paper rope comes in thicknesses from ¼in (6mm) to 2in (55mm), at ¼in intervals up to 1in (25mm) and then two further thicknesses of 1½in (40mm) and 2in (55mm); it is sold by the metre or by the coil. You can also purchase wired versions of it.

Paper rope can be used for any number of projects and materials and works particularly well with card construction and papier mâché and wire frames – in fact, with any project that needs that extra bit of shape or bulk. In theatre it has been used for years to create decorative mouldings on sets and arboreal plant effects, but it can also be used in costume props and for prototyping ideas for these, due to its relatively low cost. Originally created for use in GRP work, where it is used to provide reinforcing ribs to large projects when glassed over, it has become a staple product of the prop maker due to its versatility and absorption properties. You can even use offcuts to make an improvised papier mâché pulp once you remove the cotton sheath.

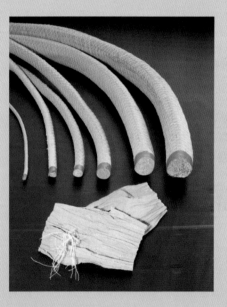

ABOVE LEFT: A very handy and inexpensive product, paper rope is sold by the metre or the roll. The rolls range in length from 200m for the 6.5mm (¼in) diameter, to 25m for the 55mm (2in) diameter.

ABOVE RIGHT: Paper rope sizes and sample breakdown. From the smallest diameter on the left of the picture: 6.5mm (¼in), 13.8mm (½in), 18mm (¾in), 25.5mm (1in), 40mm (1½in) and 55mm (2in). In the foreground is a section of paper rope that has had the cotton sheath removed and then been opened out, revealing a buff tissue-like paper that can be moulded and formed with water or glue.

edge to the marked point that you have just made, mark parallel lines that are half the card thickness away from the divide line.

12. On each of the ball profiles, mark a parallel line from one of the tips of the ball profile, either side of the centre line, that is half the card thickness away

from it. Draw these lines to the centre point of the of the ball profile and no further.

13. With a sharp knife, cut between the previously marked lines of all the pieces of card, removing the thin strips that are created. Make sure that you do not cut away any more card than you have marked.

14. Slide the two ball profiles onto each other via the half-lap cutaways. Looking end on at the joined pieces, you should see a regular cross or 'X' profile.

15. Paying attention to your markings for each piece's position, slide each of the card halves into the previously cut slots on the outer edges of the ball profile so that the flat edge of the semi-circles line-up with the pencil marks on the uncut ball profile. Use small pieces of masking tape to fix the pieces into position as you work. Your construction should now be looking like a skeleton ball.

16. Carefully apply PVA and tape to each of the joints and allow to dry.

17. At this point you have many options available to you, regarding how you progress from here. You could:

- Tightly pack between the semicircle ribs and the ball profile pieces with screwed-up newspaper, and then papier mâché over the whole thing
- Cut thin strips of shaped card and glue them along the outer surface of the structure from end to end, like planking, and then apply a few layers of papier mâché over this
- Cut pieces of polystyrene to fit into the gaps, glue them into position and then shape and sand them to the profiles of the ball, finishing off with either papier mâché or scrim.

Further options include expanding foams, fabric and glue or GRP top coats, soft foams and latex scrimming. It all depends on the brief and what you need to achieve.

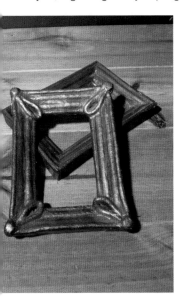

ABOVE LEFT: Picture frames made using card construction with modelling card to form an open-backed box structure. Paper rope was used to provide the internal detail and dressing (the ball corners on the top frame being made from shredded paper rope rolled into balls using PVA to bind them). Layered papier mâché was then applied over the whole structure (the larger the frame, the more layers – three layers were used here), topped by layers of gesso, which were sanded once dry, then the finished frame was base coated and dry brushed.

ABOVE MIDDLE: Everyday household objects and hardware can be incorporated into prop making, as seen here with a standard ballcock. In this instance card construction and papier mâché pulp have been used to create the base form over the ballcock. The card can be glued to itself with PVA but gluing it to plastic is best achieved with Araldite/epoxy resin glue.

ABOVE RIGHT: Jam tarts, anyone? Three layers of thin card were cut into discs, the edges snipped and laminated into a pie case shape. Rings of paper rope were added. Two discs of corrugated card glued into the middle of the tart were the 'jam'. Papier mâché was applied to the whole thing, with further papier mâché pulp crimping detail added around the pie top when dry. The completed tart can be finished as desired.

# 4
# FRAMES, CANES AND WILLOWS

## WIRE FRAMES

Wire frame construction processes are a natural progression from card construction. The main difference is that the result is a largely hollow structure, although it can be filled. The wire being referred to here is single-strand galvanized wire, which comes in a variety of thicknesses, or gauges. What we can create with wire is not limited by any real physical dimensions, like sheet materials. Wire can be bent into any shape that we require and through any angle. We can coil it, twist it, create smooth curves, sharp corners, zigzags and all sorts of wonderful shapes. In truth, with such simple methods as using hoops and ties and joining them at specific points, we can create any shape that we need to as a stable structure.

Single-strand galvanized wire and masking tape.

OPPOSITE: Large pear and pumpkin made from wire frame.

A more modern take on the wire frame idea is computer modelling, most notably, from our point of view, in film, television and computer games to create imaginary characters and worlds, but also in architecture. Although there is no actual wire used, the principle is the same – a series of lines and curves connected by nodes to create a bigger, more stable shape – and is known as 'wire frame polygons'.

The thickness of the single-strand galvanized wire required will very much depend on the size of the project that you are to undertake. However, a good general stock size is 1.6mm. The galvanized aspect protects it from rusting, and the single strand means exactly that – this is one piece of wire wound up into a spool. It is also very cost-effective, as you can get a 31.6m spool for under £3. The 1.6mm is suitable for small and medium-sized projects, as it has sufficient rigidity that it can support itself well enough without being accidently bent out of shape, is easy enough to shape, either with the fingers or with pliers, and it can of course be combined with either thicker or thinner wires for flexibility in working. If, however you are working on larger projects then either a 2mm, 2.5mm or a 3.15mm may be more appropriate, although they take a little more effort, and tools, to manipulate.

### Joining and Fixing

There are various ways to join and fix the wires.

#### MASKING TAPE

Half-inch (12mm) masking tape is a very quick fixing method for single-strand wire and it works particularly well with 1.6mm. Masking tape may seem like an unlikely fixing medium for wire frames, but it is amazingly robust when used as a binding material with wire. You should also keep in mind that, when binding at all of the nodal points, each wrapping of tape adds strength to the previous and subsequent wrapping. Longevity of the tape fixing is generally not a consideration, as the whole thing is going to be covered in products that give further strength and permanence to the object.

### STRING AND GLUE

String and glue can also be used to bind the wire, and if you use a glue like Rosco FlexBond you will end up with a very secure join, although make sure that you use a natural, non-synthetic string or twine like Coats Barbour 3-cord linen upholstery and mattress twine (thicker twines can be used for the thicker wires). There isn't any knot-tying with this process – just apply glue and wind the cord around tightly, add a little more glue, rub it in (with gloved fingers) and it's done. This is the same process that is used with flexible canes.

### THIN WIRE AND GLUE

Thinner wire can be used to bond around the thicker wires; anything up to 1.25mm diameter is suitable, as these are very easy to bend in small, tight coils. By applying a layer of something like FlexBond over the top after binding, you can prevent slippage once the glue has dried, though this takes longer because the glue is not being absorbed by the binding. You can, of course, use epoxy glues over the wire but this can prove expensive, and is best done after the structure is finished or at key points so that you are gluing several joints and are not constantly having to stop and mix the glue for each one.

### THIN WIRE

If using thin wires for intricate shapes, you can use them to twist and bind what you are making as you go. It is not recommended to use wire that is over 1.25mm diameter for binding, as it is very difficult to get the binding tight enough with thicker wires and it starts to look too cumbersome; and it is not worth the trouble when there are other, easier, fixing methods. You can use thinner wires to bind thicker wires and steel rod, but the binding must be tight and even, and this is not a technique suited to load-bearing structures, where welding is the norm.

## Ties, Hoops and Strainers

There are a few approaches that we can use to create wire-frame objects, but they are all basically just variations upon a theme and follow the same principle that we applied to achieve the ball challenge when looking at card construction. What we are concerned with is shape and form, and that can be broken down into profile and bulk (as with the ball profiles and the card half-circles, for bulk). With wire-frame construction it can be very useful to use pencil and paper to plan what you are making, with each stroke of the pencil on the paper representing a length of wire.

We can refer to the elements of wire-frame construction as 'hoops, ties and strainers'. The hoops provide the bulk of the object, and are attached to the ties, which make up the height/length of the object and provide the perceived profile/shape. Strainers are employed to lend additional cross support (diagonally), reducing flex in the structure.

Pigeon made of wire frame with latex and calico skin.

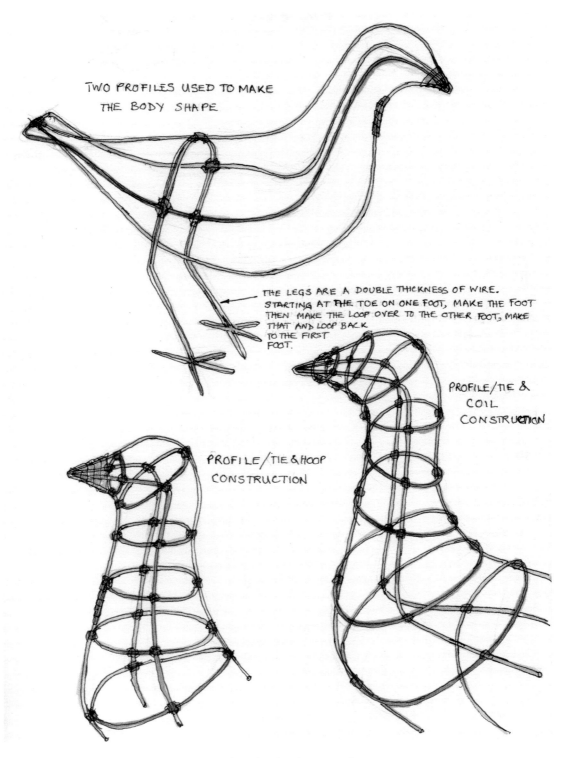

TWO PROFILES USED TO MAKE
THE BODY SHAPE

THE LEGS ARE A DOUBLE THICKNESS OF WIRE.
STARTING AT THE TOE ON ONE FOOT, MAKE THE FOOT
THEN MAKE THE LOOP OVER TO THE OTHER FOOT, MAKE
THAT AND LOOP BACK
TO THE FIRST
FOOT.

PROFILE/TIE &
COIL
CONSTRUCTION

PROFILE/TIE & HOOP
CONSTRUCTION

Fig. 17 Pigeon line mark-out showing frame layout based on the photo opposite.

## TIES

Ties can be simple lengths of wire that join the hoops together, or they can be more intricate shapes that can provide top and side elevations of the profiles required to make the shape. If, for example, you were to create a bird as a wire frame, at least two ties would be required: one to create the look of the bird from the side, and one to create the look from above/below. These two wire shapes would be simple representations of a bird, looked at from two angles, from beak to tail. The two forms/ties would be fixed together, one slotted into the other, where they meet at either end. Hoops would then be used to fill out the bulk of these two sets of ties, from head to tail of the form.

## HOOPS

Hoops can simply be that – regular rings of wire – or they can imbue a sense of shape and profile themselves, where an object might have corners, additional curves or integral protrusions. A variation on hoops is to use a coil or coils of wire that wrap around the profile pieces in a continuous spiral, adjusting to the parameters of the profiles as you go, working from one end to the other to create the bulk look of the object (as with the wire frame pigeon shown in Fig. 17). This is a quicker way of creating the shape of simpler forms, and you can add more structure by adding a second coil, starting from the opposite side and coiling the wire in the opposite direction to the first, creating a diagonal-mesh look. This can be taped at strategic points of crossover with the previous coil and the strainers.

## STRAINERS

A strainer is a little like a tie, although its primary purpose is to give added structural integrity by preventing the object from twisting or distorting. A strainer is generally applied diagonally across a structure (top to bottom), with multiple strainers being used to counter opposing forces at strategic points to either side, or around the object. Not all objects will require strainers, but they can be very useful in larger structures, where they can aid in producing a very robust result.

Wire-frame bowls – start and finish.

## L Bends

The L bend is the method used for securely fixing the unattached end of a tie to a hoop on objects that have openings, such as, mugs, jugs, vases, and open-mouth shapes on masks and puppets, to name but a few possibilities. Bending the loose end of a strainer into an L shape provides a larger contact area for the tape to do its work. Without this, the joint would lack stability and the strainer would be at risk of pulling free from the tape and the hoop. The 'foot' of L bends will also vary in length depending on the size of the object that you are making, being shorter for smaller objects and larger for bigger objects; practice should make this more apparent.

When using thicker wire to create your structures, thicker masking tape (18mm/¾in or 25mm/1in) will need to be used, or even twine and glue.

## Wire-Frame Construction

### Materials

- Paper for drawing
- 1.6mm single-strand galvanized wire
- 12mm (½in) masking tape

**WIRE-FRAME TASK**

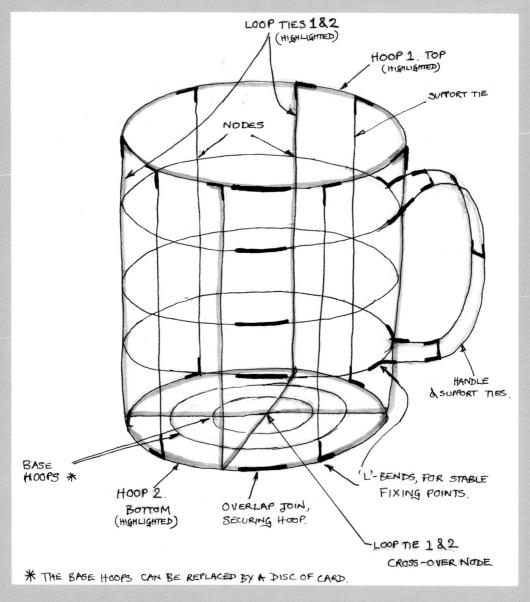

Fig. 18 Mug – line drawing of the wire frame.

Have a close look at a household object: a bowl, vase, mug, lamp base, for example. Try to envisage how you could make it using single-strand wire. Draw a 3D representation of the object on a sheet of paper and then start to draw your wire framework onto it. For now, think in terms of hoops/bulk and ties/uprights. The ties/uprights run from top to bottom of the object, across the bottom and back up to the top on the opposite side, and represent the profile – the visual shape of the object as a simple line drawing. For now, we only need to think about drawing two ties (profile pieces) for the object, but we will add more into the actual structure as it progresses. The hoops stack horizontally from the bottom to

*Continued overleaf*

**WIRE-FRAME TASK** *continued*

the top of the structure, within the ties at about 18mm (¾in) to 25mm (1in) intervals, and represent the variations (or not) in diameter/bulk of the object.

When your drawing is finished it should look like a framework representation of the original. We can, of course, add further structural elements to our drawing, but that can be done later. Handles and so on are additional pieces that can be represented on the drawing but are added independently of the hoops and strainers. Remember: each line represents a piece of wire. This process can be used for pretty much any object.

These hoops or coils are taped to the wire profiles that are a '1D' representation of the shape of the object. We normally start with two wire profiles and slot one into the other and secure with cross-taping where they meet at top and bottom of the framework. (Remember, this is the same principle as for the rugby ball task, just using a different material and process.)

Having done a rough sketch, it is now possible to take this and determine what size you want your object to be. Will it be larger, smaller or the same size as the original object? If it is staying the same size, you could take the construction measurements from the object itself and mark these onto your sketch, or simply use the object to determine your measurements. If it is going to be larger or smaller, you would be best served by creating a scale drawing of the object using a scale rule or a ruler.

The simplest way to make regular hoops is to wrap the wire around a handy cylindrical shape, like a paint pot, bucket or rolling pin (depending on the size of hoop required), allowing for an appropriate overlap on either end. The amount of overlap is very much dependent on the size of the hoop being made: starting at 12mm (½in) overlap for rings smaller than 75mm (3in) in diameter; increasing to 25–38mm (1–1½in) for ring sizes up to 20cm (8in) diameter; while rings of 60–90cm (using thicker wire) require overlaps of 15–20cm (6–8in). The aim of the overlapping wire is to minimize the risk of the hoops coming apart and eliminate any flexing at the joint.

## SCALE AND SCALE RULERS

A scale rule is a special ruler that allows you to render working drawings accurately to a scaled-down size that you can comfortably fit onto the paper that you are working on, and to a size that enables you to more easily visualize the whole project. For example, if you were making something that had a basic profile of 200cm (78¾in) × 150cm (59¹/₁₆in), and you wanted to draw this out onto a sheet of A4 paper, then a scale of 1:10 (one-tenth of the size of the actual object) would provide a drawing that would comfortably fill the page, leaving room for measurements and a title, but not much more. If you wished to represent front, side and top elevations on the same piece of paper, then a scale or 1:20 (one-twentieth the size of the actual object) would be more appropriate, unless you did these on separate pieces of A4. You can of course use larger scales on larger pieces of paper, or smaller scales on smaller pieces of paper, or even larger-scale 'detail' inserts of specific details of your working drawings

To use a ruler to create a scale drawing is simply a question of determining what the measurements on the ruler are going to represent. For example, if 10mm = 10cm, then 100mm (10cm) on the ruler = 1m (1,000mm); if 5mm = 10cm, then 100mm (10cm) on the ruler = 2m (2,000mm) and so on.

Using imperial measurements is a little more fiddly because there is not a direct correlation between the increments that make up an inch and those that make up a foot. An imperial scale rule resolves this issue; failing that, we can use generalized terms and then busk it. For example, if ½in = 1in on the ruler, 6in = 12ft (144in); if ⅛in = 6in, 4in = 16ft (192in).

We can also reverse the process to make smaller items bigger; so, for example, if 5cm (2in) = 10cm (4in), something that is 5cm tall will be visualized and drawn up as 10cm tall. We have effectively doubled the size of the object, either to make it easier to draw or because we literally want something that is twice the size of the original.

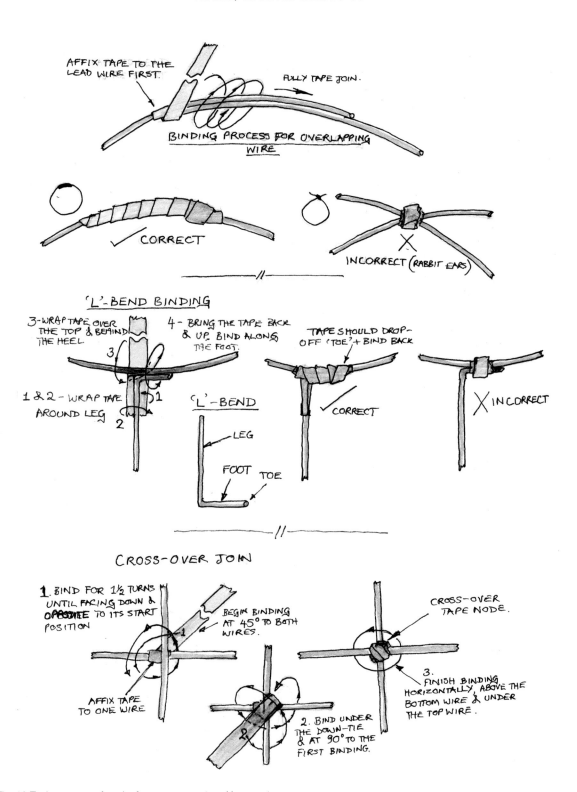

Fig. 19 Taping process for wire frames – correct and incorrect.

**Equipment**
- Pencil or pen for drawing and marking-up
- Flat-nosed pliers with a built-in wire-cutter
- Long-nose pliers for intricate shapes (optional)
- Ruler or tape measure (this could even be a rule that is attached to the table edge)
- Flex curve or piece of string for finding actual lengths

## Hoops vs Ties

The choice of whether you make the hoops or the ties first is up to you. Each object will come with its own challenges, depending on shape, and this should dictate to you what would be a more appropriate starting point. For an object like a jug or a lamp stand, it would probably be easier to start with the hoops and then join them with the ties. For an object like the aforementioned bird form, the profile-tie gives you an easier starting point as it provides a visual reference, particularly if you are just working from reference and free forming it. For a circular ball shape, there might not be any ties as such, because you can make the form, in its entirety, from hoops!

## Making Hoops

For a circular hoop, measure the required length – if you only have the diameter, multiply this by three (a gross simplification of pi), or six if using the radius – and add additional length at either end to create the overlap. Shape the hoop, removing irregularities with your thumbs and forefingers or using a firm curved surface, and overlap the ends of the wire until you have achieved the correct diameter/ circumference; then tape the join with the masking tape. The taping is done by taking a length of masking tape, long enough to wrap the join from one end to the other when spiralled around it. If the tape length is too short, simply add some more tape until the whole overlap is covered. Start your wrapping by sticking the masking tape just before the end of the overlap and at a 45-degree angle to the wire, so that as you wrap the tape, it will naturally spiral along the joint. Use thumb and forefinger to make sure that you achieve a good tight wrapping.

Once bound, hold the hoop between thumb and forefingers of each hand, either side of the taped joint, and firmly pull to see if the two wires will come apart or not. If they don't separate, you have made your first hoop, and can now repeat the process for all the others. If the wires do separate, you have not made your binding tight enough and will need to start again.

Once each hoop is made, make a tag of masking tape by folding it over the wire of the hoop and mark it with its location number and its size.

## Making Ties

Measure the length of each tie from your drawing, making sure to take into account any curves or irregularities in the tie to get the correct length (to assist you with this you could use a flexi curve or a piece of string, or even your wire). Then add additional length to cater for the L bend at both ends of the tie. If you have made a model, or can use the original object, measurements can be taken from these and used directly, or scaled up or down to make the prop larger or smaller. For open objects – such as jugs, bottles and amphorae – it is recommended that two of the ties form a continuous U-shaped loop from the opening on one side, down to and across the bottom hoop (attaching all intermediate hoops in the sequence as you go), and back up to its final position on the opposite side of the first hoop, with the second U tie being set at 90 degrees to the first, creating a crossover node in the bottom-middle of the object (see Fig. 18). The easiest way to achieve this is to make the U ties and then attach the hoops into the first of these, starting at the bottom and finishing at the top, at the L bends, then adding the second U tie to this structure. Further ties can then be added to the structure, although these need only start and finish at the top and bottom hoops, being taped to all hoops in between, without crossing over the base hoop, as this can cause an unnecessary build-up of wire at the base.

Depending on the size of the structure, you may need to add strainers at this stage for reinforcement.

Maquette (preliminary model) of Priscilla for the panto *Mother Goose*. The actual build used flexible canes, but the principle is the same as that used for wire frames.

## JOINING HOOPS AND TIES TOGETHER

Taping the L bend of the tie to the hoop is done by attaching a length of masking tape to the 'leg' of the tie, about 25mm (1in) up from the foot of the L bend (more for thicker wire) and extending beyond it, allowing for sufficient tape to bind the foot to the hoop. Where the tape is attached to the leg, this is folded around the wire, tightly overlapping itself like a sheath. The foot is then lined up with the hoop, with the tape overhanging it, and this is then wrapped over the hoop and back over the top of the foot for the first wrap and then onto the hoop behind the heel of the foot, taking a full wrap around it before taping back around and over the foot and the hoop. Continue a spiral wrap along the foot and hoop, dropping off the toe and spiralling back onto the foot for a couple more turns of the tape to finish off.

Where the length of the ties pass over the hoops, make a crossover node. Tear off an appropriate length of tape and place it on the top wire (tie) at 45 degrees to the point where the two wires cross over. Wrap the tape for one full turn around the two wires until the tape is contacting itself again (on top of the tie). Take an additional half turn and bring the tape up on the other side of the tie, deliberately missing the hoop so that you can wrap the tape in the opposite direction (at 90 degrees) to the first wrap for a full turn and then repeat the process twice more. For the last couple of turns, you will take the half-turn under the hoop wire, come up and across the tie wire at 90 degrees to it; then back under the hoop on its opposite side, coming up and over the top of the tie the other side of the hoop but on the same side of the tie wire, over it and under the hoop wire again on its opposite side. Then wrap the tape horizontally, between the two pieces of wire, pulling the applied binding tighter in the process. Finish by pinching the tape binding onto the wire with thumbs and forefingers. Your join should be firm and secure. This is basically a fusion of the diagonal and square lashing principles used in rope work.

## ADDING EXTRA STRUCTURE

Adding additional features such as handles, spouts and the like, is simply a question of forming the shapes with wire and attaching them to your base

Wire-frame teapot with chicken wire for enhanced shape, Modroc and PVA for the skin and a dressing of Fillite monkey dung to refine the shape.

structure. Card and paper rope can be used for additional support and bulk where required. Paper rope is very useful for creating lips and bases for a full range of objects, and as with card, can be affixed to the framework with masking tape or a variety of adhesives, or both.

## FINISHING OPTIONS

Once again, how you finish your wire-frame prop is up to you. You can add laminated layers of card to it; use it as the base for a papier mâché sculpt; apply layers of Modroc and PVA mix over it; or glue or sew fabrics onto it. Wider masking tape can be taped over it to bridge the gaps prior to coating with your chosen method. Stuffing the object tightly with scrunched-up newspaper will give a more regular surface for your finishes. This stuffing can be left in or removed after the prop's surface is dry. Stuffing and taping make it easier to apply structural finishes like plaster and scrim, Jesmonite and GRP. For larger objects, chicken wire can be used to wrap the object to help with shape and support.

Dead pigeon wire frame with coir fibres inserted for filling out.

Dead pigeon crafted from wire frame with masking tape. This was made for sewing onto a hat.

Dead pigeon wire frame with additional masking tape to help form the coir fibres.

Mummified hand. A wire-frame base was constructed for the hand and forearm, with bamboo over the wire to make the radius and ulna. This was covered in turn with thin foam wrapping, then calico, dipping latex and paint for the skin. A cut-up, translucent plastic tub supplied the nails. The bindings were made from muslin, PVA and paint.

Comedy bomb – when hoops become ties. Only hoops were used here to make the base structure of a round object.

# STEEL FRAMES AND PROPS

Constructing steel frames follows essentially the same approach that is used for wire frames, except that we use steel rods – either MS (mild steel) bright round or MS black (2–13mm in diameter), as well as square-section and MS flat steel – which require a different approach when cutting and fixing together. It is still possible to use twine/string to bind the steel, although this will need to be of a thicker grade (something like a 6 cord), with FlexBond or Araldite, and we can also use thin wire (twisted tightly around the steel) and Araldite, but anything over 6mm (1/4in) in diameter should ideally be welded with custom-made L brackets (cut and bent up from the same steel). This is because the steel frames tend to be used for more robust, weight-bearing media and large-scale constructions.

Your choice of welding equipment will depend on what you have available, and what you have experience of using. The advantage that welding provides is intrinsic strength with a minimal increase in weight; the downside is you may have to invest a fair amount of time and effort in the preparation of the framework and its many components, and this should be factored into the build, along with the purchase/hire of any equipment you do not have.

Box steel, tubular steel, sheet steel and even scaffolding can be used to create reinforcing elements where the structure is being use for someone to climb on or up. An example would be having to make an oak tree, from one of whose boughs hangs a swing seat that must be practical (able to be used), or there may be a requirement for people to climb the tree and sit in the branches. In this instance, the first part of the build would be to fabricate an engineered sub-structure specifically designed to take the stresses that are going to be placed upon it – any footings can later be disguised as roots. This can also be constructed so that it can come apart and be socketed back together for transportation.

The steel-frame construction can be built around the exterior of this very precise and utilitarian structure and will become a part of it. The idea is to

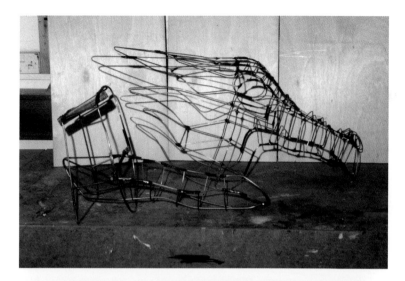

ABOVE LEFT, ABOVE RIGHT AND LEFT: Dragon costume prop for *The Magic Flute* made of a lightweight steel frame with chicken wire, dressed in hessian. The head was scrimmed in hessian and size, and the body, neck and lower jaw in hessian, with a textured slush latex and paint mix for the skin effect.

create a symbiotic relationship between the structures so that they support and strengthen each other. The exterior framework provides the basis for the 'reality' of the tree, and this will then be dressed. Note that when you make the steel frame you would need to consider how the sub-structure comes apart. After that, it is just a question of deciding if the exterior structure is permanently fixed to the various sections of the support structure, or whether it is removable (perhaps being bolted into position during the fit-up).

Steel-frame construction can seem like arduous work, and indeed it can be. However, if you have the skills, it can present you with more options than timber construction methods, as well giving you more scope to build larger, lighter and stronger structures. This is due to the difference in strength to weight ratios of the two materials. You would need to use more timber to build the same structure to get the same strength you would get from steel, and the steel will be of a much lower profile than the timber that you would have to use. If you don't have the required skill set there is always the option of freelancing that element out to someone who does, but make sure they have very clear working drawings with full specifications.

Where an object is largely decorative, the only requirement that we have is that it fulfils the brief. Large, proportionately lightweight structures can be made as steel frames, and what we decide to do over the top of the framework can render what it is supported by irrelevant, as it will not be seen.

Support structure for flying teacup and saucer for *Salad Days*. Weight rated and tested structural frame with additional welded steel support frame for the polystyrene sculpt.

Finished flying teacup and saucer for *Salad Days*.

# Welding

In metalworking, welding is the process of fusing pieces/sections of a metal together through

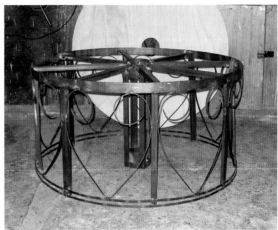

Steel frame tree base seat.

the application of extreme heat at the areas to be joined. A variety of metal types (ferrous and non-ferrous) can be welded by the following welding processes, although the equipment required will vary depending on the metal; for the purposes of this book, we are looking at mild steel.

The most common types of welding used in the small workshop are arc, MIG (metal inert gas) and TIG (tungsten inert gas), the latter two being a variant on the older arc welding process using gas cylinders containing non-volatile gases, designed to protect the molten metal from impurities as it forms. Arc welding uses welding rods (flux-coated electrode cores) that produce their own gas shield as the electrode transfers electrical energy to the workpiece, causing the metal of the join and welding rod to melt and fuse at the point of contact. Arc welding produces a coat of 'slag' over the weld, which is chipped away from the weld once it has stopped glowing, and as such is the messiest of these processes.

Equipment for these three processes is available in portable or more heavy-duty models. Although arc is the most easily portable, requiring no gas bottles, and is the cheapest to use, it is not suitable for use on thin metals such as those used for car bodywork. For domestic electrical supplies it is best not to exceed 2.5mm (⅛in) welding rods, especially for long welds. MIG welding is a cleaner, and arguably easier

Tree base seat with artificial tree prior to finished paint job.

## Materials and Equipment

Like wire-frame construction, steel construction is based around hoops, ties and strainers, so the same

Fire box being 'snuffed'.

Steel fire box with removable tripod and sliding-hinge closing 'snuff' lid.

and more precise welding form than arc, using a motorized spool to feed a thin wire core to the point of contact as the inert gas is released around this via the same nozzle. TIG requires the most practice, as it involves having to use both hands and a foot pedal, but it is the most versatile and can produce very high-quality welds – at a price.

Another welding process is oxyacetylene/gas welding. Gas welding has the disadvantage that it takes up a fair amount of space due to the size of the equipment and uses volatile gases, supplied in two separate cylinders, so is generally not viable for the small workshop.

It takes quite a bit of practice to master these techniques, although the essentials can be picked up quite quickly, and it is recommended that if you are a beginner you undertake an introductory course that provides you with practical experience and guidance on what equipment is most suitable for your needs.

preparation can be used here, just on a larger scale. Measurements are taken, the materials are cut and prepared for joining. However, because welding is being used to fuse the metal together, there is no need to allow for L bends and overlaps on any of the ties or hoops, as a properly applied weld should produce a joint that is as strong as the parent metal. Where there are crossovers at the ties and hoops, an L bracket is clamped into place (*see* illustration), and then welded to create a permanent fixing.

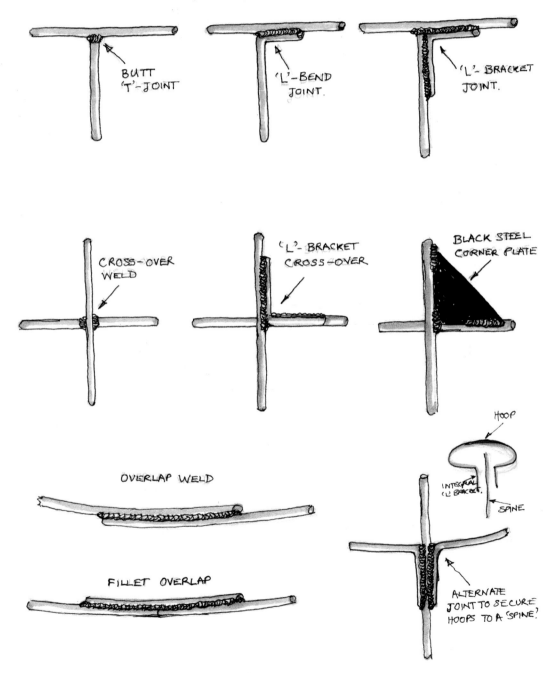

Fig. 20 Steel frames – examples of welded joints.

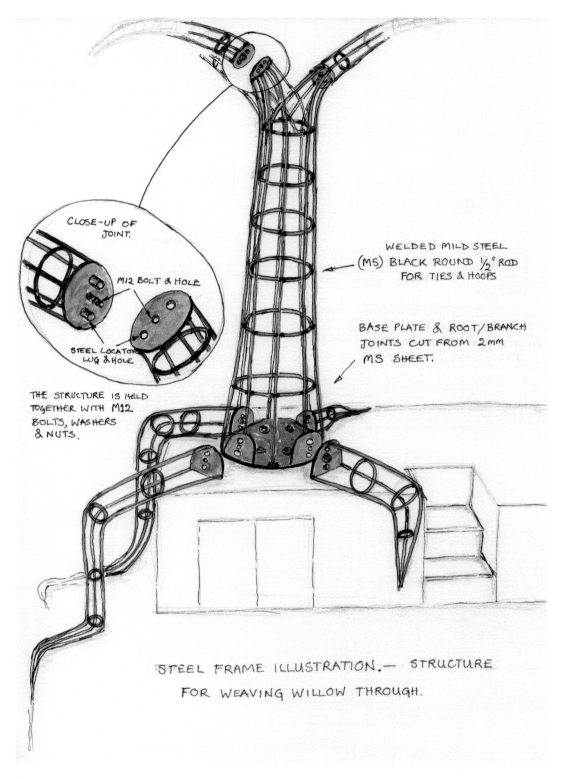

CLOSE-UP OF JOINT.

M12 BOLT & HOLE

STEEL LOCATOR LUG & HOLE

THE STRUCTURE IS HELD TOGETHER WITH M12 BOLTS, WASHERS & NUTS.

WELDED MILD STEEL (MS) BLACK ROUND ½" ROD FOR TIES & HOOPS

BASE PLATE & ROOT/BRANCH JOINTS CUT FROM 2mm MS SHEET.

STEEL FRAME ILLUSTRATION.— STRUCTURE FOR WEAVING WILLOW THROUGH.

Fig. 21 Example of steel-frame tree with hoop steel disc and tie construction.

## Materials

- Steel rods to cut into ties, hoops, strainers and L brackets
- 1.5mm–2mm mild steel sheet (optional, but it can be cut into discs to replace hoops)
- Dressing: 12mm (½in) chicken wire, paper rope for detail, poor man's fibreglass, or other preferred covering

## Equipment

- Tape measure
- Marker pen
- Welding equipment
- Welding mask
- Welding gloves
- Fume mask and/or direct extraction
- Welding apron
- Robust footwear
- Hacksaw and files or an angle grinder with grinding and cutting discs
- Mole grips, magnetic clamps or old G-cramps
- Heavy-duty metalworking vice
- Ball pein metalworking hammer
- Length of steel tube to assist with bending the steel rod

Shaped steel, welded rowlocks for Ratty's boat in *The Wind in the Willows*.

Steel manacles and shackles with sliding bolt locks for *Our Country's Good*.

# TIMBER FRAMES AND CARPENTRY

What timber provides us with is the ability to create a very strong sub-structure that will support

Timber-frame mangle made for the laundrette scene in *Aladdin*. It was dressed in rope and cord for the cast iron moulded details.

whatever we throw at it. By using sheet materials, we can shorten the build time and therefore increase the time we have available for dressing and finishing. This process can be used for rock and ground formations, trees, pillars – in fact, pretty much any medium to large structure that you can think of. Cast your mind back to the barrel the prop maker was asked to come up with in Chapter 1: that was done with a variation on this process, the only difference being that a 3.15mm single-strand wire was used as a support for the hessian skin rather than chicken wire.

The same methods as used for card construction can be employed here when using sheet materials: a combination of hoops, ties and strainers and edge half-lap joints, as with the barrel. We can also use plywood shapes, cut to the exterior dimensions of our object (the equivalent of hoops) and lengths of pine timber as our uprights/ties (50mm × 25mm, 50mm × 50mm, 75mm × 25mm); the same timber would be used for structural cross-bracing/strainers. The principle is the same, but with the materials being less yielding and requiring cutting with handsaws and jigsaws and fixing with

Barrel timber frame with epoxy bead welding.

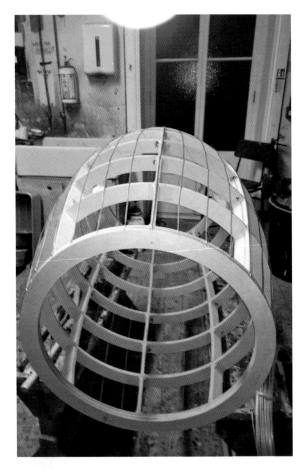

This frame was for a cable-operated animatronic sleeping pig. The head had to move up and down and from side to side, and its stomach move in and out as it 'breathed'. Other than the breathing, the body remained immobile.

Barrel with added 3.15mm single-strand galvanized wire to support hessian covering and provide detail for the barrel slats.

ABOVE RIGHT: Mr Toad's car from *A Wind in the Willows*. It has a plywood box structure, tacked together with PVA and panel pins then bonded with epoxy resin and milled cotton fibres using epoxy bead welding.

RIGHT: Mr Toad's car finished: a simple box-fame structure, made to be very durable and with a nod toward the team who made it!

Gondola collage. The timber frame with channelled and shaped plywood gives the support, with polystyrene sculpt, paper rope and epoxy resin GRP to finish.

glue, screws, nails and bolts, the process is more involved and requires a different skill set.

## Timber Props

Being able to work with wood can be invaluable for a prop maker. There are many items that can be made using carpentry and even woodcarving techniques. At a rudimentary level, it is possible to make entire items by simply cutting the timber to the required dimensions and securing it together with nails, screws or other proprietary fixings, but learning how to use mitre, half-lap, mortise and tenon, tongue and groove, scarf and dovetail joints, to name but a few, means that the props you make can be more elegant and made even stronger. Choice of timber is also an important factor in this regard, and it is useful to have a good general awareness of which wood is best used for which task.

### CHICKEN WIRE

It is worth mentioning at this point that chicken wire is a very useful product, but you may have noticed that it was not included in the section on wire frames. That is because to use it effectively it requires a support framework, without which it is unpredictable. Yes, wire frames can be used to provide that framework, but the chicken wire is not intrinsic to wire-frame construction. Chicken wire is used to help fill out the shape of the object and provide support for the overskin; it can be used to cover the whole framework or only parts of it in any of these 'framework' procedures.

It is better to use chicken wire with 12mm (½in) holes, rather than larger ones, because it will retain its shape better. Here is another point to consider: when you are looking at a piece of chicken wire, what you see is mostly air, which is very difficult to stick anything to! If you use the smallest-holed chicken wire, you are effectively increasing the amount of wire, providing more support for the skin and reducing the amount of air that you can't stick the skin to. The drawback is that the

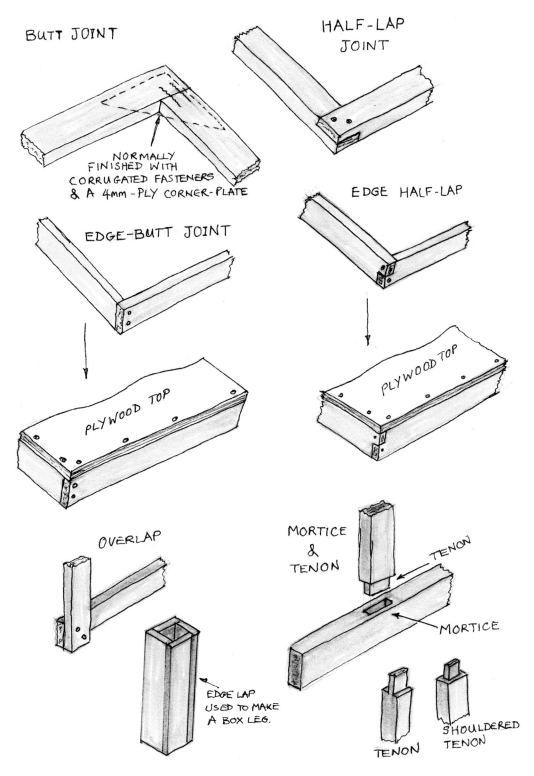

Fig. 22 Carpentry 101 – useful joints.

smaller-holed chicken wire is heavier and more expensive because it has a higher wire content than an equivalent-sized piece with larger holes – say a 50mm (2in) version. This is not to say that you shouldn't use chicken wire with larger holes, as it depends upon the job that you are doing, but anything over a 25mm (1in) hole is not conducive to these construction processes.

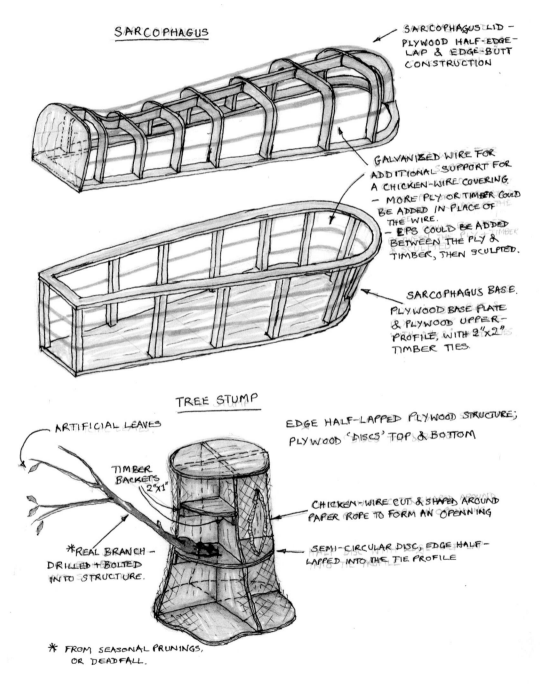

SARCOPHAGUS

SARCOPHAGUS LID – PLYWOOD HALF-EDGE-LAP & EDGE-BUTT CONSTRUCTION

GALVANIZED WIRE FOR ADDITIONAL SUPPORT FOR A CHICKEN-WIRE COVERING.
- MORE PLY OR TIMBER COULD BE ADDED IN PLACE OF THE WIRE.
- EPS COULD BE ADDED BETWEEN THE PLY & TIMBER, THEN SCULPTED.

SARCOPHAGUS BASE. PLYWOOD BASE PLATE & PLYWOOD UPPER-PROFILE, WITH 2"x2" TIMBER TIES.

TREE STUMP

ARTIFICIAL LEAVES

TIMBER BACKETS 2"x1"

*REAL BRANCH – DRILLED + BOLTED INTO STRUCTURE.

EDGE HALF-LAPPED PLYWOOD STRUCTURE; PLYWOOD 'DISCS' TOP & BOTTOM

CHICKEN-WIRE CUT & SHAPED AROUND PAPER ROPE TO FORM AN OPENING

SEMI-CIRCULAR DISC, EDGE HALF-LAPPED INTO THE TIE PROFILE

* FROM SEASONAL PRUNINGS, OR DEADFALL.

Fig. 23 Sarcophagus and stump – timber-frame construction.

## Timber

Timber can be used for making many things, from puppets and boxes through to furniture and gondolas; mine carts and sedan chairs to occasional tables and Viking long ships – to list but a few. Any of these can be built in an authentic manner using time-honoured skills, or they can be built theatrically, made quickly (in comparison) and using… time-honoured skills. The principle of construction remains the same for all these techniques though: observe the shape and form and replicate this with frameworks, support structures and surface dressing.

Of the many types of woods that we can use, what we choose will depend upon the type of thing we want to make, how durable it should be, and the finish that we are after. For example, something we use frequently in prop making is a dowel, and we can choose between softwood and hardwood varieties. If you are going to use

The challenge chests from *The Merchant of Venice*, constructed form birch ply with slats of ply used to make the curve of the lid. A treatment of monkey dung was given to each chest.

A timber-frame automaton. As it was pushed along, the chaindrive operated the cam, which caused the piston to move up and down. A manikin head was attached to the top of the piston.

A simple ply cut-out of a trout, fixed to a length of dowel and painted for *The Wind in the Willows*.

A timber-frame and chicken wire tree being covered in hessian. The first layer was stretched around, stapled and Copydexed, providing a much easier surface for the rest of the scrimming process.

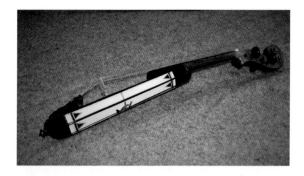

A Pochette violin. The neck was a gift, the body was carved from a piece of mahogany to take the made and painted 'ivory' inserts. The fingerboard was also made from mahogany, as was the carved tailpiece. The belly was fashioned and shaped from modelling ply, into which the f-shaped sound holes were cut.

Forms turned in oak for silicone rubber moulding for a series of six candlestick telephones. The oak is finished in shellac white hard varnish to seal the wood prior to moulding.

it purely for decoration or light use, then a pine dowel (softwood) is a cheaper option. However, if the dowel is needed for support work, is part of a structure, or something that must carry real weight, then it would be better to use a hardwood like ramin.

You can easily test the durability of softwood and hardwood dowels by doing a simple 'flex test'. Take a length each of hardwood and softwood dowel of the same diameter, say 25mm (1in), and length and place them onto two trestles or stools so that they are only supported by the two ends resting on the trestles. With the fingers of one hand press down gently but firmly at the midpoint of each dowel in turn and see which flexes more and which feels more durable. The result should be conclusive.

This additional strength to weight ratio of hardwoods vs softwoods means that we can opt to use thinner-profiled hardwood for more intricate projects that require structural integrity rather than the standard kiln-dried, modestly priced softwood, traditionally used in rep theatre, as the density of the wood enables us to use joints and fixings that may not work in softwood. There is, of course, an element of generalization here, because other factors will also come into play, such as the type of softwood or hardwood you are using, how well seasoned the wood is, and the tools you have available to you. The terms 'softwood' and 'hardwood' can be a little misleading, moreover, as some softwoods can be very hard while some hardwoods can be very soft (for example balsa wood).

Mr Toad's gypsy caravan from *The Wind in the Willows* – a plywood box structure with 'leaded' bay window.

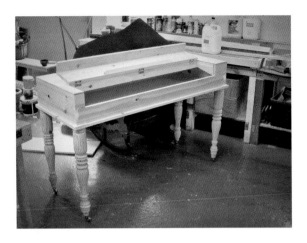

Harpsichord made from timber with turned legs. It was made as a shell, into which an electric keyboard could be inserted. It's seen here in bare wood, the finish a water-soluble wood stain.

# FLEXIBLE CANES

This is a generic term given to a variety of giant grasses also referred to as 'rattan' or 'furniture cane' (bamboo could also be included in the cane category, as a close relation to the rattans, although it has some very different properties). However, what we are specifically referring to here are Palembang, Kooboo, Tohiti and Manau. These canes range from 4mm (³⁄₁₆in) in diameter (Palembang) to 45mm (1¾in) diameter (Manau), and they all have good flexibility and resilience.

Canework is closely linked with wire-frame construction and steel frames but has its own niche. Canes are ideally suited to making frameworks, especially for large costume constructions and large puppets (where the issues of weight and durability

One of four Tudor tables that converted into market stalls. This one was for a purveyor of feathers and has calico pockets for the feathers and a slide-out surface for display and purchase. The table featured turned legs, dovetail joint construction and an inset slatted wood base. Pegged and strung storage for baskets was provided across the leg rails.

Priscilla the goose, a costume prop made for *Mother Goose*. The body was of cane construction, with foam to help create clean lines, dressed in a 'broken coat' faux fur fabric. The head was a clay sculpt, two-part plaster mould, latex casting reinforced with latex and glass-fibre chopped-strand mat. The eyes open and close independently or together, the mouth opens and closes and the wings are flappable.

Various cane sizes.

Three weapons, three materials: a long bow made from Manau; a Roman pilum (javelin) made from oak and steel; and a breakable halberd, made from bamboo and reinforced with hard brass tube, internally, at the breaking point.

should be considered), items not too far removed from the furniture origins for which the cane is mainly used. Because they are resilient, lightweight and – being fibrous – resistant to snapping, flexible canes can prove ideal for stage weapons. Lengths of Manau can be used to make good bo staffs after a little trimming and sanding around the nodes (growth sections); it is used in certain martial arts for this purpose, as well as dual stick work, for example. It can be used for the handles and shafts of cod war hammers, battleaxes, maces and clubs, which require greater rigidity to support the larger heads. It is also possible to fashion bows out of Manau, which work effectively, but do not have the pulling poundage of bows made of more traditional materials. The thinner Tohiti, meanwhile, can make good cores for role-playing and theatrical cod weapons, which are then padded with outer coatings of dense foams to prevent injury.

## Selecting Rattan

The rattans can be bought with the skin/bark on or off. You can buy lapping/binding/wrapping cane

that is used for binding the joints in cane furniture after soaking, and comes in two types: centre cane, where two 'sides' have been stripped off to create two flat surfaces; and half-glossy rattan peel or lapping cane, which is the outer edges of the centre cane. Generally, these latter two are used for decorative purposes, not necessarily just in canework.

## The Difference between Bamboo and Rattan

On the outside, bamboo and rattan can look very similar, since they both come from the grass family. However, on closer inspection, the nodal growth sections of bamboo form what looks like a knuckle, whereas the rattans produce a slightly

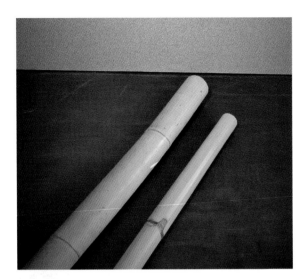

Comparing bamboo and rattan. Note that the node in bamboo is more of a knuckle, whereas the rattan is more an overlap.

A look at the end sections of bamboo and rattan, showing that bamboo is hollow and rattan is solid.

irregular overlap (like the effect of inserting drinking straws into one another to make a longer straw). Internally, the differences are even greater, as the bamboo is made up of a series of hollow chambers between each of its nodes, whereas the rattans are solid throughout. For this reason, we can use certain carpentry tools on the rattans, such as saws, chisels, spokeshaves and drawknives,

to shape and joint them. With bamboo, we must apply more caution as it tends to split if you are over-zealous with it, but it has had many uses throughout human history because of the characteristics it offers.

## Cane Splitting

Rattan can either be used whole or you can split it, which can be done very effectively by holding a cane splitting knife/glazier's putty-hacking knife (a classic example of a tool that is used in one trade, finds a different use in another and acquires a name change to boot) against the end of the cane and tapping it soundly with a hammer. As the knife enters the cane, close to the handle, keep a firm pressure on the handle as you continue to strike the exposed back edge of the knife until you have split the cane all the way down or far as you wish to. Because of its long, straight grain, you can attain some very regular split sections down the cane, especially with a little practice.

Hoops, ties and strainers are again used to achieve the shape and volume that we require. Twine and glue is our binding medium. Using an adhesive such as Rosco FlexBond will provide us with a much longer-lived joint/bond than either Copydex or PVA because it has the advantages of both and none of the negatives. Hot glue can be used for tacking as a temporary hold but should never be used as the only joint-bonding medium with cane – certainly it can be quick to use, but it is not a long-term solution. Cable ties can prove just as effective, if not more so, for a temporary fix until the glue and string have been applied.

Alongside the twine and adhesive, we can use wire or steel pins, or even pegs of cane, bamboo or dowel inserted into pre-drilled holes – for the thicker canes. This, in conjunction with strainers, provides a very strong and robust jointing system that will see your canework, costume or puppet last for years.

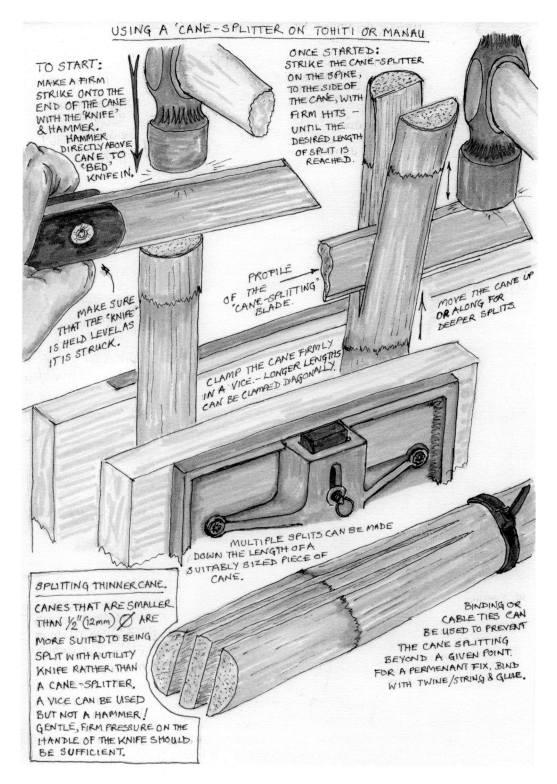

USING A 'CANE-SPLITTER' ON TOHITI OR MANAU

TO START:
MAKE A FIRM STRIKE ONTO THE END OF THE CANE WITH THE 'KNIFE' & HAMMER.

HAMMER DIRECTLY ABOVE CANE TO 'BED' KNIFE IN.

MAKE SURE THAT THE 'KNIFE' IS HELD LEVEL AS IT IS STRUCK.

ONCE STARTED:
STRIKE THE CANE-SPLITTER ON THE SPINE, TO THE SIDE OF THE CANE, WITH FIRM HITS — UNTIL THE DESIRED LENGTH OF SPLIT IS REACHED.

PROFILE OF THE 'CANE-SPLITTING' BLADE.

MOVE THE CANE UP OR ALONG FOR DEEPER SPLITS.

CLAMP THE CANE FIRMLY IN A VICE. — LONGER LENGTHS CAN BE CLAMPED DIAGONALLY.

MULTIPLE SPLITS CAN BE MADE DOWN THE LENGTH OF A SUITABLY SIZED PIECE OF CANE.

SPLITTING THINNER CANE.
CANES THAT ARE SMALLER THAN 1/2" (12mm) Ø ARE MORE SUITED TO BEING SPLIT WITH A UTILITY KNIFE RATHER THAN A CANE-SPLITTER. A VICE CAN BE USED BUT NOT A HAMMER! GENTLE, FIRM PRESSURE ON THE HANDLE OF THE KNIFE SHOULD BE SUFFICIENT.

BINDING OR CABLE TIES CAN BE USED TO PREVENT THE CANE SPLITTING BEYOND A GIVEN POINT. FOR A PERMANENT FIX, BIND WITH TWINE/STRING & GLUE.

Fig. 24 Splitting cane in single and multiple splits, with a cane-splitting knife and hammer.

The cane here has been split with a cane-splitting knife, and one of the sections has been steam bent.

Priscilla Goose cane framework – a mix of Kooboo and Tohiti canes. This structure follows the patterns on the maquette of Priscilla shown on page 101. Foam rubber strips and pipe cladding have been added so the 'skin' goes on smoothly and for the performer's comfort, respectively.

## Bending Cane

The thinner canes can be bent and looped quite easily; however, if you require a more predictable or permanent bend then you will need to apply heat via steam or hot air. There are advantages to both processes as well as certain risks. Good workshop practice and awareness of what you are doing should reduce the risks, so it ultimately comes down to preference and speed of working, but it is worth making provision for either process. Steam has an advantage in that it is a wet heat, which encourages the cane to flex and bend as it gets into the fibres of the cane. Hot air can dry the cane out as it forces it to change shape, and this can cause scorching and splitting if you are not careful; spritzing with a water spray as you heat the cane can reduce the chances of this happening.

The cane here has been split to facilitate the insertion of a helmet for simple movement control of the Jabberwocky neck and head when fixed into the costume in an adjustable pivot.

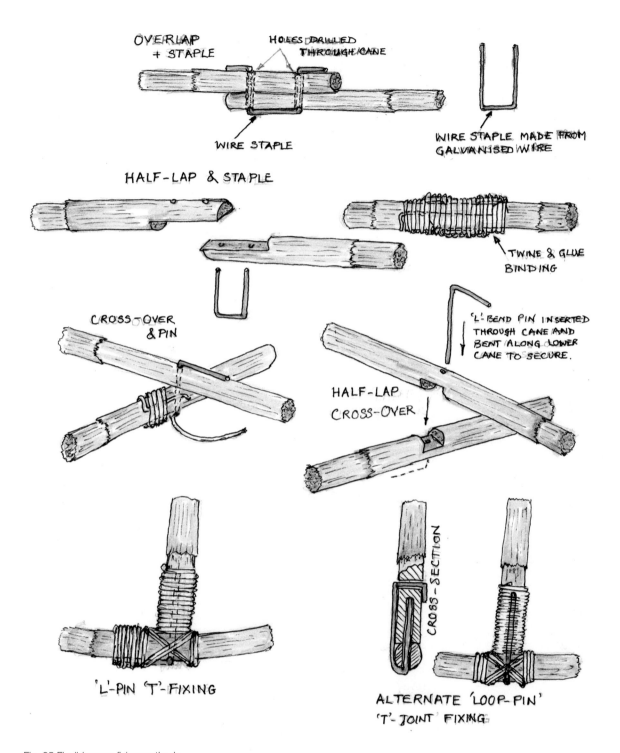

Fig. 25 Flexible cane fixing methods.

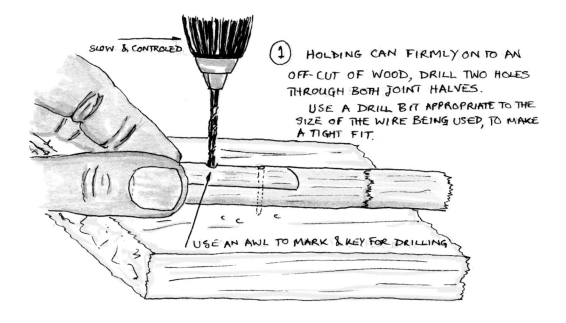

SLOW & CONTROLED

① HOLDING CAN FIRMLY ON TO AN OFF-CUT OF WOOD, DRILL TWO HOLES THROUGH BOTH JOINT HALVES.

USE A DRILL BIT APPROPRIATE TO THE SIZE OF THE WIRE BEING USED, TO MAKE A TIGHT FIT.

USE AN AWL TO MARK & KEY FOR DRILLING

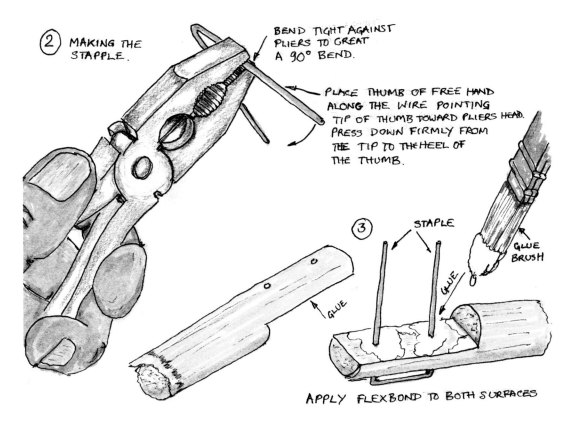

② MAKING THE STAPPLE.

BEND TIGHT AGAINST PLIERS TO GREAT A 90° BEND.

PLACE THUMB OF FREE HAND ALONG THE WIRE POINTING TIP OF THUMB TOWARD PLIERS HEAD. PRESS DOWN FIRMLY FROM THE TIP TO THE HEEL OF THE THUMB.

③ STAPLE

GLUE BRUSH

GLUE

GLUE

APPLY FLEXBOND TO BOTH SURFACES

Fig. 26 Drilling cane and making galvanized staples to fix flexible canes.

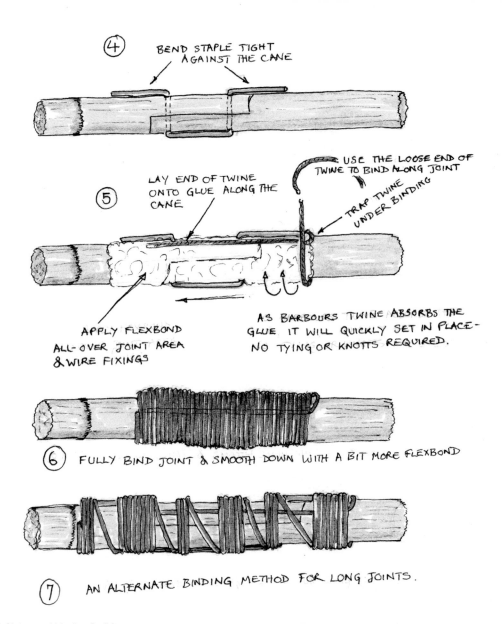

④ BEND STAPLE TIGHT AGAINST THE CANE

⑤ LAY END OF TWINE ONTO GLUE ALONG THE CANE

USE THE LOOSE END OF TWINE TO BIND ALONG JOINT

TRAP TWINE UNDER BINDING

APPLY FLEXBOND ALL-OVER JOINT AREA & WIRE FIXINGS

AS BARBOURS TWINE ABSORBS THE GLUE IT WILL QUICKLY SET IN PLACE - NO TYING OR KNOTTS REQUIRED.

⑥ FULLY BIND JOINT & SMOOTH DOWN WITH A BIT MORE FLEXBOND

⑦ AN ALTERNATE BINDING METHOD FOR LONG JOINTS.

Fig. 27 Gluing and binding flexible canes.

RIGHT: Two devices for steaming cane: an old-style kettle with modified handle (the kettle's low centre of gravity makes it more stable than taller models); a wallpaper steamer with custom-built steam nozzle.

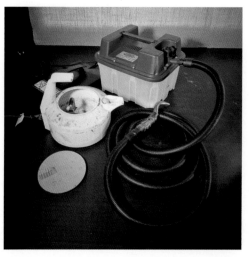

Thinner canes can be bent freehand over a source of steam or hot air; once cooled, the bend will be permanent. It is quite likely that you will need to set up a jig for thicker canes or use a vice (padded to avoid damaging the cane). The cane must be held securely in place while being steamed/heated, as the process of bending it puts the cane under considerable stress. As you heat it, gradually increase the bend of the cane

## STEAM BOX

If you are planning on doing a lot of wood or cane bending, then it might be worth considering making a steam box, a traditional piece of equipment more commonly used for bent-wood furniture and mouldings. The advantage that a steam box provides is the total immersion of the cane in the steam heat, which allows for a more even penetration of heat and moisture into the cane fibres, leading to full plasticization of the cane over time (depending how thick the cane is), at which point it can be quickly removed, placed into the jig, clamped and left to set.

A steam box is simply that, a box that is long enough to take the length of cane you wish to bend. It should be large enough to be able to accommodate multiple lengths of cane, in the interest of work progression, but not too big that it requires a huge volume of steam to fill it. A convenient size would be somewhere in the region of 1.8–2m (6–8ft) long and 15–20cm (6–8in) wide. It will need a steam inlet at the bottom on one end and an outflow vent or holes on the top side of the other end, so that the steam flows in and rises, moving though the box, and exits through the vents at the other end. It is a clever idea to have some heavy-duty galvanized mesh or lengths of 12mm (½in) dowels fitted across the width of the box to lift the cane away from the base of the box so that the steam can fully surround it. A lid on top, or a door at the end of the box allows you to put the cane in.

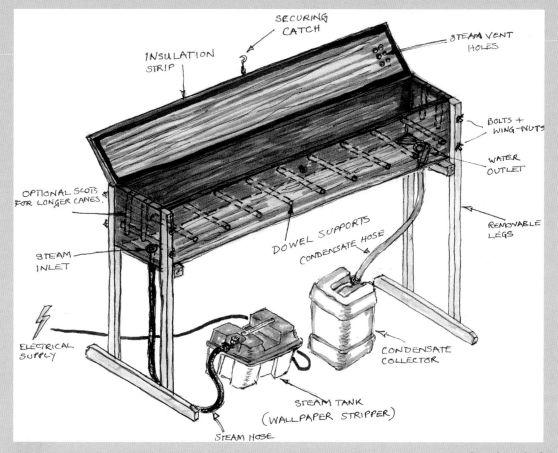

Fig. 28 A steam box.

*continued overleaf*

## STEAM BOX *continued*

The other requirement is that you have some way of providing sufficient steam via a heat source and a suitable 'kettle' that can be topped up as the water in it evaporates. One suggestion is a professional heavy-duty wallpaper steamer, as this comes as a complete unit, there is no naked flame, and it is just a question of connecting it to the box, filling it up, turning it on and keeping an eye on the water level. A shorter steam box could be constructed for longer canes, where you wish to do controlled bends at specific points on the cane, with the non-steamed ends protruding from either end of the steam box through flexible seals.

Steam boxes vent steam, which, because it is extremely hot, can soon turn a workshop into a sauna. Steaming outside, under cover, can resolve these issues, but you need to be close enough to the workshop so that you can get the work in and clamped before it 'sets up' and must be re-steamed.

until it is slightly beyond the point that you wish it to achieve. Make this bend in increments and you should feel the cane 'relax' as the heat penetrates the fibres. Forcing the cane too quickly can cause it to split or crease and bend at the main stress point. Make sure that there is no risk that the cane can suddenly spring free, releasing stored up energy, before the heat has had the opportunity to reform it, by keeping an eye on the entire length of cane as you work it. Steam/heat not only the point that you wish to bend, but either side of it as well to provide more plasticity within the fibres, making it easier to achieve the required bend. Endeavour always to apply gradual pressure, applying no more than necessary, letting the heat bend the cane and then apply further pressure when the initial load has eased. When first trying out canework, use Kooboo (more pliable and cheaper to buy) to get a feel for how it works before to using Tohiti and Manau, which require more time to work but increase the options available to you.

With the thicker Manau, you can employ the technique of splitting the end of a cane down the centre to just beyond where you intend to start your bend (you can even split it twice, producing three evenly spaced tongues), which will allow the heat to penetrate to the heart of the cane through the splits – and each section being thinner that the whole cane, it will bend quicker. Keep the bends even, using cable ties to temporarily secure each section as you go. As you bend the

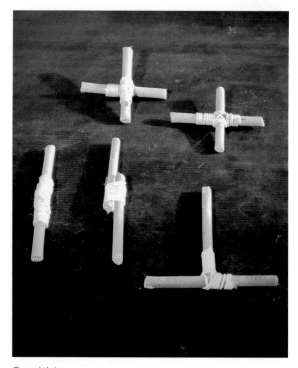

Cane joints.

cane, you will see that the inner thickness of cane appears to hold the curve, where the outer thickness (thicknesses) appear to draw back or drop behind in steps – simply the effect of the different diameters that the cane's sections are passing through. Once cooled and set, the cable ties can be cut or released, glue teased between the sections of cane with a brush and then it can be re-cable tied and strategically bound with twine and glue.

Kooboo bent with wet heat and dry heat.

Palambang plaited after soaking for a couple of days.

Steaming cane to make a umiak (canoe-style boat used by the Inuit), using a modified kettle and an improvised jig.

Laying out the base, marking, cutting and fitting the halving joints.

Once cut, the halving joints were glued and clamped with G-cramps until set, then they were drilled, pinned and bound.

The end pieces of the base frame were drawn in tight with sash cord ready for drilling, pinning and binding.

The side uprights drilled and pinned into position. Note the grooves cut into the tops ready to take the gunwales.

Gunwales and side rails being fitted and attached.

ABOVE: The finished frame with seats in place ready for final binding of tops and support.

LEFT: The seating rails being measured in. On cane structures, it is not unusual to overcut the length of the piece being fitted and trim away after fixing due to the organic nature of the material and construction process.

## WILLOW WANDS

Known variously as withies, willow wands and Somerset willow in the UK, these are the current season's whippy shoots from willow trees that have been pollarded just for this purpose. They are wonderful for use in rustic applications, such as baskets, brooms, screens, sculptures and so on. With regard to durability, the more you interweave the willow, the more robust it becomes and the more self-supporting. Willow-work can be used in conjunction with hazel staves/wands, as well as steel- and timber-frame constructions.

In theatre, willow wands are usually used to create a visual statement and, as is often the way, you can find yourself using them production after production and then not at all for what seems like years.

The fresher your willow is, the easier it is to work with. The older your willow is, the more likely it is that you will have to soak it to shape it as you would like. However, once soaked (a process that can take a few days), the willow becomes very pliant and, using the simple expedient of running each length over a slightly rounded table edge, you will be able to coil it and plait it relatively easily.

Reinforced willow-frame hobby horse, showing multiple-hoop construction for the head. The bindings were made with laid cord and willow for a rustic effect.

Steel-frame tree with soaked brown willow withies woven through the framework.

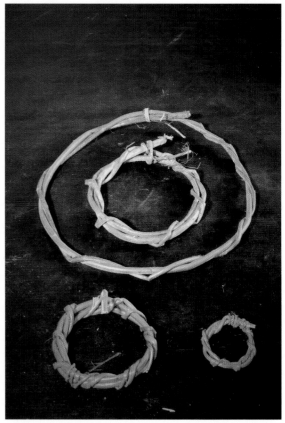

Multiple withies bound with willow to produce a more robust framework.

Soaked willow rings. Once the willow has been properly soaked, it can be bound into tight rings and plaits, with the thinner ends of the willow making a very efficient 'string' for binding to itself.

## Types of Willow

The three basic willow types are:

**Green** Freshly cut green growth that is still fully pliable

**Brown** So called because it still has the bark on and has also been dried

**Buff** Willow that has been soaked to remove the bark and then dried. It has an orangey-brown colouration caused by the natural tannins in the bark that soak into the wood as the bark is being removed. This is also the most common type of willow that you will see in commercial basketry sales for baskets, hampers, laundry skips and picnic baskets

What you end up using will come down to what the design concept is, but will usually be brown or buff willow. Remember, green willow is only available when the willow is ready to harvest, which, from a theatrical point of view, is unlikely to be when we need it.

ABOVE RIGHT: A large bear head puppet made for a production of *The Tempest*. The frame and teeth are green beech wood. Willow was bound through and interwoven, and moss and artificial leaves added for dressing. The illuminating eyes were battery powered.

A willow construction horse head for *The Mysteries*. Hoops and ties were interwoven with withies using basic basketry principles.

## FLORAL CHALLENGES

Theatre, film and television tend to do things out of season, and this can be a challenge for the creative teams. Thankfully, there is an entire industry that has evolved to produce artificial flowers, shrubs, trees and foliage to supply this demand. It originally sprang up to service shopping malls, hotel complexes, theme parks, theme pubs and wine bars, but has been readily embraced by the arts entertainment industry. This helps us indirectly as it makes it possible, for example, to use brown willow (which is more readily available year-round) for the main element of a design, and then add paint and artificial willow wands, leaves and catkins to create the illusion that it is a green willow structure.

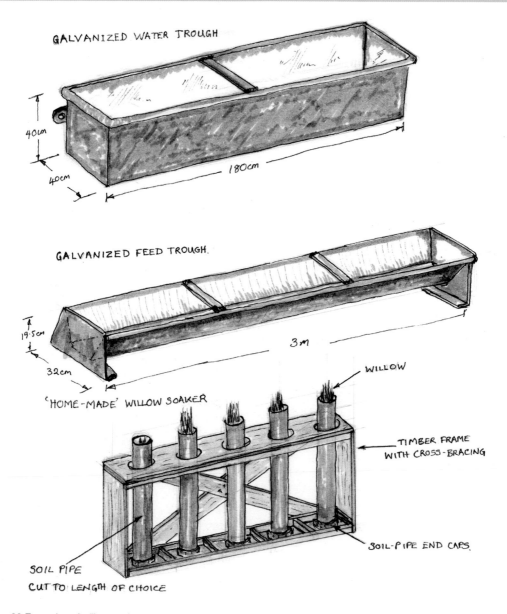

Fig. 29 Examples of willow soakers.

## Soaking Willow

One of the more interesting challenges is how you soak your recently acquired dried willow, assuming you don't want to forego having a bath until you have finished your willow-work project! For a relatively modest price it is possible to pick up a galvanized steel livestock feed and water trough from a farm suppliers. Simply select one that is of the length and depth that you want, and you have an ideal large-capacity soaking container. Another option is to use cut lengths of drainpipe or soil pipe, with an end cap sealing one end. You can make a support stand for these or stand them in an old dustbin or similar container that has been weighted at the bottom to prevent it tipping over.

Place your willow into your chosen receptacle and leave for two or three days (brown willow takes longer to soak), then you should be ready to go. If you find the cane is still a little stiff, leave it for another day or two. It is usual for a scum to form on the surface of the water, but this can be skimmed off, and the water can be replaced if doing an extended soak.

The next challenge is planning for a continuous supply of soaked willow for the duration of the project.

## Willow Used with Frameworks

As mentioned, willow can be very effectively used with the various framework processes, the individual requirements and your imagination once again determining the path that you might take. The photographs shown here illustrate frameworks and other structures using willow as dressing.

Steel frame and willow rainbow fan for *The Mysteries*. The fan is made up of three sections. Note that, as well as being interwoven through the frames, the willow is also bound to the frame with willow.

Willow and Varaform hare. The base shape for the hare is polystyrene, over which Varaform has been worked. Soaked willow is bound round and into the Varaform.

Willow and Varaform camel. The 'skin' effect was achieved with calico, glaze and water-soluble wood stain.

Papoose made for a production of *Pericles* set in 1860s America. This prop is constructed from a combination of flexible canes and willow, with 'animal skin' made using calico and a dipping latex, matt glaze and water-soluble wood stain mix.

# 5

# SCULPTING MATERIALS

Sculpting is one of the mainstays of prop making because it enables us to create precise shapes that are exact representations of the final piece. Some sculpting mediums, like clay, are simply used as 'a means to an end': they are usually moulded, and then castings are taken from the mould using more durable materials than the original clay. Others, such as expanded polystyrene, tend to be used as a sculpting medium that is then 'dressed' with other products that will protect the sculpted shape, but the expanded polystyrene remains intrinsic to the overall sculpt. Of course, as it's prop making we're talking about, it is only natural that there be variations upon these two basic concepts, but these come down to a greater understanding of the materials.

## CLAY

Clay is available in many forms, but from a prop making point of view we are interested in what is best suited for sculpting, moulding and casting. In general, we don't fire the clay we use and would tend to use air-drying varieties if the clay sculpt were to be the finished prop.

## Types of Clay

**Water-based clays** There are distinct types of processed water-based clays available in assorted

OPPOSITE: Clown head sculpt. Note the shape and form and the life that is brought into the caricature of the clown through observation of skeletal structure as well as the depth of the sculpt.

colours that can be used for specific objectives. From a cost and modelling perspective, a water-based clay that is ideally suited to sculpting is grey clay, although if you prefer the colour you could use terracotta, which also has excellent modelling properties.

**Oil-based clays** These use oil as the binding medium for the processed dry clay minerals. Plasticine is the original. It comes in a variety of colours and is well suited to certain aspects of claymation. Some, but not all, oil-based clays contain sulphur, which can have a negative effect on some moulding and casting materials: latex and silicone products are sensitive to certain oils that may be present in some varieties of oil-based clays. Check the product details and use barrier sprays and release agents to protect products that may be affected.

Chavant NSP sculpting clay and Le Beau Touché (terracotta-coloured) are both non-sulphurated sculpting clays; the latter is an oil-based clay with wax added into it to make it smoother. Chavant products are specifically designed for sculpting and casting. The Chavant NSP comes in three different grades (hard, medium and soft), all of which are grey/green in colour.

**Wax-based clays** As the name implies, with these clays wax is used as the binding medium for the clay minerals and other ingredients. These clays have an advantage that they can be melted down completely and poured into moulds, which is useful when you require a clay positive from a flexible mould such as silicone, for the purposes of remoulding or alteration. An example might be taking a life cast using Skinsil (a silicone rubber moulding compound that can be used on the skin following application of a release agent).

Plastilin is an excellent example of a wax-based clay and comes in soft (ivory-coloured) or hard (grey-coloured) versions; the two can be worked together to create a mix to suit the project you are undertaking.

## Sculpting Techniques

The approach you take when sculpting clay, whichever variety, should start with the objective of getting to the fine detail as quickly as possible, while allowing time to put care and consideration into the base sculpt. Shape and form are paramount. Looking at your reference material in detail enables you to see the required base shape for any object; the only task then is deciding what method to employ to create this.

### A Note on Cost

It is worth bearing in mind that the cost differences between buying a water-based clay and an oil- or wax-based one are huge. You can buy 25kg (55lb) of grey clay for what it would cost to buy two 1kg (4lb 2oz total) packs of Plastilin and 900g (2lb) of Chavant. This can have a severe effect upon your budget, but the wax and oil clays do have the advantage that they do not dry out and can therefore, with diligent handling, be used again and again with minimal loss.

Water-based clay, however, is easier to sculpt with, and providing you spray it with water and wrap it tightly with plastic, it will remain workable right up to the point that you need to mould it.

It is worth having both water-based and wax- or oil-based clays in a props workshop. Non-water-based clays are well suited to small sculpts that would dry out too quickly due to their small volume when using traditional clays. Ultimately, as always, it comes down to budget and what you prefer to work with.

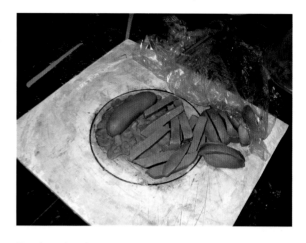

Rough sculpt of sausage, egg, beans and chips. The rough-formed chips were made by making a clay potato and 'chipping it'. Each bean was cut in half to make two beans in the 'sauce'.

Finished sausage, egg and bean sculpt. Note how the through-cuts and undercuts have been reduced or eliminated for moulding and casting purposes.

### Process

1. Is the object large or small? This can affect choice of clay and preparation methods for doing the sculpt.
2. Does it require an armature? Even small sculpts may require armatures to hold the position of the shape as it is being sculpted. The armature can be made from a variety of materials, including armature wire; armature wire fixed to a bolted bust peg and covered with expanded aluminium mesh;

galvanized wire; copper wire; timber; timber, wire and chicken wire/expanded aluminium mesh; or any combination of these. Any object that is fully 3D is likely to require an armature fixed to a modelling board. Whichever process you choose for your armature, the construction will follow the same principles used for wire-frame, card and timber constructions.

3. Bulk. A lot of clay means a lot of weight, which is another good reason for using armatures. Another option is to use a plaster or polystyrene base shape that can be sculpted over to reduce the bulk of the clay. One way of creating a durable, hollow plaster form would be to create a shape in clay that is roughly 25mm (1in) smaller than the finished plaster form needs to be. Using basic alpha plaster (a harder, denser plaster) and plasterer's scrim, shape the plaster over the clay form and let it set. Once set, remove the clay, re-bag it and spray with water, clean the excess clay from the plaster, and set the plaster form aside for a day to rest it.

4. Having created your armature (if needed) or selected your form to work over (if needed) apply the base layer of clay, roughing out the shape in general terms and keeping an eye upon dimensions as you go. What you are trying to achieve, if we use a parallel of drawing with pencils, is a rough sketch, something that has the essence of the final image but is not a finished piece. To achieve this with clay, use a cheese wire/clay cutter to make strips and lumps of clay that can be quickly and tightly pressed around the armature/form (if being used), or can be free formed into the desired shape. Pay attention to shape and form, observing accuracy of proportions, including dimensions, concentrating on getting these correct. Do not attempt to add any detail at this point; just create a suggestion of key points by using your thumbs, fingers and palms to manipulate the clay into the general contours of the shape.

5. The next step is to progress to a generalized refinement of the shape. If you are using water-based clay, lightly cover it at this point with polythene or damp rags, clean your hands and have a break, or get on with another task. Forget about the sculpt

Harpy mask sculpt. This is modelled onto a life cast to achieve accurate proportions for the actor to wear. The life cast is not of the actor but from stock and a good general representation of size and facial proportions. The clay is wax-based.

for at least the time it takes you to take some refreshment. On coming back from your break or other activity, you will be able to look with fresh eyes at what you have already achieved. Compare the reference material to the rough sculpt and rework the form where necessary.

6. Having reworked the basic form (and you can repeat this process as many times as is necessary and you have time for), you can now start refining the sculpt, adding and taking away pieces of clay as you get closer to a more precise 'sketch' of what you need to achieve. Again, allow yourself time to view the shape with fresh eyes before proceeding to the next stage.

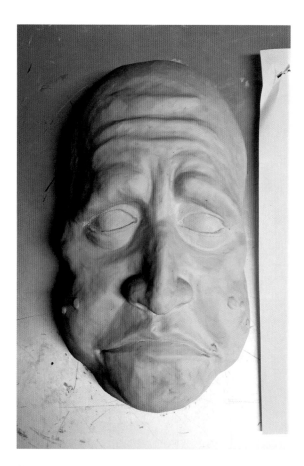

Simeon puppet head sculpt. The sculpt for this was modelled over a generalized face-shaped dome without facial features, sculpted from polystyrene. The clay is wax-based.

7. The refined sculpt. This is where you start using modelling tools in earnest to smooth and refine the form of the sculpt. Comb tools are particularly useful here as they can be worked over the surface of the clay to reveal areas that need building up or taking down prior to being smoothed out for the final finish. Become aware of the fact, that rather like the 'multi-tool paintbrush' we used for papier mâché work, a clay modelling tool has several different surfaces and edges that can be used to help you achieve your ends. These can be used for smoothing, lining, marking out, creating the angles where planes meet, pressing into the clay to form specific shapes, texturing and scraping away. Basically, the more you experiment, the more you will find out what you can do with them.

## Texture Mapping

For most of our sculpts we will want to create a surface texture to breathe life into the object when it is finished, otherwise it can appear flat and uninteresting. Surface texture influences the way that light reacts to an object, via reflection, refraction and the creation of shadow, in conjunction with the shape and form you have already created. The smoother a surface is, the more likely you are to have light reflect and glare off it. The more texture a surface has, the more the light will be refracted, giving the object in question greater depth.

Texture can be added in many ways, but two simple methods involve sponges/foam rubber offcuts and pieces of polythene sheet, preferably clear and in a variety of thicknesses.

## CLAY MODELLING TOOLS

Clay modelling tools can be invaluable for sculpting clay but there are literally hundreds of different tools and brands, made out of hardwood, bamboo, stainless steel, wire… but you only need what works for you. The wonderful thing about clay modelling is that it is literally hands on, enabling you to feel the shape and form of the clay as you work it. The more you get used to this way of working, the easier it becomes to start adding the modelling tools you need into your repertoire. The likelihood is that you will find that you only need a few trusted 'friends', maybe in assorted sizes, to see you through, and the odd special tool.

A selection of clay modelling tools showing the variety that are available.

The polythene pieces can be used to effectively create crease lines of varying depths in the surface of the clay. Lay the polythene over the clay. Choose an appropriate clay tool, like a knife edge tool, press it into the polythene and draw the tool along it to create your seam, scar or crease. When you lift the polythene, you will see that the edges of the crease have been softened out by the plastic, creating a more natural seam. If you try it without the polythene, you will find the effect is much harder to achieve. Try using different thicknesses of polythene to see how you can vary the effect. The polythene can also be used to soften out other effects by, again, using it as a barrier

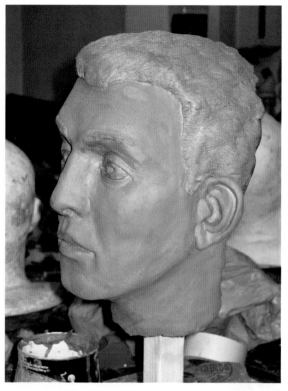

Texture-mapped head sculpt. The head is on a bolted bust peg, with aluminium armature wire and expanded aluminium mesh. Texture is achieved by spritzing with water, using foam and clay comb tools. Fingers can be used to smooth and create highlights.

Red deer stag head sculpt with real, shed antlers. The head is modelled onto 12mm (½in) birch-ply horizontal and vertical half-lapped profiles, screwed to a 50mm × 50mm (2in × 2in) bust peg secured to the modelling board. The antlers are removable for moulding and casting purposes.

between the tool and the clay when stippling with a stiff-bristled brush (such as a scrubbing brush), or a pointed clay tool, a comb tool, or the tines of a fork.

By scrunching or folding a piece of polythene, it is possible to created subtler, multiple creased effects by pressing it against the clay or rubbing down on to the scrunched plastic. You can even reposition it and try multiple overlays and differing pressure applications.

With sponges/foams of different densities, even abrasive pads, you can create a variety of textures and skin pore effects, and the simple expedient of plucking the sponges gives you even more options. These effects work best with prior preparation of the clay's surface:

For water-based clay you should spritz the area to be textured with water from a spray bottle (such as a hand-held plant mister), and then the sponge can be applied in a dabbing motion that will 'lift' the texture from the clay. Experiment with the amount of water sprayed on and the coarseness and density of the foam.

For wax- and oil-based clays, use a hairdryer or hot-air gun to gently warm and soften the surface of the clay, and then use a dabbing motion as detailed for water-based clay above.

For oil-based clay, you can use lighter fluid on the surface of the clay, but this obviously raises several H&S and COSHH considerations, such as fumes and fire risk to name but two.

Texture mapping can also be achieved by using silicone impression putty. This can be applied to a wide number of surfaces to create a negative moulding of a specific texture, or shape that you might like to impress into the clay. A product like Tiranti's T40 Silicone Rubber (Fast Set) can be used for taking impressions from the skin with the use of a suitable barrier cream. It sets in a couple of minutes and is removable in 8–10 minutes. It can also be used on many other surfaces but is most suitable for small-scale impressions due to its short pot life. Although silicone products can be pricey due to their specialist nature, the resulting texture mapping appliances can be used for many years, if looked after.

With texture mapping the only rules are that it needs to work and you must be able to replicate it should you need to use the same effect again.

Suitcase corners, eight per case. Think ahead to the mould and make the sculpt capable of producing multiple castings.

Suitcase buckle. Detail gives you more to work with when it comes to the paint.

Face sculpt. Observe shape and form in your reference material.

Pillar capital detail. When using a flexible casting medium from a rigid mould, careful consideration can allow you to achieve greater undercuts than might otherwise be the case.

## OTHER 'CLAY' PRODUCTS

**Paper clay** This is clay with a cellulose additive that adds bulk, reduces weight and reinforces the clay. Although it can air dry, you get more durable results if you fire it. Newclay comes in off-white or terracotta and has two hardeners that can be used with it, H1 and H2, aimed at, respectively, providing a hard exterior, or durability throughout. It can be baked at a mere 200°C.

**Polymer clays** These products, generally, contain no actual clay, but have been designed to have similar sculpting properties. They are ideal for small sculpts and remain malleable until baked in a domestic oven. This is an ideal medium for creating jewellery, such as brooches rings and pendants, and for small figurines and marionette parts – heads, hands, feet. Polymer clays are pricey compared to water-based clay, but they are aimed at providing a finished product. For jewellery, with the wide range of colours that you can get these products in, you can also use the clay as settings or mounts for other items like synthetic precious stones, pearls and the like – just remember not to bake the polymer clay with the jewels in: simply use your faux decoration to impress the position into the clay, and when it is baked you can then glue the jewels into place.

The main brands for these clays include Sculpey (an American product) and Fimo (German). Both come in a wide variety of colours and it will ultimately come down to availability, price and preference as to which you might use, if any. From a prop-making point of view, they add options but are unlikely to be the mainstay of your construction requirements.

# EPOXY PUTTY

Epoxy putties are a very useful product to have in your workshop and are relatively cost-effective. They can be used in conjunction with many other products, including wood, metals, plastics, GRP, ceramics and papier mâché. They can be used to sculpt and repair, can be smoothed with

Milking cow door knocker used for *Jack and the Beanstalk*, made from 4mm ply cut-out with hard brass tail. Apoxie Sculpt was modelled onto the ply and tail, then sprayed with PlastiKote metallic gold spray paint.

water and when cured can be drilled, tapped, machined, sawed, filed, sanded and painted. Do not be tempted, however, to use epoxy for tapping threads and supporting structural joints in place of more appropriate fixings, especially where there could be risk of injury or loss of life. These products are strong but they have their limitations, though you can of course use them in conjunction with other more conventional products where appropriate.

## Sculpting with Epoxy Putty

From a sculpting point of view, you can achieve some very fine detail with epoxy putty. There is no shrinkage, so it can be used over armatures with no risk of cracking as it cures. It cures at comfortable room temperatures and gentle heat can be used to speed curing. Because this is a two-part putty product that works on a 1:1 ratio mix,

Apoxie Sculpt is a very durable epoxy putty with a good working time.

it is vital that you get as near to equal quantities as humanly possible. To avoid waste, only mix up the amount that you require for the job in hand, remembering that each part will provide half the volume that you require. Use workshop hygiene principles to measure out the parts to avoid cross-contamination, and tightly wrap or seal the products after you have what you need.

Once you have your equal parts of Part A and Part B, the next process is to knead them together. This process takes a bit of time if you do it properly, but it is essential that you achieve an even mix throughout. The manufacturers have been very considerate in providing the two parts in either different shades or two distinct colours, depending on the product that you have chosen to use. As you knead the two parts together, you will observe streaks of the two shades/colours appearing through the product; keep kneading until the whole mass is an even blended colour throughout. Here is a tested and tried kneading method that has been used over decades and that produces a relatively quick and even mix:

1. Measure out equal portions of Parts A and B epoxy putty, being careful not to cross-contaminate by using separate instruments for cutting the quantities required (half of each making the final volume).
2. Seal up the bags or containers and put to one side. Remember, you can always mix up more product if you need it but, if you mix up too much, you cannot uncure it.
3. Roll each of the two parts into separate equal-sized, even sausage shapes, and place them side by side so that they are touching.
4. Pick up the two sausage shapes and, starting at one end, twist them together into an even spiral all the way to the opposite end.
5. Fold the spiralled epoxy putty in half and roll together between the palms of your hands, or on a clean work surface/modelling board it you prefer, making a single sausage shape that is about twice the length of the originals.
6. Fold the sausage shape in half and twist into another even spiral and then roll out into a sausage again.
7. At this point, to add variety, using your thumbs and forefingers squash the putty into a flat, wide strip. Fold one of the outer edges so that it is a third of the width away from the other edge, and then fold the other edge over the opposite edge so that the putty is folded onto itself in three layers.
8. Fold the putty in half, end to end, twist into an even spiral and then roll it into a sausage shape.
9. Roll the sausage shape into a ball, flatten it out, fold it in half and half again, and then roll it into a sausage shape, fold in half and twist into a spiral.
10. Repeat stages 5–9 until the epoxy is an even shade/colour throughout, at which point it will be warm, pliable and tacky, and ready to use for whatever you have planned for it.

## Water and Epoxy Putty

As mentioned previously, water can be employed to smooth the surface of the putty so that your fingers and modelling tools glide across the surface without dragging. It only requires a very small amount of water to do this, and it makes working with the putty very satisfying. However, when used to excess, the water can have a detrimental effect upon the intrinsic strength of the putty. A good technique is to dip your finger, or modelling tool, into a conveniently placed pot of clean water, shake away any drips and proceed with the sculpt. Re-dip into the pot as needed, once again shaking off the excess water before returning to work on the sculpt/repair. The object is to facilitate an easier working of the putty, not drown it!

Water can also be used to adhere pieces of the pre-mixed putty together. It is best to create a lug and socket type of join to increase the surface area of the joint, but the exact shape and size will depend on the task you are undertaking. If you are simply applying an extra layer of the putty mix, then it can simply be smoothed onto the lightly wetted surface of the previously applied putty.

# EXPANDED POLYSTYRENE (EPS) OR STYROFOAM

In Britain, we refer to it as polystyrene (a bit of a misnomer as it comes in expanded and non-expanded forms), in the USA and Canada it is known as styrofoam, but it's the same product (Styrofoam is actually a brand name for extruded polystyrene). Extruded polystyrene products can be used for sculpting, and are very good, but the cost tends to be substantially higher than other materials for the same quantity. Still, for smaller products this could be a viable choice. Styrofoam comes in a variety of product types; for sculpting either the blue or pink sheet materials can be used, and this comes down to personal preference on texture and resilience.

Buying your polystyrene is best done through the manufacturer, especially if you build up a good relationship with them. The advantages of buying from a manufacturer far outweigh the expedience of popping down to your local builders' merchant

Candle holders made from assorted bits and Milliput. Milliput comes in a range of colours, but the yellow/grey is the cheapest and is a good base for sculpting and repairs.

Poly lathe-carved cauldon. Creating your own polystyrene lathe and using it to create a whole host of turned items is very satisfying. It will make the workshop look like it has been hit by a snowdrift, though.

and picking up several sheets of a less suitable product from them:

- You can save as much as 50 per cent on the retail price
- You may get a discount for bulk orders
- You can select the exact product and density that you want
- You can have it cut to a size that suits you
- They will create bespoke products for you at additional cost service – this can be useful when time is against you
- You can collect or have it delivered for a fee
- You may even get a card each festive season, thanking you for your custom!

## Ordering Polystyrene

As with a lot of products, abbreviations are often used when ordering polystyrene products, for example:

**EPS** Expanded polystyrene
**XPS** Extruded polystyrene
**VB** Virgin beads, the raw materials used to make EPS and XPS
**SD** Standard density
**HD** Hard density
**EHD** Extra-hard density

**ENVIRONMENTAL AWARENESS**

Polystyrene has many uses commercially and because of this there is a lot of it around. The problem is that it is a potential threat to the environment since a lot of it is 'single use', such as packaging. This is also how it is often used in theatre, where, due to the high-pressure 'get it made and move on' attitude, polystyrene is a very useful product. Over the years production methods have changed to make the manufacturing of the product more environmentally friendly, and research continues into the disposal of waste polystyrene.

**UHD** Ultra-hard density
**FRA** Fire-retardant additive

A line on an order or delivery sheet would look something like this:

8 × sheets, VB, EPS, HD, FRA @ 1,200mm (48in) × 2,400mm (96in) × 100mm (4in)

This means that you are ordering eight sheets of virgin bead expanded polystyrene with a fire-retardant additive, which will be 1.2m (4ft) wide, 2.4m (8ft) long and 10cmm (4in) thick. A standard sheet size is 1,200mm (4ft) × 2,400mm (8ft) and you can order a thickness from 25mm (1in) up to 600mm (24in) in 25mm (1in) increments.

The density of the material you need will be determined by the job that you are intending to do, but for general sculpting purposes hard density produces a very good result at a reasonable cost. The difference in density is down to the quantity of virgin beads that are placed into the mould: the more beads, the tighter the cell structure, because they have less room to expand. Conversely, with the packaging grades of EPS, there are a lot fewer beads and a certain amount of recycled material, which results in a much larger, looser cell structure.

There are other grades below the SD, but these should not be considered as viable sculpting mediums as they are too soft and fragile to work with at a professional level. As they say, 'once you have tried HD you won't go back'. The XHD and the UHD are superb mediums to work with as they have very good resistance, are light in weight but solid, and you can create very fine sculpts with them. The UHD has the advantage that it can be the base for sculpts that the actors must walk and climb on, especially when used in conjunction with timber structures and poor man's fibreglass.

## Gluing Polystyrene

There are a range of products that can be used to glue expanded polystyrene, but 'polystyrene

A comparison of EHD EPS and SD EPS polystyrene. Note the tighter cell structure of the top piece.

cement' is not one of them, as it is intended for non-expanded polystyrene products such as those used to make model aircraft, cars and so on. It works by effectively welding the two parts of plastic together in a controlled melt. When used on expanded polystyrene it will melt it in a more extreme way because there is less substance to the EPS than the non-expanded polystyrene products.

There are products that are specifically designed for use with EPS, however, and others that work with a variety of materials. These products include those with water and solvent bases and certain skeleton gun application tubes as well as spray expanding foams, which can also be used to fill gaps in the polystyrene sculpt and then be shaped and sanded to blend in.

Of the many products that can be used to secure polystyrene sheets and blocks together, the one that can't be beaten on price, coverage and

sheer magic is latex adhesive (for example Copydex, Flints…dex, Sticcobond F1).

Now, there are advantages and disadvantages to using latex as an adhesive. Latex is a natural product, harvested from trees, and as such it is a water-based organic product. As a result, it takes longer to dry than the solvent-based adhesives, but this is only noticeable if your drying conditions are cold and damp. If you have a warm, dry workshop and the adhesive is applied properly, you can expect the product to dry within 10–15 minutes.

The application of the latex adhesive is key. A light, even layer should be applied to both surfaces when applying to non-porous surfaces such as expanded polystyrene. You can use a spreader to do this (improvised from the side of an old glue tub if you do not have a spreader to hand), or an offcut of foam rubber, but it is important that you do not apply it too thickly, or leave streaks and splodges of glue that will take longer to dry than the rest of it. The glue can be tipped from the pot onto one of the surfaces, and any excess can be scraped straight onto its paired surface after spreading (with practice, you can turn this application method into an art form). You can also apply the adhesive from a pot using the sponge to transfer it onto the work or use a combination of the two methods.

Once applied, leave the latex adhesive to dry… completely! Unlike with solvent-based adhesives, you are not limited to a 'tack' point and open time. With forward planning the latex adhesive will usually be dry when you need, and it doesn't matter how long you leave it. Even if you have an extended break, when you do get back to the workshop, all you need do is align the various pieces in their marked order, pressing them together as you go, and they will bond tightly (as long as the surfaces to be bonded are evenly matched at the point of contact).

## Tools for Working Polystyrene

There are many tools that can be used for carving and shaping expanded polystyrene – but which

*Salad Days* tea cup and saucer, clad in polystyrene, glued into place with Copydex.

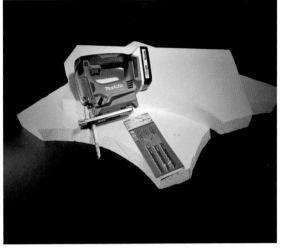

Jigsaw and Bosch EPS cutting blade.

tool you use will ultimately be determined by what stage you are at. The chances are that you will already have many of the tools that could be used with EPS, and it is a relatively painless process to make other, more specialized tools.

To cut large sheets down to size, you can use woodworking jacksaws or multi-purpose saws that are designed to cut through a variety of materials, and different blade types can be bought for them. These latter come with a stiffer blade than a standard woodworking saw and are therefore less prone to going off-line through the thickness of the sheet, but the blade length is shorter. Both saws work well, and you will give yourself a good workout while using them.

## KEYHOLE SAWS

These are useful for cutting intricate patterns through styrene up to 100mm (4in) thick. Bosch make EPS jigsaw blades for the same purpose, which are very good on 25mm (1in) and 50mm (2in) sheet thicknesses but require a slower, more considered approach on the 75mm (3in) and 100mm (4in) sheets, otherwise the bottom of the blade will take its own path on the bends. With the 100mm (4in) sheets, there is a good chance that if you rush it, the Bosch polystyrene cutting

blades could punch out chunks of EPS from the underside of the sheet because the blade will be working at the extremity of its depth capability.

## GENERAL SHAPING TOOLS

For general shaping it is difficult to beat the Stanley Surform range, all of which are excellent and invaluable for different points of working on the EPS. You can also use standard woodworking rasps for shaping, or affix coarse grades of abrasive paper to offcuts of timber and dowel for specific tasks. Tongue depressors and lolly sticks can have abrasive paper stuck to them for more intricate jobs – you can even use emery boards (intended for manicures, but useful in prop making).

## 'THE IMPLEMENT'

Simply put, this is a hacksaw blade that has had one end ground down, on a bench grinder, into a knife point. It is then sharpened using a whetstone or oilstone, at which point it becomes a very useful multi-purpose tool for sawing, cutting and intricate work in the fine-tuning and detail stage of your work. Using a blade designed for cutting mild steel will give you the advantage of flexibility and reduce the risk of it breaking as you work with it. 'The implement' is often made up from older

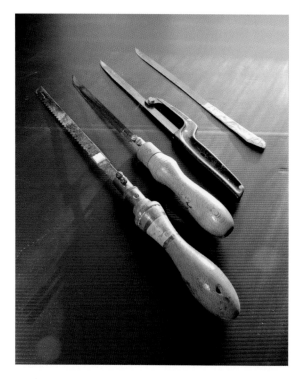

Variations of 'the implement': the blade on the left is from an old electric carving knife.

a quick way of bringing an edge to a knife. You can also use an oil- or whetstone to produce this edge, especially if the knife has been neglected. Learning to sharpen your own blades properly will serve you well for years to come. Alternatively, you can use a knife sharpening service and suffer the inconvenience of not having your knives available at certain periods.

I mention bread knives here, but not all bread knives are made equal because some have a weak connection where the blade enters the handle. With all your knives, you should make sure that the 'tang' (the part of the blade that enters the handle) is robust. The most secure knives are those where the tang is the same profile as the handle, and the handle is made up of 'scales' that are riveted to each other through the tang in a sandwich effect. Bread knives – and some carving knives – have a serrated edge, which can be useful for trimming when you want a more rigid blade than that provided by 'the implement'. Whatever you decide upon, it is good to have a choice of straight and serrated edges for quick working.

blades that are being replaced because their steel cutting days are over, but they are still plenty sharp enough to deal with polystyrene. The advantage of using a saw blade that is 30cm (1ft) long incorporating a knife blade at one end will become obvious as soon as you start using one. Extra comfort can be provided by purchasing or making a handle for one end to save your fingers becoming abraded by the saw teeth.

## CARVING KNIVES, BREAD KNIVES AND PARING KNIVES

These should be bought/sought out specifically for use in your workshop. Once used for prop making, any kitchen instrument should no longer be considered fit for food purposes, due to the risk of ingestion of contaminants used in the prop shop. You do not have to buy expensive knives – going around charity shops can produce some very nice blades that will serve you well for years. It is also worth getting a knife-sharpening steel, as this is

## ANGLE GRINDERS, ARBORTECH WOODCARVER AND FLAP DISCS

These require good tool control and maximum concentration, or severe injury could occur. You will also need to be relatively fit and be wearing full safety gear, including a leather welder's apron and sturdy work boots. A face shield is preferable to goggles as it is a more comfortable option when wearing a dust and fume mask and less prone to steaming up.

The Arbortech woodcarver kit, which includes a polycarbonate blade guard, is designed for use with any 100mm (4in) or 115mm (6in) hand-held angle grinder, for carving and distressing wood much more quickly than could be achieved by conventional methods. It is therefore hardly surprising that it has come to be used by some for sculpting large EPS projects as a method of quick reduction, once all the initial pieces have been cut to size by more conventional means and glued into place.

## H&S AND POLYSTYRENE

As you work, you will produce a lot of waste material, even on small jobs, and the effect can be like working in a snowdrift without the cold. It is at this point that it is very easy to lose track of where your tools are, and this can lead to injury when you kneel, sit or lean over and discover a hidden blade, or twist your ankle on a sanding block hidden beneath the polystyrene. It is not only personal injury that is a risk here, but the fact that you could irreparably damage a very useful tool.

Good workshop practice should be brought into play. Either have a designated space, within easy reach, that will be the home for the tools you are using (this may be mobile, like a wheeled trolley, tool caddy, or just a tray), or in the case of knives, make sure the blades are covered (make sheaths or scabbards for them), while 'implements' can have the sharp end stuck into an old cork. A spare block of polystyrene can be used to stick all knives and 'implements' into, or, for quicker access, you can stick them into a section of the workpiece that is not currently being worked on.

When using the Arbortech blade, the same principles apply for EPS as for wood:

• You control the tool
• Only work the blade in the direction that the disc is spinning: to the right with the blade angled down to the left; to the left with the blade angled down to the right; or back toward the handle with the blade angled down toward the front. Do not work against the blade direction – that is, towards the angle and direction that the blade is pointing – or the blade will catch and bounce back or kick aggressively, damaging your workpiece and causing injury to you if you do not have a secure grip on the grinder
• Move the workpiece or yourself into the best working position – never use the tool at the extremes of your control capabilities or injury may occur

This may sound a bit like a disaster infomercial but applies to pretty much any tool, especially power tools; and, as with any other tool, if you do not feel confident or comfortable using it, seek proper training and guidance or do not use it.

The Arbortech blade and guard are moderately expensive but can prove to be very useful for wood shaping and polystyrene carving. It is important to make sure that your workpiece is well secured and not able to break free. In the case of smaller EPS pieces, these can be glued to some 18mm (¾in) plywood and either clamped or screwed to trestles, saw horses or a workbench.

Arbortech also produce a purpose-built Mini Carver, a grinder with an extended working arm that takes a 50mm (2in) carving blade (and other assorted blades and disks of the same size), capable of delivering a more precise and controlled sculpt. This is not cheap.

If you can't afford an Arbortech blade, then a flap disc, which is an abrasive disc with overlapping flaps of abrasive material that is designed for use with angle grinders, can be used instead and will cost a fraction of the price. The discs come in two grit sizes (40 and 60), and for EPS work they do not need to be fresh discs but can be left-overs from other work.

## POLYSTYRENE CUTTER/ HOT-WIRE CUTTER

If cutting sheets thicker than 100mm (4in), it is worth using an industrial hot wire, which can be bought or hired depending on the amount of polystyrene work you intend to do. Although you will have to contend with fumes by using extraction and fume masks, the effortless way that the hot wire goes through EPS is like a hot wire… going through EPS. There are two thicknesses of wire that can be used with these machines, a thin cutting wire and a thick sculpting wire; the machine will have specific settings for each. The thin wire will enable you to cut thicknesses up to 2.4m (8ft) relatively quickly (check the specifications of your machine to see the maximum depth of cut), while the sculpting wire is good for general reduction and precise shapes but is limited in the size and depth of cut that it can make.

Polystyrene hot-wire cutting – making hundreds of 'coins' for four pillars.

The polystyrene cutter is set up in the bench to facilitate clean, straight cuts and various disc sizes. Note the 'turntable' to the left.

Hot wire refining the pig's head core. The hot wire is very useful when working freehand, whether with the thin cutting wire or the thicker sculpting wire.

Whichever way you work with polystyrene, you will produce fumes and dust. If you are working it manually, you will release fumes every time you cut; when sanding it, you will produce, as well as the more visible large particles, fine particles that can hang round in the atmosphere for quite a while, especially if you are working without a decent-quality LEV rated extraction system.

Despite its name, a polystyrene cutter/hot wire cutter works by melting, rather than cutting, the polystyrene in a controlled way, and as such will produce a lot of fumes, visible and invisible. Without a good extraction system, unless you can work outside, this can make the workspace a very unpleasant and hazardous space for anyone not wearing proper organic fume protection equipment. To reduce excess fumes, it is important that you never use the cutting wire beyond the range that your equipment instructions state (once set correctly, the wire should be a brick red colour in dull light, or have a hot, blackish appearance in bright lighting conditions). Tempting as it might be to crank the temperature up to cut even quicker, your cuts will be less precise, and the fume increase will be substantial.

## Sculpting Polystyrene

Sculpting polystyrene is the opposite of sculpting clay. EPS is not a malleable product like clay, and

### THINK OF OTHERS

Just a reminder: if there are others working in the workshop, be considerate of them, clearing up mess regularly, and using extraction systems to create a better working environment. Never consume food and drink in the workshops, as any contaminants in the atmosphere can get into these, and through them, into you – you should have a separate place, away from the immediate environs of the workshop, for eating, drinking (non-alcoholic drinks) and relaxing.

Stone jug – mark-out and cut perspective 1.

it takes a different mind set to use it. It is perhaps easier to think of clay as a modelling and moulding compound that you build up, and EPS and XPS as compounds that require cutting and carving in a reduction process. Looking at it like this, it is possible to see why some people have an initial affinity with one but not the other process. However, each requires a similar approach in preparation when a larger object is being created.

Preparation is key. Make sure that the image you are trying to extract is firmly in your mind and that the piece of EPS you are working on is large enough to accommodate it… if it isn't, add a bit more.

The following process assumes you are sculpting from a regular block. When starting out with EPS carving, it is better to start with something that will prove a manageable challenge: something cylindrical like a mason jar is ideal. The whole thing can be sculpted from the polystyrene, or just the body of the jar, with other elements being added on with a cardboard tube and paper rope for the neck and lip, and a card strip and paper rope for the handle… your choice.

1. Mark onto the front of the polystyrene an outline of the image that you are going to sculpt. This marking-out should be as precise as you can get it. If dealing with very regular objects, use measurements and straight edges to assist you in being accurate. When cutting a cylinder, start with a rectangular cuboid that is the height and width of the finished piece.

2. On the top of the polystyrene mark the position that the object occupies within it, relative to the image that you have carefully marked onto the front surface. In the case of the mason jar, draw two diagonal lines from opposite corner to opposite corner so that you have an 'X', indicating the centre point of the square top surface of the rectangular cuboid. With a compass, inscribe a circle around the marked 'X' that touches the four outer edges of the top square surface. Repeat this process on the bottom surface, as this will make it easier to achieve accuracy with the cylinder later.

3. At this juncture, it should be possible to see what is and isn't needed. Any polystyrene outside the boundaries of your two images is excess material that will need removing before you can deal with the sculpt proper. Although the front image (elevation) of our cylinder appears to take up the whole of the block, it can be clearly seen by looking at the top surface of the block (or top elevation), that it is only where the circumference of the circle touches the outer edges that this is *actually* the case. Because of this, it is the top surface that will be used for marking the areas that require cutting away, and from these we can mark extended lines from top to bottom of the cuboid to facilitate the removal of the block's long corners, as shown in the illustrations.

4. Where the circumference of the circle faces a corner of the bock, draw a diagonal line across the corner of the block, touching the circumference and at right angles to the 'X' line that bisects the circumference as it travels from corner to corner. Repeat this process for the other three corners, and on the underside of the block.

5. Using a straight edge, join up the extremities of the lines you have drawn across the corners on the top edge of the block to those that you have marked on the bottom surface. As you look at the block now, you should see four long triangular sections at the corners, which, when removed, will leave the block looking octagonal.

FRONT
ELEVATION

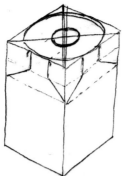

FRONT, SIDE &
TOP ELEVATION

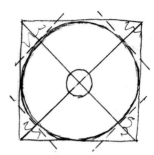

MARKING OUT WHAT
CAN BE REMOVED / CUT AWAY

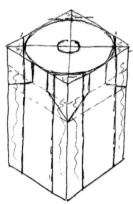

CUT-AWAY MARKED
AROUND THE BLOCK

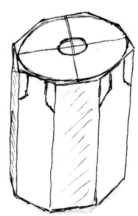

EXCESS MATERIAL
REMOVED

REFINING THE
REMOVAL OF THE EXCESS
TO REVEAL THE CYLINDER

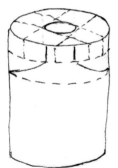

CUTTING AWAY THE
EXCESS FROM THE NECK

CUT AWAY THE
EXCESS FROM THE
SHOULDER

THE BASE SHAPE
FINISHED

PAPER-ROPE & CARD
USED TO BUILD-UP
LIP + HANDLE
FINISH AS DESIRED.

Fig. 30 Marking out and reducing a polystyrene block to make a mason jug.

## IMPROVISED MARKING METHODS

If you do not have a compass large enough you can use a piece of string tied to either a large nail or an offcut of 6mm (¼in) dowel shaped to a point at one end. This can be pushed into the styrene to half its length. Tie a marker pen to the other end of the string at the required distance and then inscribe the circumference of the circle while keeping the string taut.

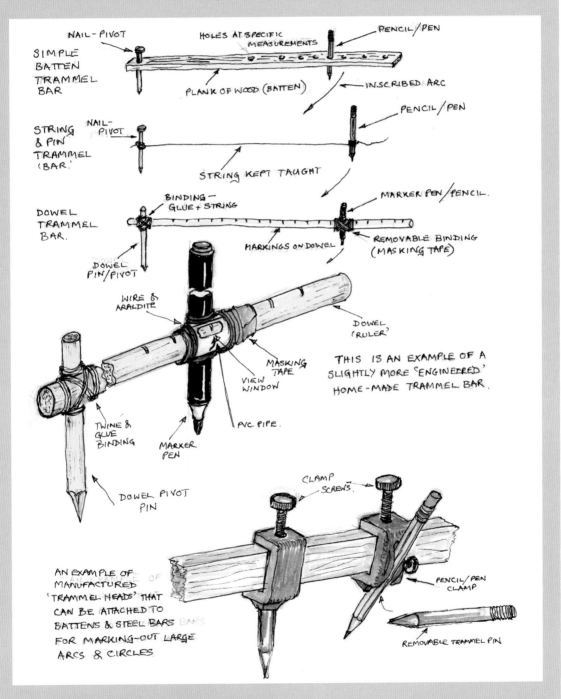

Fig. 31 Improvised trammel bars for marking larger arcs and circles.

*continued* overleaf

## IMPROVISED MARKING METHODS *continued*

A more accurate way of achieving the same result is to use a trammel bar. The pin and the marker are still used but the string is replaced by a length of wood, dowel or rod that the pin and the pen can be attached to or through. If using a piece of wood, you can drill holes into it for different radii up a marked centre line form one end of the wood to the other. The pin goes in one end and the pen is inserted into the relevant hole for the radius required. If using dowel or rod, you secure the pin to the outer edge of the rod just short of one of the ends (this can be achieved with tape, glue and string or rubber bands), and the pen is attached to the same side of the rod as the pin in such a way that its distance from the pin can be adjusted. Increments can be marked up the length of the rod for different radii, and the pen can be taped to a specified measurement, or you can create an adjustable scale by taping/fixing the pen to a short piece of tube that fits snugly over the dowel/rod, and you can use masking tape on either end of the pen tube to hold it in place until it needs moving. With this latter example, there will need to be a little tweaking on the rod markings unless a 'view' window is cut into the pen tube opposite the pen, at its mid line.

6. Taking a saw, cut across each of the corners in turn, making sure that you accurately follow the lines down each of the sides of the block from top to bottom. Use a steady approach and a correct grip on the saw (forefinger pointing down the length of the saw whilst the other three fingers and thumb grip the handle). The hand and forearm should be in complete alignment, the elbow being able to clear the ribs without obstruction, and adjustment of the yaw of the blade achieved by rotating the radius and ulna (bones of the forearm) of the cutting arm, not the wrist.

7. Once all four corners are cut away you will have turned the cuboid into a cylinder with an octagonal profile. The next stage is to cut away the eight smaller corners, which can be done by eye, or by further marking across the corners against the circumference and drawing more lines down the block to create shallower triangles that will be cut away as before. You will then have a cylindrical shape with sixteen sides.

Polystyrene turning lathe. This has been built out of a budget drill press.

8. At this point, a saw becomes too cumbersome to use, but you can use a sharp knife for further reduction; or a Surform drawn down the corners will quickly remove them. Your cylindrical shape will now start to emerge in its true form. Sand/abrasive paper, stapled to a 20cm (8in) piece of 3in × 1in offcut timber, can be used to then refine the shape.

9. To turn the shape into a mason jar, or any other similar shape, is then just a question of shaping the shoulder, dimpling the base and forming a neck and handle, which, as mentioned earlier, can be part of the sculpting process. How you achieve it is up to you, because it is your capabilities and experience that will grow and develop as you make these choices. This basic cylindrical shape can be turned into a whole host of objects, including vases, pots, urns, decorative legs for tables (with a timber or steel core) and so on.

If you have access to a hot wire cutter then you can create the cylinder by setting up a jig, creating a simple turntable and cutting the whole block or a series of discs that can be glued together. It is also possible to build a polystyrene lathe, which can create fantastic results, but you will end up looking like a yeti in a winter wonderland.

Giant polystyrene cotton reels made for a costume exhibition. They were turned on the poly lathe, then simply painted and wood grained as they were purely decorative. For a production they would have been scrimmed.

Altar legs, designed to fit around 25mm box steel legs. They were turned, sliced in half and channelled out with a shaped sculpting hot-wire.

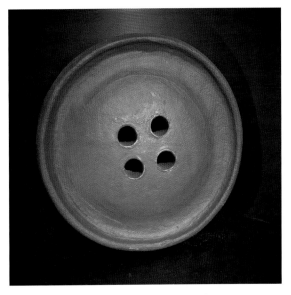

EPS giant button for a panto. It was hand sculpted but a 6mm (¼in) plywood disc core gave it added weight and durability.

Polystyrene coin pillars. Each of the four pillars is 4.3m (14ft) high with capitals attached. That is a lot of coins, so the hot wire was invaluable.

An EPS sculpt of a suit of armour, starting with refinement of the shape.

ABOVE LEFT: This pumpkin was on a pole, so it has a 20mm (¾in) plywood core profile that the pole was fixed to. Polystyrene was glued either side and sculpted around the core. Then it was finished with scrim, gesso, paint and glaze.

ABOVE RIGHT: The Madam Macadam peat bog sculpt. Working outside due to space issues means having to be on top of the clean-up.

Pig timber frame with Copydexed rough block sculpt. Note this is a hollow sculpt for a number of mechanisms.

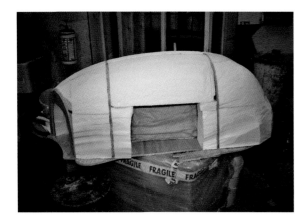

The refined pig sculpt, ready for a foam skin. The square hole in the front is for a large custom-made air bladder so that the pig is seen to be breathing.

A practice sculpt in EPS. This is a useful way to explore the possibilities of polystyrene, to feel form and flow as you sculpt.

A talented student making a beautiful sculpt of a fan shell for a door portico. Note the appropriate dress and PPE.

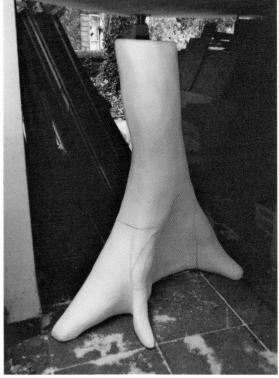

Poly-carved tree for a panto. It's simple, but note the flow of the form.

# FOAM RUBBER SCULPTING

It may seem improbable, but upholstery foam can be used as a sculpting medium for soft/cod props – props that need to be made of materials that are robust but flexible and won't cause injury. These can include items like costume props and puppets, certain types of weapons and foodstuffs. The foam comes in a variety of densities, denoted by colour, and can be bought in cushion or sheet sizes; purchased from a reputable seller, it will be fire retardant.

Foam rubber sheets can be glued into thicker sheets and blocks with various adhesives, including Copydex, which works particularly well due to its flexible nature. Gluing foam rubber has its challenges, namely that the glue requires a light application so that it is not forced into the foam, where it will cause the foam to scrunch when the glue dries. You may need to apply two of three layers of adhesive to get a good bond. Application should be done with a pot and an offcut of foam, with the Copydex being applied with the foam, not poured on! The foam should be treated as a non-porous object so the adhesive will be applied to both surfaces (and, in the case of Copydex, allowed to dry completely before bonding).

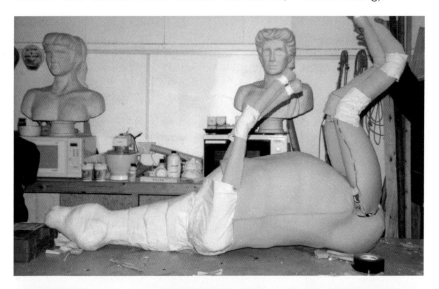

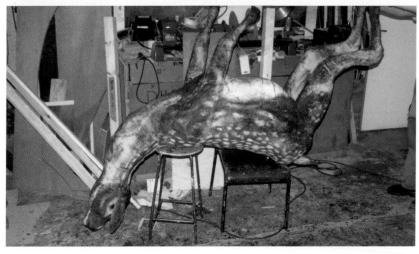

Articulated dead fallow deer foam sculpt over EPS and epoxy resin GRP forms for *The Merry Wives of Windsor*. It was skinned in calico and dressed in faux fur.

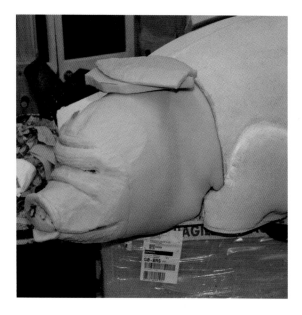

Pig's head foam sculpt, achieved by gluing foam onto the GRP core, drawing the detail on and using a sharp carving knife to shape. Note the two Copydex lines where the foam has been added on to follow the shape of the core.

The finished face of the foam pig's head with a skin of slush mould latex.

Sculpting/carving can be done with very sharp knives and 'the implement'. To create clean lines, do not open the foam out as you cut through it, as this will create a more irregular cut through the depth of the foam and could cause jagged edges at the surface. To create a clean cut, draw a sharp long-bladed knife along a pre-marked line in a confident and steady motion, endeavouring not to over-extend your hand and arm with the knife. Always try to keep your body in good alignment with the knife so that you are never over-reaching, because this can result in inaccurate cutting. To make your cut deeper, simply place the knife into the previously made incision, attempting to maintain the same blade angle, and draw it through the foam, repeating the process until your cut is complete.

Curves can be successfully achieved in several ways. One way is to place the foam onto a level surface. Mark out your cutting line with a marker pen. Hold the knife vertically (this can be done with the knife in your fist, thumb at the top, blade pointing down, or in a more conventional hold

depending on preference), with the blade edge perpendicular to the cut to be made, not the spine of the knife (otherwise the tip of the blade ends up chasing the upper part of the blade, which will cut further ahead as you create the curve, resulting in an irregular, inaccurate cut). Starting at the edge of the foam, use a downward cut – only cutting on the 'down'; do not use a sawing motion unless you require a striated effect – gently easing the perpendicular blade along the cutting line until the hilt touches the foam. Pull the knife back to the top of the cut line ready for the next incision. Proceed in this manner until the cut is complete. Do not force the knife through the foam as this will cause distortion of the foam and a bad cut. Always allow the knife to do the cutting, discover how well it works with the density of the foam you are using, and keep it well sharpened as you work.

Another curve-cutting approach is to cut straight lines and corners first, then continuing with this approach, use further straight cuts to remove the excess material (in the same vein as creating the EPS cylinder above). Then you can refine the curve line by removing the remaining material as detailed above. This approach makes it easier to see the cut you will be making at the expense of having to make more cuts and creating more offcuts of foam.

It is also possible to use a hot wire with foam rubber, but this does tend to leave a slightly tacky edge, as well as creating a lot of fumes.

## Smoothing the Foam Rubber

Refinements can be achieved with sharp knives and scissors (holding the blade edges flat against the foam and using a snipping motion to remove irregularities). Abrasive papers can also be used to advantageous effect so long as you draw/sand in one direction only, rather than backwards and forwards.

It is also possible, as with EPS sculpting, to use an angle grinder with a grinding disc, or abrasive paper flap discs to shape and smooth the foam, with a very light brushing effect. If you go down

TOP: Foam and latex house bricks. Careful, clean cutting with a sharp knife can produce convincing results.

Foam rubber and canvas-coated baguettes made for a fight sequence in *Dick Whittington*. The canvas was Copydexed onto the foam sculpt as a single layer and then latexed. Milled cotton fibres and slush latex create the bread texture in the baguette detail.

this route, the work should be well held or secured down and full safety equipment should be worn, including heavy-duty gloves. If you don't have a firm grip on the foam piece, or have it secured incorrectly, any overly heavy application of the grinder could see your work shooting across the workshop, which is far from ideal and potentially hazardous. The angle grinder technique is only appropriate for medium and large sculpts, although it is possible to use a tool like the Dremel Multitool for smaller pieces. In either case, a fume mask is essential due to the amount of fine particulate material thrown into the atmosphere, and fumes created. If you are not confident with angle grinders and the like, abrasive paper will work just as well; it will take longer to achieve the same results but, on a positive note, you won't have the discomfort of all the protective gear.

Foam rubber sea bass. For this, foam was sandwiched either side of a canvas profile. The fins are Barbour's twine between layers of muslin. A slush latex build-up has been started but a few more coats still need to be carefully sponged on.

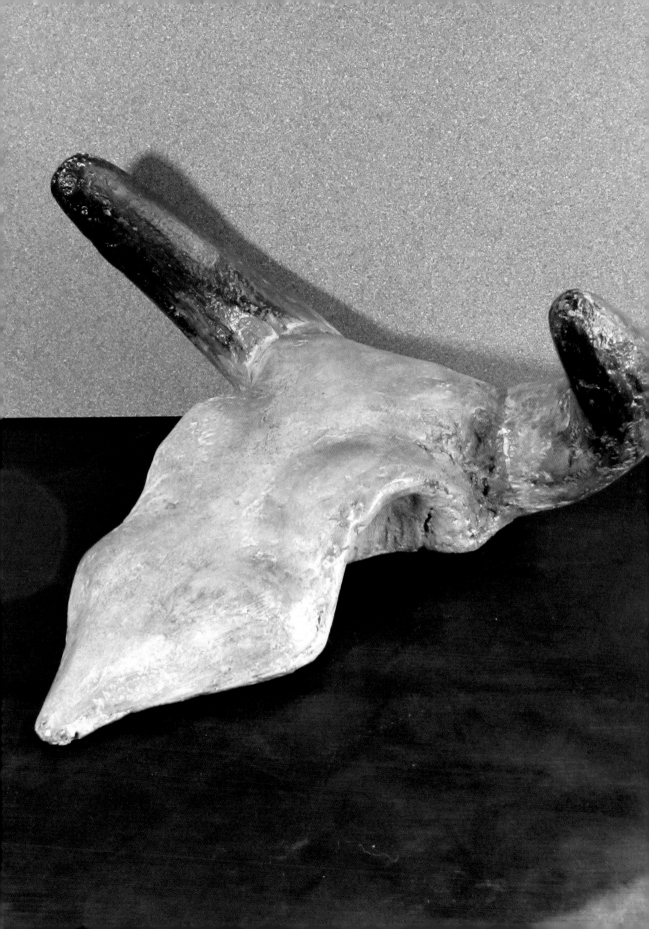

# 6
# MOULDING MATERIALS

Early moulding techniques date back thousands of years as mankind discovered ways to create and improve tools, utensils, ornaments and weapons, and make more robust versions of them. What has changed over the centuries are the types of moulding and casting materials that have been developed, and the tasks that they can be used for. Many of the original processes are still being used, particularly in the arts, jewellery making and metal smithing, but they now sit alongside products like the silicone rubbers. This section will cover a variety of materials, some of which will be covered in detail, whilst others more briefly: this is because of their more advanced nature and resource requirements, which push them into the category of advanced prop making, which is beyond the aims of this volume. However, it is useful to know that they are there waiting for a time when you are ready for them.

## MOULDING MATERIALS AND OPTIONS

When seeking to cast an object it is necessary to consider the material that the original form is made from and the material that you wish the casting to be executed in. This will help determine the most appropriate moulding medium for the job. Failure to take either of these points into account can lead to a failure in the mould, loss of the original and, by extension, any subsequent castings, and a potential loss of money in wasted time and materials. To avoid this, there are two basic rules that we can observe when deciding upon the most appropriate

OPPOSITE: Cow skull made of EPS coated in epoxy resin and milled cotton fibres (epoxy bead weld but used as a durable coating).

moulding medium for the original form and the reproduction casting/s:

- For a rigid casting, use a flexible moulding material
- For a flexible casting, use a rigid moulding material

From a basic prop-making point of view, these two observations should suffice. However, there are always exceptions to the rule, and that is where these four sub-categories come into play:

- If the form is rigid and the casting is to be likewise, then the most suitable moulding materials will be those that are flexible but with a rigid outer 'case' supporting them
- If the original form is made from a flexible or a plastic medium like clay, and the casting is to be made in a flexible medium, then a rigid mould material would be a more suitable choice
- If the form is flexible or plastic, like clay, but the casting is to be rigid, then a flexible medium would be the material of choice
- If the form is rigid but the casting is to be flexible, then a flexible moulding medium would be the logical choice, but this may require a new form to be cast in a plastic medium (like a wax-based clay) so that a rigid mould can be made from the new form and flexible castings can then be taken from the new mould. Of course, this will depend on the casting material being used in the first instance and the detail required from the casting

Why is it necessary to use flexible moulds with rigid forms? Simply put, to avoid the original becoming

Candlestick telephone – forms, moulds and castings. The moulds here are self-supporting silicones. The phone base is a very pliable silicone, but the other moulds are a semi-rigid silicone with minimal flex.

trapped within the mould. There are ways to prevent this happening with rigid forms – indeed, in the pottery industry, rigid moulds are used and reused frequently for slip-cast objects such as mugs, plates, bowls and so on, and this comes down to the next topic, mould type.

## MOULDS

Another vital consideration in mould creation is how the casting is to be extracted from the mould once cured. After all, the mould and the casting are of no use to us if we are unable to extricate one from the other. Again, there are two choices:

- A one-part mould, where the shape of the form is such that it leaves a large enough hole on the underside of the mould after casting that the object and any castings can be easily extracted

- Multiple-part moulds, which are made up of two or more sections due to the complex shape of the object being cast, which may have undercuts and through-cuts that make using a one-part mould impractical, due to the risk of the object becoming trapped within portions of the casting material

## Undercuts, Through-Cuts and Pinch Points

These are features of more complicated forms that can make casting more tricky:

- An **undercut** is a part of the form or original sculpt that shapes back upon itself, that creates realism within the object but can create a potential trapping point for the casting material within a mould
- A **through-cut** is basically a hole through the object, again creating shape and form for the object but that can lock the original form into a mould if not addressed
- A **pinch point** is where a part, or various parts, of the form come close together and then flow away from each other, like in the middle of an hourglass

Let us consider the task of creating a mould of a human figurine of about 20cm (8in) high that is standing on a slightly domed 'grass' base that is approximately 7.5cm (3in) in diameter, overlooking… whatever. The figure is standing with feet apart, the weight taken upon the left leg and hip and the right leg angled slightly out from the body. The right foot is at a 45-degree angle to the left foot, which is pointing forward, and the right heel is in line with the ball of the left big toe. The figure is wearing form-fitting clothing, short sleeves and is barefoot. They have their right hand on their right hip and the left hand across the body with the thumb tucked into the waistband of the trousers, palm hiding any belt buckle, fingers relaxed and pointing down to the right.

The 'figurine' that we are considering presents us with a few challenges. The human form is rife with undercuts and pinch points in any case, but when it adopts various stances and positions, particularly when relaxing, these become exaggerated and the whole aspect of through-cuts is also introduced. If this figure were standing rigidly to attention, chin drawn back, ready for inspection, and wearing less form-hugging clothing, then creating a one-part strippable rubber mould in either dipping latex or even a silicone rubber like Skinsil would be a definite option. This is because all the awkward challenges would be removed by closing up the body, making it more linear and filling the gaps with clothing. If it also had a rifle grasped between the thumb and forefingers of the right hand and drawn tight against the body in the attention pose, this would make life even easier, as it would make the leg section of the mould a little wider, providing more room to remove the original figure and subsequent castings. As it is, because of the more relaxed nature of our figure, a one-part mould is out of the question.

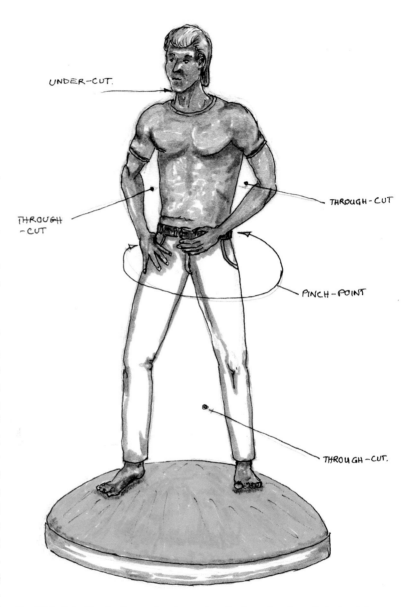

Fig. 32 A statuette of a figure, showing undercuts, through-cuts and pinch points.

We can sometimes make life easier for ourselves by adding details to the figurine by sculpting additional aspects onto it (with a wax- or oil-based clay or even epoxy putty, if it is an existing object). A cardigan or scarf tied around the neck removes/reduces a pinch point and can cover the through-cut created by the right hand on the hip, for example. Sculpting a dog or object between the figure's feet could close off that gap, if it were suitably sized. Obviously these would only be options if they tie in with the 'story' of the figurine for the job that you are doing, but they are options. They might not necessarily make it possible to create a one-part mould from that figure, but could make it easier to change a more complex shape into one that might require only a two-part mould rather than a three- or four-part one.

# MOULDING MATERIALS

There are exceptions to the rules around the choice of casting materials as well as the make-up of the original form. A very flexible casting medium, such as slush mould latex, used to create a semi-rigid casting can, once cured, be drawn through a much narrower aperture than the bulk of the form would suggest, because it can be squashed and folded in on itself to a substantial degree (although it may require a light application of talcum powder first to prevent it from sticking to itself). Another flexible material, like a polyurethane soft expanding foam, would not be able to perform the same trick since the full volume of the mould is taken up with the casting and attempting to compress it to pull it through a narrower aperture would probably distort it and cause it to tear.

It is possible to create rigid moulds for rigid castings where the shape of the form has a uniform aspect that will simply 'pop' out of the mould, such as a shallow bowl form. Where a 'one of a kind' item is required, we can always resort to the plaster waste mould option usually reserved for a detailed clay sculpt that will be reproduced in GRP or casting metals. The mould will be smashed when the casting is cured, leaving nothing but your perfect casting! This is where the phrase, 'They broke the mould when they made you', comes from.

## Plaster

Plaster, for the prop maker, is a valuable resource, as it allows us to take castings from objects with all sorts of shapes and in a wide choice of materials. There are two main types of these plasters that we use, and it is important to note that these are designated as 'casting plasters'.

The alpha plasters are also known as 'stone-cast' plasters because of their denser nature, which makes them very useful where high heat is required for setting the casting.

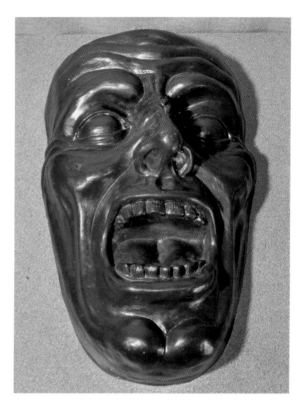

Goliath head waste mould casting, which was taken as a way of preserving the original form once the latex cast had been taken. The mould was broken to remove this positive. GRP is lighter than plaster and more durable.

The beta plasters are also known as 'fine-casting' plasters due to their ability to pick up high detail from castings.

Casting plasters can also be used as rigid supporting cases for flexible mould mediums such as latex and silicone rubbers and have the advantage that they are an inert product that will not 'attack' the rubbers.

### MIXING AND POURING PLASTER

Virtually every plaster has its own weight-to-fluid ratio, which can make the idea of using a variety of plasters a little daunting. However, as a rule of thumb, a simple 2:1 ratio of plaster to water works with both alpha and beta casting and moulding plasters. Although alpha plasters are substantially heavier than their beta counterparts, the volumes for mixing are the same – two parts of plaster to

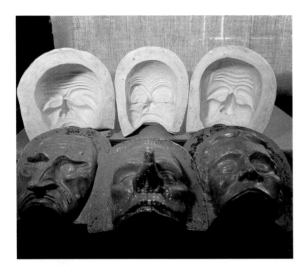

Plaster moulds turned into fibreglass forms. Plaster moulds get 'tired' and can degrade with time and constant use. One way to give new life to an old mould is to turn it into a waste mould for a GRP casting – this could be practical or decorative.

one part of water. Therefore, any casting or moulding process is the same, whichever plaster you are using:

1. Pour the required volume of water into a container.
2. Into a separate dry container, measure out twice the volume of plaster than you have of water. Best practice here is to have two identical containers that are used for dispensing plaster and water – one for each, and kept specifically for the purpose to avoid cross-contamination.
3. At your workstation, start the mixing process by adding the plaster to the water, sprinkling it by the handful over the surface of the water (quickly and efficiently) until an island of plaster is sitting on the surface of the water. Be aware that islands will appear to be forming quite early on, due to the water's surface tension, but these will sink quite quickly.
4. As the island sits there, it will gradually absorb water over a period of about 20–30 seconds and become fully wetted (a process called 'slaking'), at which point it can be mixed.
5. Slide one hand beneath the surface of the water, palm up (using your other hand to stabilize

the mixing pot), and mix the plaster into the palm of your hand while moving it around the bottom of the container; try not to break the surface of the water as this can encourage air bubbles to form. After a few minutes, you will have an even mix of plaster and water.
6. Draw your hand out of the plaster to see whether you have achieved an even mix. If the coating on your hand is the same from wrist to fingertips, you're good to go. If, however, the mix gets more watery as it nears the wrist and thicker at the fingers, a little more mixing is required, with an emphasis on mixing from the bottom of the pot to the surface of the mix… but don't take too long.
7. Plaster can be poured or spattered/flicked, depending on whether you are creating box or balloon moulds.

## Latex: Dipping/Casting and Brush Mould

Although classified as two products from the sales point of view, these are, in fact the same product except that a thixotropic additive has been introduced into the second to create the more viscous product called brush mould latex. It is possible to buy this additive separately to add to your dipping latex as and when you need it and thus save the expense of keeping a stock of brush-mould latex that you may only use infrequently.

## Modroc/Gypsona Plaster Bandage

How you buy it will depend on your supplier, but the technical name for this product is Gypsona plaster bandage, which is a gauze bandage that is impregnated with gypsum plaster. In the craft trade it is referred to as Modroc (modelling rock) because it is very useful as a modelling material for hobbies such as railway modelling, where entire landscapes can be formed with this, card or wire and chicken-wire constructions.

① MEASURE OUT ONE-PART OF WATER TO TWO-PARTS OF PLASTER INTO SEPERATE CONTAINERS.

WATER

PLASTER

② SPRINKLE THE PLASTER EVENLY OVER THE SURFACE OF THE WATER.

③ ONCE AN ISLAND OF PLASTER HAS FORMED UPON THE SURFACE OF THE WATER, ALLOW IT TO 'SLAKE' - SOAKING UP THE SURROUNDING WATER UNTILL FULLY WETTED.

④ IMMERSE A HAND BENEATH THE SURFACE OF THE WATER AND MIX THE PLASTER FROM BENEATH THE SURFACE UNTIL EVENLY MIXED THROUGH-OUT, ROLLING THE FINGERS INTO YOUR PALM.

Fig. 33 Plaster mixing – the slaking process.

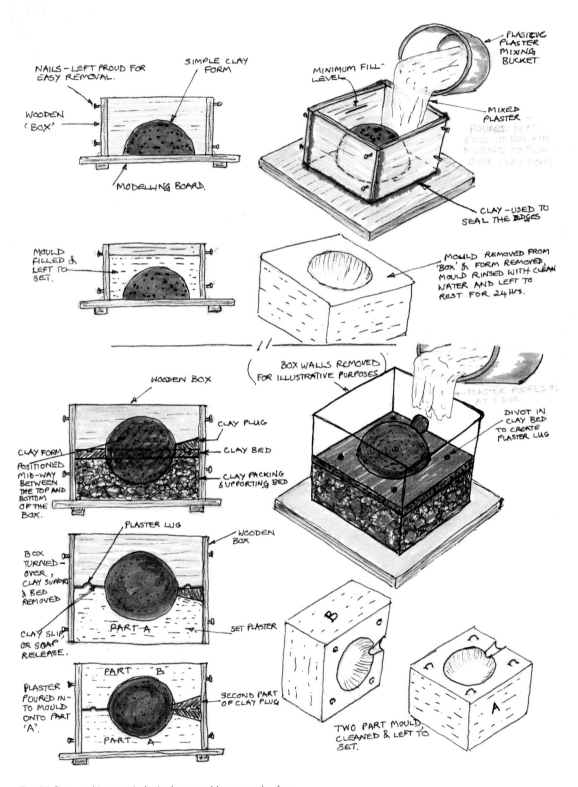

Fig. 34 One- and two-part plaster box moulds over a clay form.

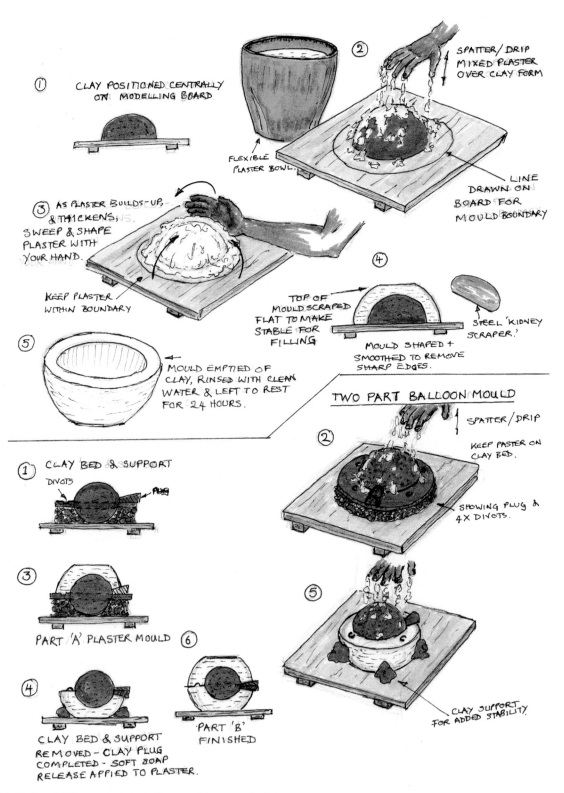

① CLAY POSITIONED CENTRALLY ON MODELLING BOARD

② SPATTER/DRIP MIXED PLASTER OVER CLAY FORM

FLEXIBLE PLASTER BOWL.

LINE DRAWN ON BOARD FOR MOULD BOUNDARY

③ AS PLASTER BUILDS UP & THICKENS, SWEEP & SHAPE PLASTER WITH YOUR HAND.

KEEP PLASTER WITHIN BOUNDARY

④ TOP OF MOULD SCRAPED FLAT TO MAKE STABLE FOR FILLING

STEEL 'KIDNEY SCRAPER.'

MOULD SHAPED + SMOOTHED TO REMOVE SHARP EDGES.

⑤ MOULD EMPTIED OF CLAY, RINSED WITH CLEAN WATER & LEFT TO REST FOR 24 HOURS.

## TWO PART BALLOON MOULD

② SPATTER/DRIP

KEEP PASTER ON CLAY BED.

SHOWING PLUG & 4 X DIVOTS.

① CLAY BED & SUPPORT

DIVOTS

PLUG

③ PART 'A' PLASTER MOULD ⑥

④ CLAY BED & SUPPORT REMOVED – CLAY PLUG COMPLETED – SOFT SOAP RELEASE APPIED TO PLASTER.

'PART 'B' FINISHED

⑤

CLAY SUPPORT FOR ADDED STABILITY.

Fig. 35 One- and two-part plaster balloon moulds over a clay form.

ABOVE: Two-part balloon mould opened for removal of the clay form.

LEFT: Plaster box mould of suitcase corners.

ABOVE: Plasterer's scrim, coarse tape. This is very useful for reinforcing a mould and reducing the amount of plaster required. Use after the detail layer has been applied and is firming up, then build up three layers of scrim over this with fresh plaster.

ABOVE RIGHT: A silicone rubber mould. Without a supporting case, the mould would be unstable. There are many choices, but arguably the easiest and quickest is plaster.

RIGHT: A scrim-reinforced plaster case for a silicone rubber mould. Note the low profile of the mould case compared to the size of the original silicone mould in previous photo.

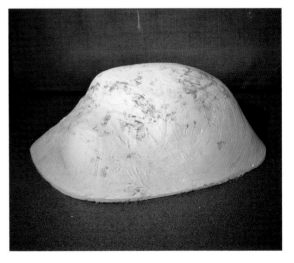

Clown form. The initial layers are in dipping latex – a few layers are sufficient to secure the detail in the form. Allow to become translucent between layers, then apply a good layer of brush mould latex.

Over the previous latex layers, scrim three layers of muslin and more dipping latex, or brush mould latex for a thicker build-up. After this, Modroc and PVA was moulded over the rubber to form a lightweight case.

In mould making, it can be used to make simple rigid moulds that can be easily stripped away but are not great on detail. More often it is used as a supporting case for flexible mould mediums like latex and silicone rubber (such as Skinsil).

## Hot-Melt Rubber

Hot-melt rubbers, such as Vinamold and Gel-flex, are mentioned here merely as a point of information, because although the concept is not particularly challenging (you melt some rubber and pour it over your form, let it cool and then take castings from it), the equipment is expensive, detail is moderate, and the health and safety issues are significant, with molten temperatures of the polymerised PVC resin at 150°C when pourable; the length of time it takes to melt the rubber is also considerable. That is not to say that this method does not have a place, but for the purposes of this book there are other, more suitable products that we can use.

ABOVE LEFT: A mould of a fist: a dipping and brush mould latex mould, reinforced with muslin and supported by a Varaform case.

ABOVE RIGHT: Dipping latex set-up with latex and coagulant poured into marked containers.

ABOVE LEFT: Lower the form slowly into the latex to avoid trapping air bubbles in the detail. Withdraw the form equally slowly.

ABOVE RIGHT: Carefully (avoid splashing), lower the dipped form into the coagulant until the latex is immersed, and then lift slowly back out and allow any excess to drip back.

Place in a warm oven, about 40–50ºC, to allow to dry fully. When dry, the latex will look slightly amber in colour and will darken with age and exposure to UV light.

The mould empty, the case in place, the case can be taped up with masking tape to provide maximum support. After a casting has been taken and has set, remove the case and use soapy water to ease the rubber off.

Once dry, for more complex shapes, a case can be made from Modroc or Varaform before the original form is removed.

A Modroc case supporting a Brush Mould latex mould for a GRP skull mask. The case is very durable because the Modroc was worked with a PVA and water mix (like papier mâché), rather than water alone.

## GRP: Glass-Reinforced Plastic/Fibreglass

It is not uncommon to hear this product referred to as fibreglass, which is a misnomer because the actual fibreglass is only one component – admittedly the reinforcing component – of the process that is more correctly named GRP (glass-reinforced plastic), which is a literal description of the product and how it works. A liquid resin with a catalyst mixed in, to facilitate a measured cure time, is used to bond layers of glass-fibre mat or fabric together in a lamination process. This can be used for making moulds or taking castings. The advantage of GRP moulds (and castings) is that they are very durable and extremely light when compared to plaster moulds of the same size but tend to be suited to forms of a more generic shape, as excessive detail could cause castings to lock into the mould.

GRP can also be used as a durable rigid supporting case for flexible mould mediums such as latex and silicone rubbers, producing a lighter and more durable case than plaster, although it is advisable to use release/barriers sprays to prevent 'styrene attack', which certain rubbers can be prone to.

Heavy 450gsm chopped strand mat. It comes in various weights, but this is the standard reinforcing component for polyester GRP. It's not suited to epoxy resin because the resin has a high viscosity.

GRP gondola made for *A Merchant of Venice* from epoxy resin and woven roving.

Glass fibre tissue is used to finish off the laying up of polyester resin and chopped strand mat (CSM), providing a cleaner finish.

## Silicone

Perhaps the most detailed moulding medium available to us, silicone rubbers are superb for taking rigid castings from a wide range of resin types, and can also be used for casting certain metals, as well as flexible mediums such as the polyurethane flex foams. They are not suitable for standard latex products, as these rely upon absorption of moisture into the mould surface, but they work very well with foam latex for puppetry and prosthetic make-up.

Silicone putty comes in various forms and is useful for creating small, quick moulds in a variety of situations, even taking impressions from objects that are on vertical surfaces or overhead.

### SKINSIL

Skinsil is another silicone product, which is comparatively new in the history of silicones, and has been designed for life-casting purposes. The aim was to get more highly detailed impressions from the model/actor that is being cast, but, also, an impression that could be used to produce repeat castings directly from the original mould, in a variety of materials, which up to the advent of Skinsil had not been possible. It is used in conjunction with

Pig's head form with polyester GRP and 300gsm CSM making the endo-skeleton for an animatronic pig.

plaster bandage, which provides a rigid support case for the Skinsil mould; once the first casting is in the mould and cured, the plaster bandage case could be set aside and replaced with a reinforced plaster case, GRP case or even a case made from a thermoformable plastic, with reinforcing struts.

## Alginate

Alginate is a very cost-effective way of taking detailed life casting impressions. Most of us will be familiar with it due to its use in dentistry for taking dental impressions of our teeth. The detail produced when using alginate is incredible, especially when you consider that it is a product that is extracted from brown seaweed – a combination of the wonders of nature and human ingenuity.

Alginate is a powder that is mixed with water and then applied to the object/subject to be moulded. Depending on the set of the alginate you have chosen, you will have between 2 and 8 minutes working time to create the mould, and once set it requires a plaster bandage case for support. A positive casting must be taken from the alginate

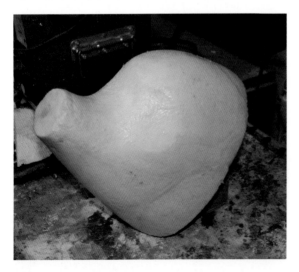

Pig's head form. It is possible to use polyester resin GRP over polystyrene if, like here, dipping latex has been used to create skin over the top of the EPS. Three or four layers should do, but you can apply more.

Pig's head endo-skeleton. Note that the EPS core has been removed, along with the latex skin, leaving a clean interior.

Humpty Dumpty made from epoxy GRP and woven roving. Unlike polyester resin, epoxy resin can be applied straight onto EPS without harming it. Note the ply core profiles. They attached to a steel fame and internal counterweight system.

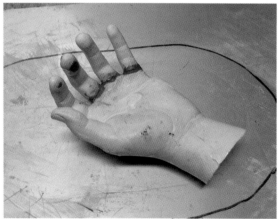

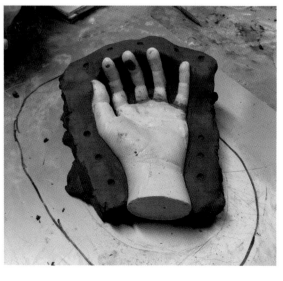

ABOVE: Polyester GRP forms made over clay sculpts to act as forms for leatherwork.

ABOVE RIGHT: A plaster life-cast hand ready for moulding.

RIGHT: The hand is set into a clay bed. Note how the bed follows the cupped shape of the hand. The hand is also raised off the board.

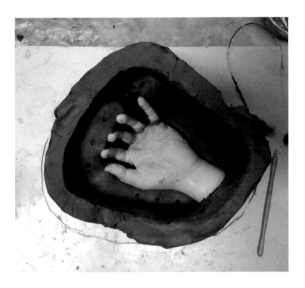

A clay wall is erected around the clay bed and carefully worked into it to eliminate leaks. Note that the wall presses against the stump of the wrist. Product will be poured in here. Spray with a non-silicone release agent.

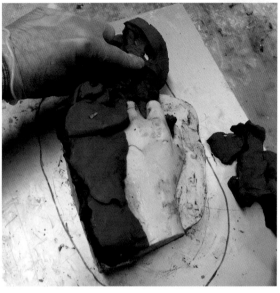

The clay bed is being removed. Remove excess clay from the silicone bed.

Part A of the mould poured. The mould can now be turned over.

Replace and tidy up the wall and check that it is higher than the hand by about 25mm (1in).

mould at the earliest opportunity due to its propensity to dry out and shrink if left for too long. Shrinkage happens over a period of hours and can be inhibited by packing the alginate mould with damp cloths or towels and covering it; but a casting should ideally be taken from the mould within a half hour of the alginate setting.

## Health and Safety

When using a new product for the first time, always be sure to read the instructions carefully and acquire a copy of the H&S and COSHH data sheets.

Weight verses volume. Note that the silicone is shipped in a 2.5kg tin but the silicone volume is lower in the tin because it is heavier than products that have a more equal weight to volume ratio. Sold as a kit, the catalyst is also part of the total weight of 2.5kg.

ABOVE: As silicone is very viscous, it can help to have an extra pair of hands when mixing. The mix should be thorough, getting right into the bottom corner to achieve an even colour blend.

TOP RIGHT: When pouring, do it from a height, producing a thin ribbon of silicone. Pour in from one point at an edge and allow the silicone to flow through the mould.

RIGHT MIDDLE: It takes a while but keep that ribbon-pour right up to the end of the tin.

RIGHT: A two-part silicone mould of a hand. Including the curing time of the silicone, this mould was produced over two days and nights. Optimally you would leave it for another week to fully cure at room temperature.

# 7
# CASTING MATERIALS

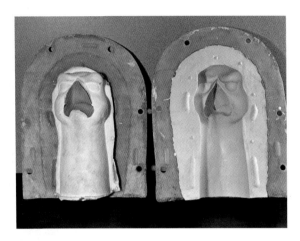

Foamed latex skin from a silicone and GRP mould. This is one of two halves of the head and neck. Foam latex is flexible and pliant and makes a good prosthetic and puppet skin.

OPPOSITE: Phoenix puppet – foamed latex over a GRP skull and beak casting.

Dipping latex and slush mould latex come in 5kg containers.

In this chapter we will be looking at a variety of casting materials, some rigid and some flexible, that can be used for taking impressions from the mould mediums covered in the previous chapter. It will become clear that certain materials that can be used for making moulds can also be used for taking castings from moulds.

## LATEX

### AL 360 Slush Mould Latex

Often just referred to as slush mould latex, this is a very useful, natural medium for taking castings from plaster moulds. The combination of latex and plaster moulds just works, and is a very useful tool in the prop maker's repertoire. Although slush

mould latex is a semi-rigid medium, it can be used to create castings that to all intents and purposes look solid. This is down to a principle mentioned in the introduction – that theatre is about illusion, and slush mould latex can help us to attain that in several ways.

Castings are achieved by pouring the latex into clean (this simply means free of contaminants like oil or grease that could harm the latex, or act as an anti-flocculant) plaster moulds and leaving it to sit for 20 minutes, after which a skin will have formed on the internal surface of the mould; at this point the excess latex can be poured back into its container, ready to be used for the next casting. The mould is then placed into a drier at between 50–60°C, or somewhere warm, until the skin has dried and can be removed from the mould. Drying times are affected by the size of the

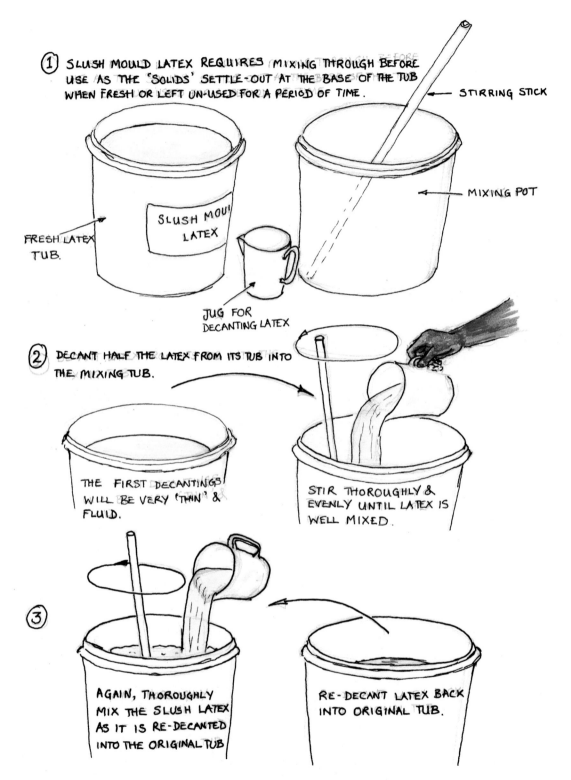

① SLUSH MOULD LATEX REQUIRES MIXING THROUGH BEFORE USE AS THE 'SOLIDS' SETTLE-OUT AT THE BASE OF THE TUB WHEN FRESH OR LEFT UN-USED FOR A PERIOD OF TIME.

STIRRING STICK

MIXING POT

SLUSH MOUL LATEX

FRESH LATEX TUB.

JUG FOR DECANTING LATEX

② DECANT HALF THE LATEX FROM ITS TUB INTO THE MIXING TUB.

THE FIRST DECANTINGS WILL BE VERY 'THIN' & FLUID.

STIR THOROUGHLY & EVENLY UNTIL LATEX IS WELL MIXED.

③ AGAIN, THOROUGHLY MIX THE SLUSH LATEX AS IT IS RE-DECANTED INTO THE ORIGINAL TUB

RE-DECANT LATEX BACK INTO ORIGINAL TUB.

Fig. 36  Preparing slush mould latex for use when new or after prolonged non-usage.

mould; how dry the mould was prior to use; and whether it is an open or closed mould – if there is a large aperture allowing the warm air in to circulate, the casting will dry quicker than if the heat needs to penetrate the thickness of the mould. To test whether the latex has set, use the 'thumbnail test'. Simply push your thumbnail into an area of the latex casting: if an impression of the nail remains, it has not set, but if the nail impression springs back, then it has.

## REINFORCED SLUSH MOULD LATEX WITH GLASS FIBRE

Slush mould latex can be made much more rigid by scrimming glass fibre mat or plasterer's (hessian) scrim onto the inner surfaces of the casting. Milled cotton fibres or cellulose fibres can be mixed into the liquid slush mould latex to form a butter in paste that can be used to thicken, or smooth out, certain areas of the internal casting for rigidity in those areas, or prior to scrimming in the fibreglass or hessian.

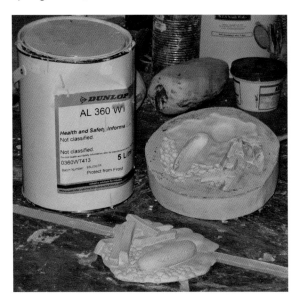

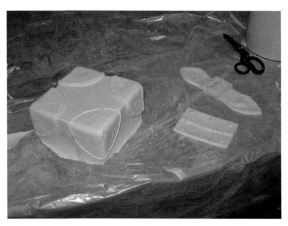

ABOVE: Latex castings being trimmed.

LEFT: Slush mould latex casting of sausage, egg, beans and chips removed from the mould.

Multiple castings. Well-thought-out moulds can increase productivity by reducing running times on the mould.

Casting of olives from a clay sculpt, ready to be painted and fitted into a bowl.

The paint job makes all the difference to these slush mould castings of cakes.

The finished sausage, egg, beans and chips.

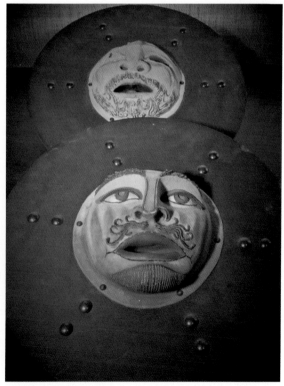

Puppet head shield bosses – Odin and Thor, for a *Beowulf* theatre in education tour – made from slush latex.

Cow skull made from slush mould latex and real horns.

Daisy the Cow made from reinforced latex. Note the cutaways, designed to reduce weight; with the glass fibre adding strength to the casting, there is no loss in rigidity. The muslin is there to support the faux fur.

Priscilla head made from reinforced slush latex.

## Dipping/Casting Latex and Brush Mould Latex

Also known simply as latex, depending upon your supplier, dipping latex is a different product from slush mould latex as it does not contain any additional additives like sulphur, or the bulking agents. Although closely related to Copydex, it is much more fluid when poured, and once cured, it does not retain any of the adhesive properties of the former. As with Copydex, if left exposed to sunlight/ UV light, this latex will gradually biodegrade.

A look inside the body of the phoenix puppet. Again cutaways reduce weight but glass fibre provides rigidity and the muslin can be seen supporting the faux fur fabric.

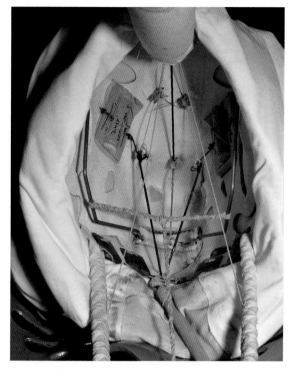

A bear head made from reinforced latex from a three-part plaster mould, for another production of *The Tempest*.

A glimpse into Daisy's head reveals mechanisms for her jaw, both eyes and neck (at top of picture). Note that everything is anchored into the reinforced latex.

Daisy the Cow.

The Goliath puppet head made from reinforced latex. The hair and eyebrows are sheepskin and the beard is rabbit skin.

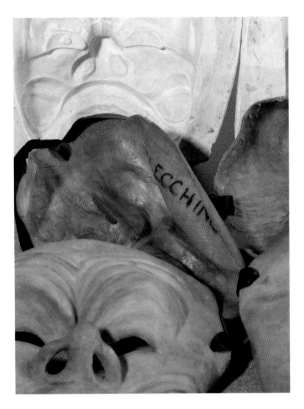

Lightweight, durable rehearsal and performance masks can be made by using dipping and brush mould latex and scrimming muslin into plaster moulds. The example here has been dyed with fabric dye and salt in hot water.

## WHAT IS LATEX?

Latex is a natural resource. Although it can be harvested from many sources, the main production is from the rubber tree (*Hevea brasiliensis*) in Malaysia and Indonesia. Latex has a distinctive smell of ammonia, as ammonia gas is suffused throughout the latex to preserve it for transportation. When the latex is exposed to the atmosphere, the ammonia disperses and the latex will start to cure.

There are many different liquid latex products, which have differing properties. In prop making the key forms are Copydex, dipping/casting latex, brush mould latex, slush mould latex and foam latex. Foam latex is ideal for puppetry and prosthetic make-up as it is lightweight, but without the proper equipment it can be a tricky product to master – though very satisfying when you do.

The main difference between the other latex products mentioned and slush mould latex is the colour when cured. Slush mould latex, due to its make-up, dries a creamy-white colour, whereas the base latex colour of the others dries to a translucent pale amber colour that darkens with age. (Foam latex becomes a creamy white colour when the other ingredients are added to it; it is 'foamed' in a mixer and then baked.)

Latex is an air-drying product and drying will be speeded up if warmth is added into the equation. Although latex is naturally temperature resistant, it is better for the non-foamed products to keep the temperature range to between 50 and 60°C, as this will extend the life of the moulds and reduce risk of damage to the forms used to make dipping latex moulds.

Dipping latex is used, as the name suggests, by dipping the object to be moulded (with a little preparation), into the dipping latex. This is done slowly, and once the object is fully immersed, it is slowly withdrawn. It is then allowed to air dry until it starts to become translucent, at which point it is re-dipped, with the process being repeated until the required build-up or desired number of layers (normally twelve) is reached.

As mentioned previously, brush mould latex is dipping latex with an additive that makes it substantially thicker, with a consistency of soft butter. It is used in conjunction with dipping latex to thicken mould walls and create a much more rigid and thicker mould than can be achieved with the dipping latex alone, and with less effort. It is applied in what is referred to as a 'butter-on' process. Butter muslin can be used with the brush mould latex to support and reinforce the exterior of the mould, like a cheese.

## Additives

### LATEX THICKENER

Latex thickener is a thixotropic additive, a translucent gel, that can be put into latex products to make the latex more viscous so that it can be buttered into moulds or onto castings until the desired build-up has been achieved. At this point it can be put into a drier on a gentle heat, or set aside to cure in a warm place.

### LATEX COAGULANT

This is a mild acid used in conjunction with dipping latex to counteract the effect that the ammonia has on the latex, allowing it to coagulate (set) quicker, so that the layers of mould build-up can be achieved more quickly. The coagulant is added as an additional dip between layers of latex: so you would dip the form into the latex, and then into the coagulant, followed by a dip into the latex and then back into the coagulant and so on until the desired build-up is achieved. Between dips, always allow the excess product to drip back into the relevant dipping container to avoid wastage and cross contamination. Latex coagulant is an inexpensive way of achieving quicker mould build-up. Its acidic strength is something akin to a white vinegar, but all precautions should be taken, as a matter of workshop hygiene, to avoid skin and eye contact and spillages.

### MILLED COTTON AND TREECELL (CELLULOSE) FIBRES

These two products can be used with a wide range of materials, but a little playing around has shown that they can make good fillers for latex products, especially when using brush mould latex, or with latex thickener, as it creates a solid but flexible casting while reducing the weight you would get from a thickened casting without the fibres. The milled cotton/Treecell also gives a spongy quality that makes it a wonderful solution for making heads, ears, noses and so on for human and animal puppets and masks. It works well with slush mould latex for reinforcement, but when used in conjunction with dipping and brush mould latex the results are more flexible. Run a few layers of dipping latex into a mould, allow each to set, then butter in a mix of brush mould latex and milled cotton/Treecell fibres and put the mould in an oven to cure. Alternatively, you can use a soap mould release on the plaster mould and put the brush

mould latex and fibre mix straight into the mould. The release is a necessary precaution to prevent the mix from 'biting' into the mould and causing surface damage to it.

## CASTING SILICONES

Silicone rubber can also be used for taking castings, and of recent years there has been a substantial quantity of new products added onto the market for model makers, craftspeople and the theatre, TV and film industries. These are suitable for prosthetics and puppets as well as skins for animatronics. They come in two parts (A and B) that are translucent, and can be coloured with a broad range of silicone pigments. They are designed to be highly flexible and tough, with the intention of replicating skin.

## POLYURETHANE PRODUCTS

This is a very versatile range of materials all derived from the same base but processed in separate

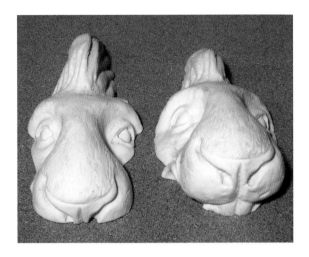

Porcupine sample castings showing the natural colour of the polyurethane.

Polyurethane flex-foam bricks, cast from a sealed plaster mould. The plaster mould surface had to be sealed and release agents applied for each casting.

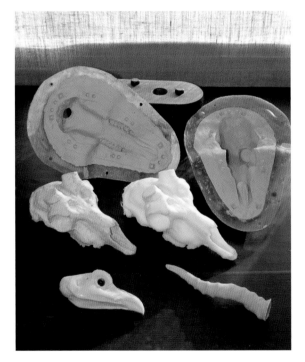

Polyurethane rigid and flexible castings. The antelope skulls are taken from the silicone mould; the paler one is a soft foam. The capercaillie head, bottom right, is from a taxidermy supplier.

OPPOSITE: Polyurethane porcupine door knocker from a clay sculpt and silicone mould. There is also an internal core of EPS to reduce resin volume when casting, which was cheaper than making a two-part silicone mould – the length is about 35cm (14in) top to bottom.

Cruciform with pained Christ. Two of these were required for a production of *Macbeth*. A trawl around an antiques market resulted in a pewter original. One mould later there were two polyurethane castings.

ways to create different properties. They come as resins or foam products, in rigid and flexible forms, non-expanded and expanded, and can suit a wide range of tasks.

# GRP – FIBREGLASS

As mentioned earlier, GRP makes a very good casting medium where a solid shell or core is required. It is very useful for producing endo-skeletal forms for puppets and animatronics, where it can be used in conjunction with foam latex, casting silicones and casting urethanes.

Head mould opened with the casting still in place.

Stippling in 450gsm glass fibre into a silicone mould.

Three layers of glass and one of tissue.

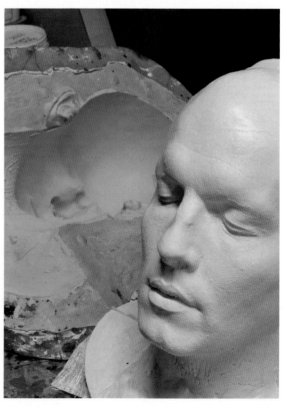

Finished casting, ready for final trim.

One mould, multiple castings, many options.

GRP wobbling clown head – finished.

A replica Series 200 GPO phone. The body is polyester resin GRP. The 'antler cradle', dial and handset are polyurethane castings, all from parts of original phones.

# COLD CASTING

This is a technique that uses polyester casting resins and various fillers such as stone and metal powders. The term cold casting refers to the task of creating statues and castings using GRP where the gel coat is loaded with metal powder. When cured and polished, the finished object can look identical to an object that was made in a foundry with molten metal, but at a fraction of the price. Cold casting is a useful way of creating metal and stone plaques and busts, statues and mouldings in very durable mediums, and has the added benefit that you can create multiple items from the same mould.

A series of ten stars from one card and Apoxie Sculpt form (bottom left) and the silicone rubber mould (bottom right). Ten stars from this mould made the silicone rubber mould at the top, which made another sixty stars.

Two castings from a silicone putty mould of a stone rosette from a public house frontage. The top casting is Fillite and the bottom one is slate powder, both mixed with polyester resin.

# GLASS FX AND SUGAR GLASS

These are products that are used for 'breakable effects' such as windows, bottles, plates and vases. They are plastic polymers, which, when heated (best done in an electric oven at a controlled temperature) to the correct temperature, become pourable and when set are brittle so they break in a glass-like fashion but without the hazards. There is also a similar silicone product available, which has the advantage that there is no risk whatsoever of cuts and grazes for the performers. Accidental breakages with Glass FX can potentially be re-melted and recycled, something that is not recommended for pieces that have been swept off the stage floor (this is due to any foreign objects and contaminants that could be mixed up with the product and cause a potential fire risk/toxic fumes when reheated).

The term sugar glass is often used to describe these products because in years gone by molten sugar was used to create the same effect, but none of these modern products use sugar as an ingredient.

# PLASTER BREAKABLES

There are times when a statuette, figurine, china cup or bowl need to be broken during the action of a play. This comes into the realm of running props. It might be possible to acquire all the china wear that you require, but this does have its risks as china produces very sharp edges when broken, and the cost may be prohibitive. Creating a mould that multiple plaster slip castings can be taken from can be a much more appropriate option. The mould, for a figurine, could even be purchased from a craft store as a strippable rubber (dipping latex) mould if a suitable shape were available. After an initial casting, you could then make further moulds of your own, or simply buy multiples, to increase production turnout.

The process of slip casting involves mixing up a beta plaster in the usual manner, pouring it into the mould until it is about third full and then rotating and tipping the mould to form an even skin on the internal surface of the mould. It will take a little trial and error to achieve the desired wall thickness. Do not rush it, and only mix up sufficient plaster for the job at hand. More plaster can be added when the first layer has set and remember to use soapy water on the outside of the strippable rubber mould to make its removal easier.

Silicone rubber, multi-part moulds can be used for larger or more complicated slip castings, and for this the plaster can simply be poured into the mould and left to set. When cured and dry, the slip castings can be painted after sealing the surface of the dry casting with watered-down PVA or glaze.

# JESMONITE

A very useful and robust product, Jesmonite is described as a water-based glass-fibre system, which is technically true, as it does use a water-based resin and a stitched quadraxial glass-fibre fabric to bond and reinforce a type of stone cast plaster. This should not, however, be confused with GRP and the reasons that you might choose a polyester or epoxy resin-based system for a job. There are indeed times where any of these products could be chosen over any other, and for a variety of valid reasons; if you require a light weight product, Jesmonite will not be your first choice, but it does have many other uses and advantages that make it worth using.

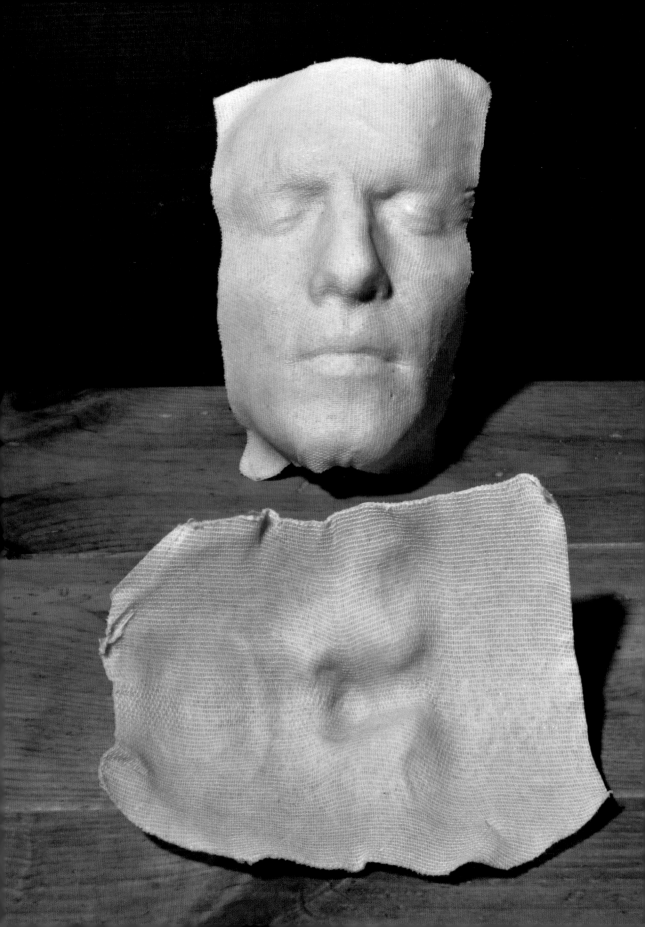

# 8
# THERMOFORMABLE PLASTICS

Celastic Greek helm moulded over a clay form. When dry, it was removed from the form and cleaned. The crest plume was made from unravelled hemp, knotted through the Celastic and sealed in.

Of all the products that have become available for use in prop making, the thermoformable plastics are perhaps the most exciting. The reason for this is that we had not long previously lost an invaluable product known as Celastic (which certainly had its health risks if used without proper precautions). It was great for masks, armour, statues, puppet bodies and heads – in fact, with the right preparation, it could be draped and moulded over a wide variety of shapes and, when laminated to itself, created a very tough shell. It could then be dressed in products like papier mâché pulp, gesso, tissue, fabrics, faux furs, jewels and so on. However, it had to be softened with industrial acetone, which meant it was potentially a COSHH high-risk product.

Thankfully the gap between Celastic going and the thermoformable plastics arriving was not too long, and soon there were Varaform, Wonderflex and Foss Shape, as well as the newer Worbla's product ranges. Thermoformable products are available from many sources, possibly even your local craft store and art supplier, but some products may only be attainable through specialist outlets or on the internet. Thermoformable plastics are suitable for a wide range of props, but are particularly useful for masks, puppetry and armour.

## VARAFORM

Varaform is a cotton open mesh that is impregnated with thermoformable plastic, and it is this open structure that makes Varaform incredibly pliable.

OPPOSITE: Wonderflex TMR 1 demonstrating the flex and stretch of the material and the detail it can pick up.

Examples of Varaform, both light and heavy. The mesh structure has both advantages and disadvantages, but it is a versatile product.

BELOW: Handbag pug dogs for the Ugly Sisters. Varaform was used to make the unseen body forms to support the head and shoulders. Both were taken as variants from existing pug dog moulds.

Cleopatra's crown modelled in Varaform. This product takes papier mâché pulp well, especially with a light pre-sanding to key.

Two half-head bird masks made from Varaform with Celluclay beaks and real feathers.

overlaps for adjoining pieces, much like papier mâché, with the joins being worked into each other firmly (which is where steam comes into its own).

## WONDERFLEX

Manufactured by Foss, Wonderflex is a solid sheet thermoformable plastic with a polyester gauze impressed into it. Foss originally trialled this in a pale blue/green colour and in six different thicknesses ranging from about 0.5mm up to about 2mm. It is currently only sold as a white product at 1mm thick.

Heating is achieved by hot-air gun, but it is also possible to heat it in electric workshop ovens, and even in hot water, or with a steamer, but with the heat required being about 70–80°C, it is advisable to wear snug-fitting, heat-resistant gloves; rubber gloves, like those used for washing dishes, work well. It is possible to work heated Wonderflex with your bare hands, but unless you have developed a good tolerance to hot products you may find it very uncomfortable, especially when working

Varaform is bought in sheets or rolls (dependent upon the quantity you require and supplier availability), in two grades (heavy or light) and a gauze membrane, a lightweight closed sheet that cuts and tears readily. Strength is gained through lamination, and all three types will bond with each other.

Varaform products are designed to be softened in hot water at about 70°C (no hotter); you can buy a Varaform thermostatically controlled bath for the purpose (at great expense), or just use a hot plate and a suitably sized pot. When heated sufficiently, which only takes a minute or so once the water is up to temperature, the Varaform can be hooked out of the water with a stick or bent wire and can be handled almost immediately, once you shake off any hot water still clinging to it, but you need to work quickly and efficiently. Steam can be used from a suitable supply, such as a milliner's (hat) steamer or a wallpaper steamer, to re-soften the Varaform as you work it. Hot air can also be used to soften the Varaform, but it is easy to overheat, at which point it becomes very tacky.

Pieces of Varaform are cut to a suitable size and shape for the area to be covered, with appropriate

Wonderflex TMR 1. The blue/green is the colour it came in when first available; the white is the current product.

LEFT: This mask was made using TMR 6. It does not pick up the same detail, but it does hold a good, solid shape in one thickness. It was finished with gesso and paint.

ABOVE RIGHT: A Wonderflex eye mask where all the added detail was also achieved with the Wonderflex, the texture of the product adding to the overall look.

Half masks on sticks. All the detail on the foreground masks and sticks is achieved with Wonderflex. The top mask has added lace and twine. The sticks were secured in with the Wonderflex and are still holding many years later.

on bigger projects. A fair bit of thumb and finger pressure is required to bond layers together and smooth and shape it, but you could use stainless steel modelling tools or improvise with 500ml drinks bottles filled with warm water. Where extra durability is required, layers of Wonderflex can be laminated together, which is particularly useful for armour pieces and armatures, as this will reduce flexibility in the piece. Once constructed, Wonderflex will oblige you by accepting a wide range of finishes.

## FOSS SHAPE

Another Foss product, Foss Shape is available in two thicknesses that have the look of a synthetic felt. It is matted down and shaped through the application of heat at around 90°C, which can be achieved with a hot-air gun and something to smooth it down, like an old drinks bottle (kept and labelled specifically for the purpose), filled with warm water. Alternatively, you can buy an electric steam iron to smooth it into shape and compress it at the same time. Steamers will also work in conjunction with smoothing tools. The trick is to have a play around and see what works for you.

A useful feature of Foss Shape is the option of stitching together a form that can be stuffed with wadding, coir fibres, old fabric or sawdust, which is then heated, turning it into a more rigid shape. Patterns can be cut and stitched together to make stiffened costumes or costume props. The degree to which you compress it will create variations in stiffness and flexibility. Foss Shape can also be used as supporting shapes beneath fabric, and when stiffened, can have papier mâché worked over it, or fabrics glued or stitched to it.

## WORBLA'S PRODUCTS

The Worbla product range lends itself well to the making of a range of props and craft products for theatre, LARP, model rail enthusiasts and so on,

An example of Worbla's Finest Art. It has the look and feel and smell of a thermoformable plastic that has been filled with sawdust. Not having a mesh or fabric structure supporting it, the product is highly malleable.

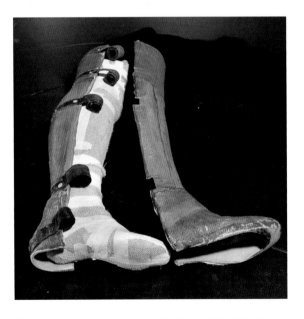

This 'wooden leg' is a mix of products, with the top layer being Worbla's Finest Art, which takes paint well. Plastazote and Wonderflex were modelled over the leg life cast, then the Worbla's. It is all secured by an interlocking overlap and one-wrap Velcro.

The finished leg being worn in a production of *Treasure Island*.

as well as providing options that Varaform and Wonderflex don't, such as colour variety, including a transparent option, and a pellet form. The Worbla's Finest Art product has a sawdust colour to it that makes a good base coat. It has no supporting mesh so can be stretched significantly when heated and can be effectively sanded before priming and painting. As with the other thermoformable products mentioned here, it can be heated and reheated as you go. Do not overheat, as this can damage any thermoform product.

## Thermoformable Pellets

Thermoformable pellet forms from Worbla's Deco Art (65°C) and Coolmorph (42°C) ranges are alternatives to sheet forms, and can be hand sculpted and used in moulds as well. They will take very good detail and are reusable, and can also have colour added to them in their softened form: the Deco Art can be dyed with acrylics when soft, and the Coolmorph with their own range of powder pigments. Both can be heated with hot-air guns, in water baths or in an ovenproof bowl in an electric oven. They are classified as non-toxic, but as with all things prop making, make sure that you are segregating the items you use for making props from those that you use for food preparation and other domestic applications.

## MOULDING OPTIONS AND LIMITATIONS

All the above products can be used to sculpt free form over frameworks or over solid forms of plaster, Jesmonite or GRP. Milliner's blocks can be used for hat shapes, but these thermoformable products must never be moulded onto the skin as this could result in, at best, extreme discomfort or, at worst, severe burns. Used safely, these are very versatile products that can be used to create a wide range of props from masks to costume elements. They can even be used to create lightweight armatures for animatronic projects. They can be finished with a full range of assorted products and paints, although some keying may be required to the surface before application of your chosen method.

## KYDEX

Kydex is a more industrial form of thermoformable plastic that has become available to the public and is being used in a range of craft areas, including leathercraft, as a sub-structure for leather products, gun holsters and protective masks, and cosplay. It has the advantage that it comes in a broad range of colours and thicknesses and is extremely durable. The detail you get out of it will very much depend on your ingenuity when moulding it, which ideally requires forms and moulding presses (which can be fabricated relatively simply), as it is not a product that is particularly well suited to freehand forming due to the high temperature that is required to mould it effectively.

## COMBINING THE PRODUCTS

Wonderflex, Varaform and Worbla's products work best when built up in tightly laminated layers, as this will produce enhanced rigidity. As with all prop-making materials, you can mix and match certain thermoformable plastics despite the difference in temperature ranges used with the specific products. Both the Wonderflex and Worbla's sheet forms can be used to overlay Varaform and each other. The Worbla's Finest Art makes a very good top dressing over both Wonderflex and Varaform because it has no internal structure, and so can be stretched and worked over forms more easily. It can also be used to cover imperfections since offcuts can be heated and pressed into a putty form that can be shaped and moulded to form detail or repair faults. At the same time, the mesh structures of Wonderflex and Varaform can be used to reinforce the Worbla's Finest Art. The pellet forms can be used for further detail enhancement of the sheet materials, although, due to their cooler temperature range, some base structure, such as wire or even forms made from the base materials, set into the parent material, will reduce the risk of these falling off.

The more shape and form that there is in an object made from these materials, the more self-supporting the product will be, especially with multiple layers of lamination; three layers is sufficient for most objects, although on smaller objects you may even get away with one layer. Laminated layers must be thoroughly worked together to prevent separation, especially when trimming, although more heat can be applied to rework the layers should this happen.

Bear in mind that it is unlikely that any one of these products will be the go-to material every time, and that experience with some or all of them can help you build a larger repertoire of materials and techniques. It is also worth pointing out that they can be costly and are basically a modern variant on papier mâché and card construction processes, although a lot quicker and cleaner to work with, and are an H&S improvement on Celastic.

Let's not forget papier mâché; it can be used in conjunction with any of these products and works very well as a top dressing for Varaform (light or heavy, depending upon the size of the project). Varaform can be used in a single layer as a base structure for a prop and make it unnecessary to apply twelve layers of paper: it is possible to use a minimum of three layers and still produce a robust product.

## PLASTAZOTE

Plastazote is a thermoformable dense foam that comes in a wide variety of colours and thicknesses from 3mm up to 25mm. It is widely used in everyday

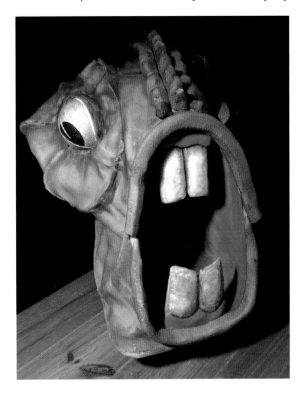

Plastazote and cane Jabberwocky head. Assorted colours of Plastazote were cut with a sharp knife, sanded and reheated to smooth it out.

life as an impact-resistant foam in martial arts dojos and fitness halls, kids' play areas and for camping and the like. It is well suited for making cod costumes and weapons, and as such has found much usage in the LARP world. Plastazote is, however, notoriously difficult to cover as it is chemically resistant to most products; fortunately, in most cases, it can be used as is. For LARP it tends to have a dipping latex skin built up on it. The latex usually has paint/pigment mixed in with it, but if the skin is not thick enough or is treated over-vigorously, it can abrade, tear and start to peel away.

Using a hot-air gun on Plastazote, up to 12mm, should warm it up nicely. It does require quite a bit of heat to warm it through, depending on thickness, so keep the heat source moving around or you might melt it. With practice you can hand form it or work it over forms and improvise 'presses' to help shape it.

Hot glue works very well as a permanent fix with Plastazote. Various solvent-based contact adhesives will work with it, as will FlexBond if you allow it to 'tack' slightly – a little trial and error may be required to find the optimal tack point.

Cutting Plastazote is best done with a utility knife with a sharp blade. Sculpting can be achieved with carving knives and woodworking rasps and abrasive paper. Having sanded Plastazote, it will take on a slightly fluffy appearance, but this can be smoothed out with heat from a hot-air gun and a heatproof glove on your hand. As with all things, experience and trial and error go hand in hand, and Plastazote, in its many guises, can prove a useful product for more than just 'fun' props.

Marking out the piece. The handle is a length of Tohiti with shaped pipe lagging around it. Some 3.15mm galvanized wire provided a core for the pickaxe head.

Cutting and building up the layers in 10mm LD 60 Plastazote, which is fire retardant.

Building sculpt thickness
and base shape.

BELOW: FlexBond was
applied between the
layers and allowed to
become tacky.

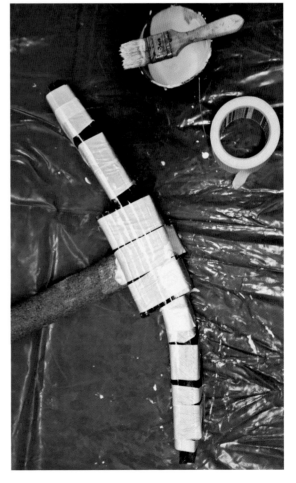

RIGHT: Tacked layers pressed and bound together to set.
Binding finished, left to set fully.

With the glue set and masking tape removed, the sculpt can commence.

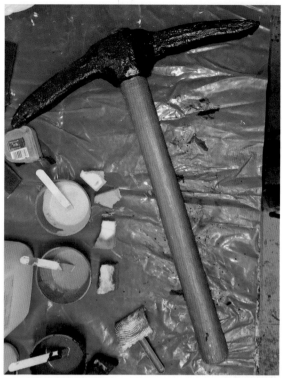

The finished sculpt being painted with a dipping latex-rich paint.

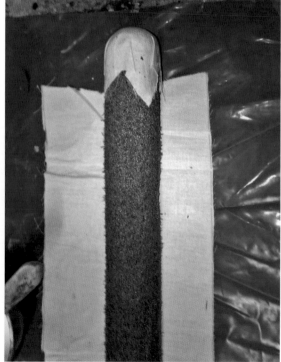

ABOVE LEFT: Wonderflex shovel head with Plastazote build-up. The Wonderflex was modelled over a real shovel head. The Plastazote will be heated and shaped to fit the back of the shovel and glued into place.

ABOVE RIGHT: Calico being glued around the handle to create a smooth look.

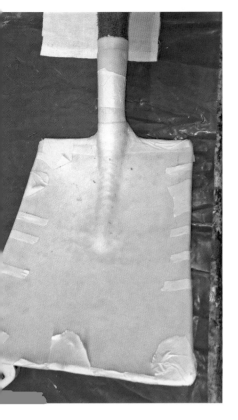  

ABOVE LEFT: The Plastazote backing glued and held in place by masking tape.

ABOVE MIDDLE: FlexBond being used to glue the calico backing over onto the front of the shovel.

ABOVE RIGHT: The finished shovel. This prop was made for the cast to promenade through the audience without causing them injury.

 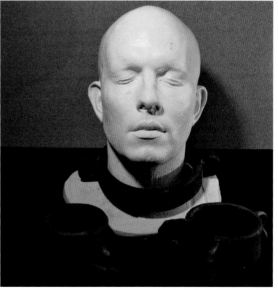

ABOVE LEFT: Plastazote knight's helm, covered in calico (for Tweedledum).

ABOVE RIGHT: Plastazote collar and manacles. A dozen sets were made for a dance sequence.

# 9
# SCRIMMING

In theatre, 'scrimming' is a process whereby protective layers of fabric are applied over an object, such as polystyrene, using a glue medium to bond the fabric to the object in laminated layers, prior to any texture and decorative finish being applied after the 'scrim' has dried. In the world of fabrics, 'scrim' is a definition given to certain types of fabric, which may, or may not, be used for prop scrimming. There are various dictionary definitions of the term 'scrim' but all appear to relate back to the fabric itself and the purpose of using it to obscure/hide something; for example, in upholstery, linen, then hessian and now synthetic scrims were and are used to cover the underside of a piece of furniture to obscure the internal structure. Scrim linings can be used to back curtain fabric, and to dress the inside of chests for storing clothes or bedding.

The process of scrimming an object in prop making is different because, although the reason for doing so does relate to obscuring the internal structure, it is primarily done to create a durable finish for the prop/scenery in question, which multiple layers of fabric (usually three) will achieve when bonded with a suitable adhesive, one layer on top of the other, in a manner reminiscent of papier mâché. Scrimming can also be used to reinforce the internal surface of an object to provide durability when taking castings from moulds, in a comparable way to how glass fibre mats and fabrics are used in GRP work. The fabrics and adhesives used for any project will vary, depending upon the result that is required, whether used externally or internally, and whether the finished result needs to be hard or flexible – not forgetting the potential cost implications of the products.

## FABRICS

There is a broad range of fabric scrims that we could choose from, but we can limit our options to those that are going to allow the best flow, absorption and lamination of the adhesives that we are going to use.

## Muslin

Muslin is a lightweight cotton fabric that is see-through due to its light, open structure. On its own

Cotton scrim has a more open weave than butter muslin, which makes it more pliable, if a little more prone to fraying when cut. It's a good, inexpensive product.

OPPOSITE: Calico clothing and detail on a bust. The bust is sculpted EPS and is scrimmed with size and muslin; the face is a latex casting from a plaster mould and clay sculpt. All the clothing and necklace detail are calico and glue.

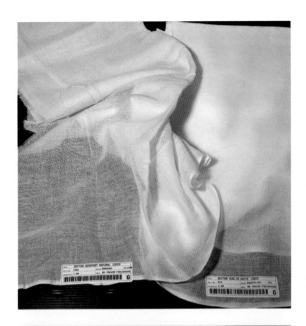

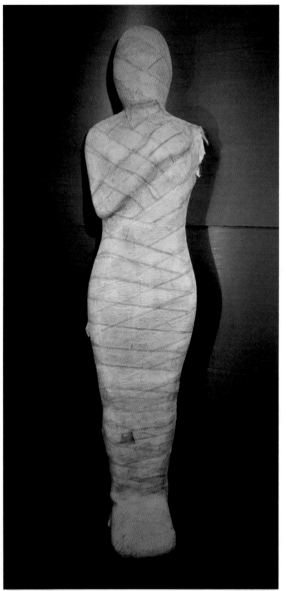

ABOVE: An EPS mummy. This was a project for a first year exercise – what better way to go than a decorative scrim with butter muslin and tinted PVA?

TOP LEFT: Cotton Westport and butter muslin. Unbleached and bleached products are both good for a refined scrim with a range of adhesives.

LEFT: Cotton scrim and glue size on EPS to make altar legs. These are awaiting fitting, when the seams will be closed up and a texture and paint finish applied.

it is not a very robust fabric as it can be easily snagged, but it can produce very evocative effects when hung to catch the light or blowing in a breeze. Muslin comes in a wide variety of weights and widths, but the two varieties that we are interested in are cotton scrim and butter muslin.

Traditionally, the preferred scrimming material in theatre is butter muslin, due to its even texture and good flow properties when used to cover objects with flowing and tricky shapes. However, cotton scrim is a very cost-effective alternative as it is about a third of the price of butter muslin and, due to its slightly more open weave, will flex and flow across the trickiest of detail leaving fewer harsh creases and requiring fewer cuts. The disadvantage with cotton scrim is that it will fray more easily than butter muslin and the texture of the fabric is not as even.

## Calico

You can buy light, medium and heavy calico (a type of unbleached cotton that is less fine than muslin). From a scrimming perspective, the easier

Calico and slush mould latex suitcase covering with piping detail. The piping was made and glued down first. Panels of calico were Copydexed into place, then slush mould latex, mixed with a base colour, was sponged on evenly.

one to use is the light calico, due to its more open weave compared to medium or heavy calico, which means that the adhesive can pass through the fabric more easily, facilitating a quicker bond to previous layers. Heavier fabrics will soak up the adhesive so more will be required before the bond will become effective, and fabrics of a very tight weave will prevent the adhesive from being worked through it and can only be glued, not scrimmed.

## Hessian

Hessian is derived from the jute plant from the Indian subcontinent and comes in a variety of forms. Innovative ways are being sought to turn what is basically a very coarse but plentiful fibre into more refined products – in upholstery and leatherworking, jute threads are being used alongside and, in some cases, instead of the more traditional linen threads due to the additional tensile strength that jute offers.

The pigeon wire-frame form covered in calico, which is glued in place with Copydex.

The finished suitcases with slush mould latex, buckles, straps and corners. They were used for an English National Ballet production of *The Canterville Ghost*.

Calico makes a very good sculpting medium for clothes and jewellery when 'dressing' props.

### SCRIMMING VS GLUING

The idea with scrimming is to 'wet' the fabric through so that it becomes a reinforcement to the adhesive, with every fibre of the fabric bonded to its neighbour, as opposed to gluing, where you simply require the contacting surfaces to bind together. This process is very akin to producing GRP, and this is why, with certain products, you may hear the term 'poor man's fibreglass' to describe something that produces a similar result but at a much lower cost and usually fewer H&S concerns.

From our perspective, we are not concerned with tactile beauty but jute's innate strength, which is very useful to us when scrimming objects that need to be particularly robust. It also takes a multitude of finishes that can easily mask the base texture of the hessian, if required. As with the other fabrics, we are after a more open weave, such as jute hessian natural, which has very good flow properties, absorbs most adhesives well and allows for good 'wetting-down'. There is a hessian called jute scrim (also known as plasterer's scrim), which has a very open weave and is better suited for creating a thicker build-up using bonding agents such as Idenden, Flints Mud, Firecheck and monkey dung, and of course plasters and Jesmonite.

These two hessian products can be combined, which is particularly useful on open structures

A dragon form for *The Magic Flute*. Hessian scrim has been used to scrim the head, using glue size, which has pulled it tight to the head shape, where the chicken wire has been used to create a decorative effect over the steel frame. Where flexibility was required, the hessian was stitched and painted with slush latex and a paint mix.

such as timber frames and chicken wire, where an initial layer of the jute hessian can be fixed into place over the base structure by stapling, snipping and gluing, getting the hessian to conform to the base shape. This layer can then be wetted through while scrimming on pieces of the jute scrim to build up a second layer. Leave this to dry, then tidy up any rough bits prior to scrimming with more jute scrim and your chosen bulking product, applying further layers if required, and then applying the finishing texture. You could also apply a final layer of jute hessian, creating a sandwich effect and providing a smoother surface scrim for a more refined finish once dry. With certain bulking products like Idenden, Flints Mud, Firecheck and so on, it is worth bearing in mind that the more

bulk you build in one go, the longer the drying time. This should not be a major problem in a well-heated workshop, but in cold, damp conditions could cause major delays.

Hessian is not suited to small fiddly props but excels when used for poor man's fibreglass.

## Canvas

Canvas comes in multiple forms and is most commonly made from linen (which comes from flax) or cotton. Cotton is the cheaper alternative, but whichever you use, opt for a variety that is a plain weave and lightweight, as these have a more open structure, which provides the benefits mentioned

Jute scrim and plasterer's scrim (medium). Both have excellent flow properties, with the jute scrim providing the more even texture.

EPS, PVA and plasterer's scrim (coarse). This mixture gives a very durable finish that provided an excellent key for the Flints Mud mix and shredded plasterer's scrim strands.

ABOVE: Plasterer's scrim (coarse) and size (poor man's fibreglass) on an EPS tree trunk with a steel core and collars to accept custom branches.

LEFT: Prototyping a jute scrim and PVA poor man's fibreglass with a Flints Mud mix with sawdust, compost and foam crumb (sugar fine).

Natural heavy floor canvas was selected for the umiak (Inuit canoe) in a double layer for durability.

The skinned umiak. The idea was to have a fabric that could be hand finished with a natural cord to provide the look of a skin canoe. This is a lot smaller than the real article.

above. Although canvas can work in scrimming, it is better suited to flatter surfaces or those with flowing contours, and the cost is slightly higher than the other fabrics.

## Glass Fibre

Glass fibre also comes in a variety of forms and densities and is specifically designed for 'laying-up' in GRP. As an inert product, there is nothing to stop it being used with other glue/resin mediums, but where it works particularly well is as a reinforcing scrim for slush mould latex castings, using a glass fibre chopped strand mat (CSM), which is the product with the best flow properties for complex shapes; the weight of the mat will depend on the size of the casting – heavier for large, lighter for small. This technique can be used for projects such as human heads, monster heads, body shapes, armour, decorative mouldings, puppet forms and the like.

The fibres are wetted into the back of the casting with slush mould latex and a cheap brush in a stippling motion (as with GRP lay-up). Three layers of CSM and slush latex, with a finishing layer of glass fibre tissue, are usually sufficient reinforcement for a casting when dry, although more layers can be applied if necessary. Slush mould latex and milled cotton or Treecell fibres can be used to smooth out tricky detail areas prior to laying up. Open moulds or multiple-part moulds allowing access for this technique are required, although you can cast and lay up into each part of a multiple-part mould and then trim and joint together once dry. The latex casting effectively becomes rigid in this instance due to the lamination process.

## ADHESIVES

### Size and PVA

As with the fabrics, there are many choices that we could go for when looking at adhesives for scrimming, but it ultimately comes down to what you want to achieve and what is reliable and safe. Traditionally there are two main choices for glue when scrimming: size (a type of gelatin) and PVA. These two products are ideal for rigid finishes and both have their pros and cons regarding use, but are hard to beat for reliability, cost and H&S and COSHH concerns.

PVA should not be mixed any higher than a 1:1 ratio with water – equal volumes of glue and water;

This is 1kg (2lb) of glue size granules, measured out and ready to start the mixing process. Granules are preferable to powder as they mix more readily.

## SIZE, GELATIN AND BLOOM

It is worth mentioning here that although size is a type of gelatin and is related to the gelatin used in domestic cookery, that is where the similarity ends. Because size is not intended for human consumption, it does not require licensing for that purpose, but the main difference is the Bloom rating (measurement of the strength of a gel) of the various gelatin products. Domestic gelatin, used for binding various foodstuffs like trifles and mousses, has a Bloom of between 18 and 20, while glue size has a Bloom in the region of 150–250, which would make your mousse nigh-on bullet-proof (but don't try it). Prosthetic-grade gelatins, used for body parts, fake food, false noses, chins, ears, scars and so on, can have a Bloom of 260–320, but require the addition of other products to produce a life-like result.

in practice, we are more likely to use a 4:1 ratio of PVA to water – four parts of glue to one part of water by volume, in order to decrease drying times and prevent too much run-off. Therefore, for every litre of PVA, we can make-up 1.25ltr of product mix, or a maximum of 2ltr if we pushed it to the highest mixing ratio of 1:1.

The mixing ratios for size (granular size or hot glue size) can vary depending upon whether you are using it to prime canvas, mix scenic powder paints or scrim with it. For scrimming we require a ratio of 1kg of granular size to 5–7ltr of water. This will provide 5–7ltr of glue product for around the same price as our 1.25–2ltr of PVA mix. Glue size does have very real advantages over PVA, but it also has some disadvantages.

## MIXING GLUE SIZE

To mix glue size takes time and additional equipment, although it needn't cost a fortune and, once you have it, it is always there to use. Basically, you require a double-boiler set-up, which can be achieved with two galvanized buckets, a half-brick (most important) and a hotplate (electric).

A bain-marie or double boiler pot. It has an advantage over the double bucket system in that it contains the steam in the outer pot, meaning it is less likely to run dry and you can always check the spout for the level of water. No half-brick required!

Traditionally, preparing the glue takes a while, soaking the granules in tepid water for an hour or more before warming through and heating. But there is an easier way, which will have the product

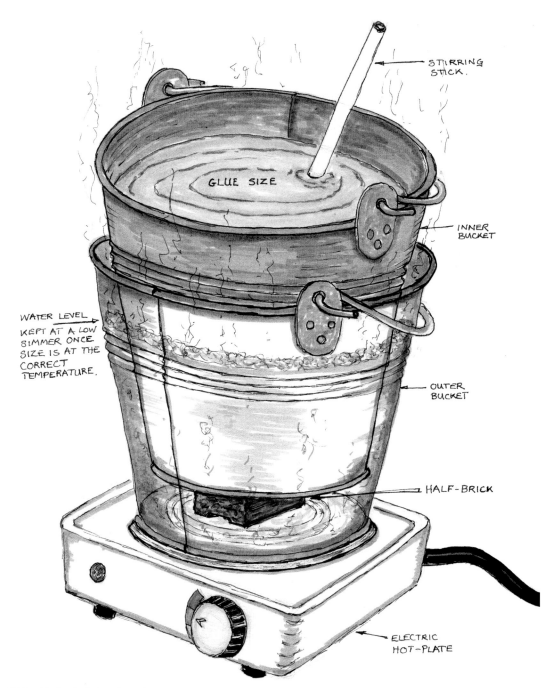

STIRRING STICK.

GLUE SIZE

INNER BUCKET

WATER LEVEL KEPT AT A LOW SIMMER ONCE SIZE IS AT THE CORRECT TEMPERATURE.

OUTER BUCKET

HALF-BRICK

ELECTRIC HOT-PLATE

Fig. 37 Double-bucket glue size set-up.

ready to use in just over an hour, with minimal preparation on your part.

The half-brick (a common red/orange house brick) fulfils two important roles:

- The half-brick is placed in the middle of the outer bucket, and the inner bucket sits on top of it. A half-brick is used so that it will fit in the outer bucket and within the diameter of the underside

A half house brick is essential to the double bucket system. This one was used for many years.

ing, which will wick the heat away from metal containers in no time at all

When using glue size for scrimming, it is good practice to dispense the size into smaller containers for easier handling and to prevent size from dripping all over the worktops and floor when moving between the size pot and the workpiece. After about half an hour, depending upon the volume of your pot, the size will start to thicken and become gelatinous. This is not a problem – simply pour, scrape or peel what is left back into the size pot, give it a stir and take out a fresh batch. If the size in your working pot should solidify because you got called away from your work, or you went to lunch and forgot to pour the leftover product back, it can once again be returned to the glue pot and re-warmed into a working consistency. Size will wash out of brushes, clothing and off skin with warm, soapy water.

## SIZE PREPARATION

If you have ever had the 'pleasure' of preparing size in the traditional fashion, you will realize why a little experimentation was necessary, and how that led to the development of this method, which is more conducive to prop making and producing 5–7ltr batches of size as and when required, in the quickest time possible and with the least amount of fuss.

### Materials
- Water
- Freshly boiled water
- Granular size

### Equipment
- Kettle (to boil 1.5ltr of water)
- Hotplate
- Double boiler (bain-marie)
- Plastic mixing pot (minimum 5ltr capacity)
- Robust stirring stick
- 1ltr jug or pot for measuring out fresh and boiled water

of the inner bucket. The effect is to stabilize the inner bucket, preventing it from bobbing around in the outer bucket and eliminating the risk of water slopping out of that bucket and onto the hotplate

- The brick acts like a storage heater, absorbing heat and releasing it over time. This is useful, because if it becomes necessary to temporarily move the size bucket to another location within the workshop, and you don't want to move the hotplate, or there are no electric sockets nearby (and you don't want to run an extension lead due to the risks inherent with that), the brick will keep the water in the outer bucket up to temperature, and the size workable for at least an hour. In colder working environments, the brick will do its best, but the working times will be reduced without some form of insulation around the buckets. The same applies when working outside on a summer's day with a breeze blow-

## Process

1. Using either the double bucket and half-brick system or a catering bain-marie, pour tap-hot water to the fill level in the outer container (with the double bucket system, this will depend on the amount of product that you will be putting into the inner bucket, because the inner bucket should sit comfortably on the half-brick when filled with the required volume of size mix).

2. Place the outer container onto the electric hot-plate on a moderate heat.

3. Boil a kettle of water, approximately 1.5ltr, and set aside.

4. Measure 1kg of granular size and place it and a robust stirring stick into a plastic bucket/container ready for mixing.

5. Using tepid water, slowly pour 3.5ltr into the bucket/container onto the size, while stirring continually. This pouring can be done a litre at a time to make it more manageable, but it is important that you stir constantly to prevent the size turning into a gelatinous mass. The granules will start to swell, but keep adding the tepid water and stirring until all 3.5ltr have been added, at which point it will be quite thick and you can still see a hint of the swollen granules.

6. It is now time to pour in the 1.5ltr off-the-boil hot water, just a half cup at a time while constantly stirring; you will see the mix gradually becoming more fluid as the granules dissolve and merge. Once the last of the hot water is in the pot and stirred in, the mix is complete and should be pourable and fluid.

7. Pour the mix into the inner container of the double bucket/bain-marie. If you haven't quite reached into the bottom edges of the mixing container you may experience a little 'vindaloo' moment as semi-gelatinous product slides into the warming pot. This isn't a problem, but just aim for a more thorough mix next time.

8. Leave the size to warm through, maintaining the water level in the outer pot and making sure that the temperature of the size does not rise beyond that of a comfortably hot bath – you should be able to put your hand in the size and hold it there without any risk of scalding it.

9. After about an hour of gentle warming, the size is ready to use. More size can be mixed and added to the pot as you progress, which is the advantage of having a separate mixing pot.

## PVA or Size?

Which should you choose, PVA or size? To a degree, the choice comes down to personal preference, but it is useful to have the option of both. It is easier to scrim with size once it is made up: because it is used 'hot' (although you now know this to be a bit of a misnomer), it helps to iron out the creases in the fabric, smoothing it down quicker, and as it cools it locks the fabric into place, meaning that you can rotate the object with negligible risk of the scrim pulling away against the work surface. If applied properly, you will get little or no run-off with size, and any you do get, can potentially be added back into the size pot.

PVA is very easy to mix up, although it costs more than size, and it produces a robust finish, arguably more so than size (but as a texture is usually applied over scrim this point can considered to be a little bit moot). It is more fiddly than size to apply, as it does not gel, it takes longer to set before it can be fully handled and there is a tendency for scrim to peel way as you are working and rotating it.

Glue application with both PVA and size should be done with a brush in a controlled manner, only adding sufficient product to wet the fabric down to the base and subsequent layers. Three layers are the norm, but further layers can be applied if desired.

## Latex and Scrimming for Flexibility

If you need to scrim a flexible surface, or a soft prop made from foam- or fabric-covered wadding, then neither size nor PVA would be appropriate. What we need is an 'adhesive' that will provide the movement that is demanded by the choice of materials for the base structure. The quotation marks around the term 'adhesive' indicate that the

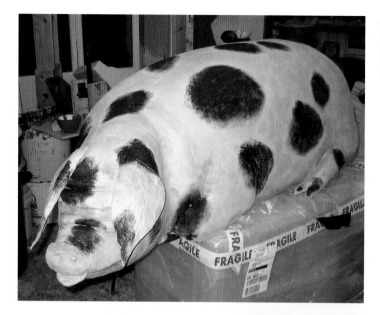

Gloucester Old Spot pig with a slush mould latex skin. Careful build-up of the latex layer prevents the foam from becoming stiff, because the 'skin' builds up on the surface of the foam.

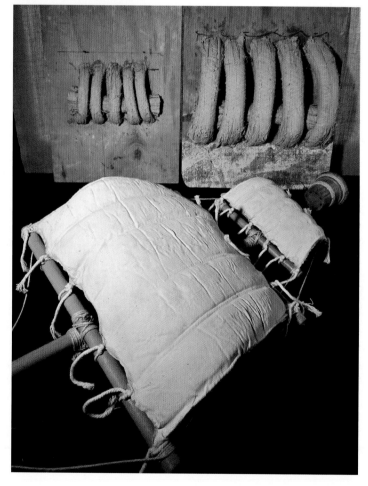

Scooter sails. Quarter-inch foam rubber was stretched over the paper rope forms in the background. Piping cord was laid in and stapled down to the boards of the form, then calico and latex were scrimmed over this. Once dry, the sail was removed from the form and scrimmed on the back surface. The fitting to the mast was done with the integrated piping cord. The crow's nest was a small plant pot.

products that we might use to scrim with may not be sold as glues or scrimming mediums, but have been found over decades of prop making to be a logical choice for certain tasks that would otherwise be difficult to achieve.

Dipping latex and slush mould latex are ideal products for providing flexible scrim coverings or linings. As mentioned in Chapter 7, any casting can be made more rigid by using fibreglass or plasterer's scrim on the inside of the slush mould latex casting. But by using muslin, calico or even canvas, a robust exterior finish can be provided to soft props that allow for a certain amount of flexibility and 'squishiness' while at the same time providing protection for the internal structure. Due to the natural durability of the latex, it is often possible to cover with as little as one layer of fabric over the sub-structure to provide that protection.

The other side of the coin when using fabric and latex to scrim with is that you reduce the stretch of the latex to that of the fabric: what you get is durability and flexibility without elasticity. This is not so different to the way that slush mould latex works anyway, but if using dipping latex, the loss of stretch will be quite noticeable, although it is unlikely to be a problem.

After scrimming, further layers of latex can be applied to the scrimmed surface to create further build-up and skin thickness, but remember that as latex products dry, particularly dipping latex, they can exhibit Copydex-like properties, so prevent the different surfaces from contacting each other until the latex is fully dry.

### Scrimming Without Scrim!

It is possible to cover soft, flexible props with a built-up skin of latex without using scrimming fabrics. This works very well on foam rubber props and is simply a question of lightly sponging the latex onto the surface of the foam, being careful not to force it through the surface, allowing it to touch dry, then applying further light layers until the 'pore' structure on the surface of the foam has been sealed. Once sealed, you can apply the latex more vigorously until you have created the

desired skin thickness, at which point all that is left is to create any texture with a latex base and any paint finish with a latex or FlexBond binding medium. Achieving this effect is easier with slush mould latex than dipping latex due to the latter's higher fluidity, but if you use a thixotropic additive or brush mould latex any potential problem should be resolved, and skin build-up will be achieved more quickly.

## Silicone Rubber

Silicone rubber can be used as a binding medium for scrim and subsequent skin build-up, but this is a much more expensive and specialized process and, despite having many positive attributes, it can add substantial weight onto larger props, such as costume props.

## Modroc

Gypsona plaster bandage, or Modroc, has been used in the entertainment, craft and hobby world for years, due to its ease of use and relatively cost-effective aspect. You can buy it as Gypsona plaster bandage, and it will come sealed in a paper wrap in a box, or you can buy it at lower cost in a slab or unsealed rolls in a plastic bag at a given weight. The difference between the two products is quality control. What you get with Modroc is the bandage that did not pass the test for ratio of plaster to gauze for a medical application, but which is still perfectly serviceable for the purposes for which we need it.

There are two main application methods for plaster bandage; both require a bowl of lukewarm water, and, if you wish to speed plaster setting times, a pinch of table salt in the water.

**Method 1** This is how plaster is used medically. While keeping hold of it, immerse the whole roll slowly in the water for ten seconds or so (or until the air bubbles have stopped), lift it out, give it a moderately firm squeeze to remove any excess water, and then bind it around the object that you are covering by unrolling the bandage around it. Use your gloved hands to smooth the plaster bandage down, removing irregularities as you go. The plaster has a creamy texture while fluid and your hands should glide over it until it starts to set. Multiple rolls can be applied until you have achieved the desired build-up.

**Method 2** Cut the bandage into specific strips, sizes or shapes, until you have what you need for the coverage and number of layers desired (usually three). Dip each piece into the bowl of water, then hold it above the water bowl with one hand and run it through the index and forefinger of the other hand like a squeegee; then apply it in a scrimming-type process in whole layers until the required build-up is achieved (the scrimming adhesive, in this case, is simply the chemical reaction between the plaster and the water).

Plaster bandage can be used for sculpting and covering, for masks and flowing shapes, and can be added as dressing to other props… but it lacks durability and can start to break down if handled too much or it gets knocked around. This can be partly resolved by adding products like gesso, varnish, PVA or even resins over the top of the fully dry product, or following the procedure below.

## The 'Modern Twist' on Modroc

Simply replace the lukewarm water with our previous PVA/water mix, used for papier mâché and scrimming (you can increase the water content slightly for this to make it a little less viscous). Individually dunk your strips of plaster bandage into the glue mix, immediately drawing the bandage out once fully immersed and, as you draw it back out, squeegee the strip between your index and middle finger of your other hand, making sure the excess glue drains back into the glue pot. Open the bandage out if it has become folded, and smooth it over the object to be covered.

Modroc and monkey dung bowls. Any finish can be used on this process. The Modroc is old, less than perfect stock that won't work with water but works well with a slightly watered-down PVA.

This process can be used for masks, sculpting over frames covered with chicken wire, card constructions, wire frames, papier mâché and timber, and can be used with Varaform, even Wonderflex, Worbla's and Foss Shape, if desired. Once fully dry (a process that will take about a day in optimal conditions), it can be coated and finished in many media to suit your desires and imagination. Because the PVA soaks into the plaster, it makes it much more robust with a much higher impact resistance than when activated with water and, combined with the gauze, makes a product that will last for years.

There is another advantage. Unused Modroc has a limited shelf life that is affected by atmospheric humidity – in other words, the drier your workshop and storage areas, the longer the plaster bandage lasts. If the bandage has been

## THINGS NOT TO DO WITH MODROC AND PVA

PVA with plaster bandage must not be used for life-casting purposes due to the risk of casts becoming stuck and severe injury being caused. This process is purely for making props and rigid, lightweight mould cases for non-life-casting purposes.

Moulds made using plaster bandage and PVA are not suitable for taking slush mould latex castings because the moulds are non-porous, due to the PVA taking up the void space that would otherwise be present in the plaster particles and would allow for the passage of moisture and air. Slush mould latex requires a porous mould to enable a skin to be built up on the internal surface of the mould, caused by moisture being absorbed into the mould at the point of contact, which makes the latex coagulate.

Hessian scrim being stretched over a barrel frame. Strategic cuts were made to create an overlap and remove wrinkles and creases. The hessian is being stapled to the top surface.

compromised, it will feel gritty when you use it and will not bond as well, and the resultant piece can lack strength and rigidity. However, when used with the PVA/water mix, although the Modroc will still feel gritty, the finished dry prop will be just as robust as if you had used fresh plaster bandage because the PVA mix soaks into the plaster and bonds all the plaster particles together.

## Poor Man's Fibreglass

The traditional poor man's fibreglass uses size as the 'resin' compound and hessian as the 'glass fibres'. The process is one of lamination, as in GRP and other scrimming-type processes (layered papier mâché and so on). The advantage is that it has much lower health and safety and COSHH risks than either polyester or epoxy resin GRP. It also has the advantage that, once dry, there are few limits with regard to the type of products that can be used to build on or texture it, especially if you wish to use more traditional products.

The hessian is, as with all scrimming tasks, cut into manageable pieces that will suit the object

The dry hessian layer complete. The top edge is glued down with PVA.

being worked upon, but as large as you can comfortably work with. A little tip, if you are working over a timber-frame and chicken-wire construction, is to tack the first full layer into place with a

An open log section showing the timber-frame and chicken wire construction, with paper rope for the opening, held in place by the chicken wire, jute scrim and hessian poor man's fibreglass. Such a build is extremely durable.

PVA is applied to the dry layer of scrim on half the upper surface. A fresh half-side of scrim is drawn over the newly applied glue and smoothed down, then more glue is applied over this to get the two pieces to laminate. The hessian is folded back at the other end and the process repeated. The barrel is turned over and the same process is gone through again. Another half-section is applied to each upper half of the barrel to make a full three-layer total.

staple gun and Copydex. Stretch each piece of hessian into place to form it as snuggly as possible around the object. The trick is to overlap the pieces slightly as you staple them to the framework, where possible, or tack them together with a light application of Copydex, which will bond almost instantly when smoothed down, until each area is completely wrapped and held in place by its contact with pieces fore and aft, above and below. Once the whole object is covered by this first layer, wet it down with your prepared glue size and then follow up with a second layer of hessian, scrimmed through onto the first in manageable

sections. Apply size, apply hessian, apply more size, until the second layer is complete and then move on to the third layer.

With a polystyrene form, it is simpler to apply the size directly onto the EPS and then overlay each piece of hessian as you progress with a 50mm (2in) overlap. The size on the form will prevent the hessian from slipping around while you add more size to it to wet it through to the size and EPS form beneath. Only apply sufficient size to the form to suit the dimensions of the piece of fabric that you will be scrimming on to it, as you want the size beneath to be wet so that it will be drawn into the hessian as you work it from the top side. You can use your gloved hands to quickly smooth the hessian into place over the freshly sized form, firmly rubbing it down prior to brushing more size onto the newly applied hessian. Apply your second and third layers as for standard size scrimming.

Poor man's fibre glass: A large timber and chicken-wire tree trunk section showing the first jute scrim layer being stretched and 'Copydexed' into place, prior to the application of glue size the and scrimming on of a further two layers of the jute fabric.

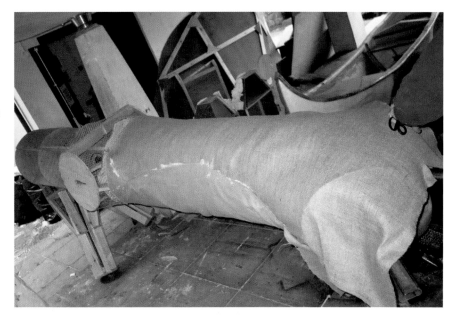

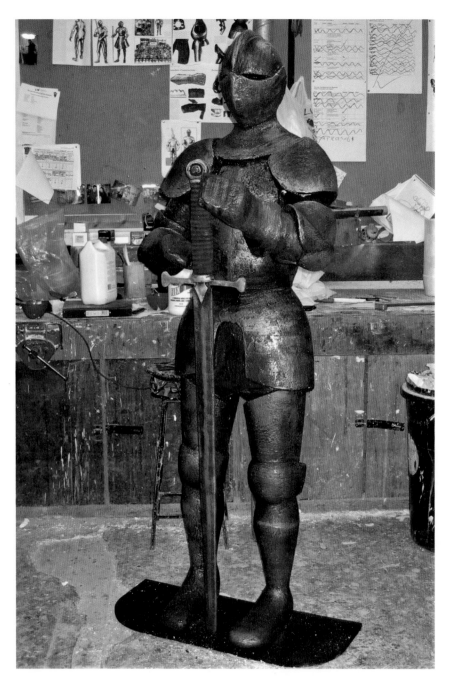

Suit of armour. The finish on the armour is a black monkey dung smoothed with wetted spatulas, then adorned with a dry brushing of silver paint and a graphite paste polish.

# 10
# TEXTURE MEDIUMS

The number of texture mediums available to prop makers and scenic artists has increased exponentially over the past decade, although choice of product is going to come down to what you can afford, especially if you have to buy or hire additional equipment to use a specific product.

There are a lot of texture medium products currently being used that have become standard to the workplace and fit into the affordable bracket. Texture mediums usually involve something to provide the texture, from smooth to coarse, and something to bind it with, although the higher priced products are pre-mixed to provide an all-in-one convenience product. It is the more traditional 'mix to please' products that will be addressed here.

## MONKEY DUNG

Monkey dung is an excellent and extremely durable texture medium that won't break the bank and can produce hard, smooth finishes and hard, rough finishes. Monkey dung can be applied over a wide range of surfaces, including expanded and extruded polystyrene, but works particularly well over scrimmed surfaces, especially poor man's fibreglass, where it masks the texture of the hessian, which in turn provides an excellent key for the monkey dung to grip into.

Monkey dung comprises three constituent parts: PVA, paint and sawdust. Without the paint, it isn't monkey dung. Any colour of paint can be used as the base colour for monkey dung, which makes it an extremely useful and relatively inexpensive texture medium. The final texture of the 'dung' can be varied enormously by altering the coarseness of

the sawdust used. By repeated sieving, the texture can be made smooth enough to pipe through an icing bag, and a wetted spatula or spreading tool, even a tongue depressor for smaller projects, can be used to smooth and shape the surface of monkey dung (particularly useful for cake icing).

## Mixing Monkey Dung

To mix monkey dung you will need a container/mixing pot, preferably plastic, (with some flex for cleaning out dried product; an old PVA or glaze tub works well for this once the top of the tub has been removed) and of an appropriate size for the job at hand.

1. Pour a quantity of PVA into the mixing tub to make up about a third of the overall target volume; for example, if you were aiming for a litre volume of product, then you would add in approximately 330ml of PVA.
2. Add the paint to the PVA and mix in thoroughly at a ratio of about one tablespoon of paint to every litre of PVA if using super-saturated scenic colours (if using non-super-sats, you may have to use up to 0.25ltr of paint to every litre of PVA). If you are mixing a specific colour, or shade of paint, then do this in a separate mixing container and then add it to the PVA. This is because, although the PVA will become translucent when dry, in its liquid state it is white, which will cause the paint to look creamy or even pastel and make it difficult to get an accurate colour mix if you try to achieve the mixing of your colour in the PVA itself.
3. Pre-sieve the sawdust, if required, and add it by the handful to the PVA/paint mix, stirring it in with a

## PAINTS

These techniques rely upon paints that are water-based – that is, they use water in the clean-up process. It is possible that some non-scenic paints, such as some varieties of household emulsions, may cause your PVA to coagulate or separate, which is something we wish to avoid. If in doubt, do a small test mix of the PVA and paint to determine whether this is likely to happen.

It is possible to rely on household emulsions for black and white, especially when cheap primers are needed, but use test pots to ascertain whether there will be problems when mixing with products like PVA, FlexBond and dipping latex.

stout mixing stick, until the desired texture/thickness is acquired. There is no rocket science involved in this process – the trick is simply not to make the mix too dry, as this will prevent it from adhering to the intended surface. If in doubt, try applying a sample, and if it falls/rolls off as you apply it, it is too dry. On the other hand, if it slumps and runs and won't hold the texture, it is too wet. If the mix does become too dry, simply add, and mix in, sufficient PVA to make it tacky again. If it is too sloppy, add more sawdust. If you want a sculptable texture then make the mix thick enough that the stirring stick can stand up in it and that peaks and troughs can be made in the mix without collapsing. If you want a more fluid mix that will create a thinner, smoother coat, then hold back on the sawdust. It is up to you to decide on the texture you are after, and you can mix and match different textures to provide extra depth to the prop, letting each layer dry before applying the next. If using a predominantly pine sawdust, it will not alter the colour of the paint significantly as the sawdust absorbs the glue and paint becoming one with the mix, which is why it is so versatile and durable.

4. Apply the monkey dung to your project, building and adjusting the texture as you need it.

Different textures on papier mâché. From top: a coarse monkey dung; a fine monkey dung; a smooth Fillite monkey dung; first layer of gesso (note the crazing, caused by moisture being drawn from the gesso by a porous surface. This is normal and after sanding and a few more layers will disappear); slush latex and milled cotton fibres.

Application can be done with spreaders, spatulas, and even gloved hands and improvised sculpting tools – you will find what works for you as you experiment with the product. If you decide to use bought modelling tools and other equipment, make sure that you clean them thoroughly before the dung dries on them.

5. Once dry, a light sanding can further smooth or eliminate particularly rough areas, prior to adding paint finishes and dressing.

Monkey dung can be used for all sorts of projects, from trees and rocks to cast metal items and rust effects as well as mosses and lichens and the icing of decorative cakes, on base structures of card, timber or EPS. In the hobby world it is excellent for creating dioramas, tunnels, gorges, bridges and so on for model railways or tabletop gaming. It can also be used as a 'mortar' for visibly bonding items together. As with most prop-making materials, your imagination is the determining factor.

It is possible to swap out the sawdust for products like Fillite, sand and glass bubbles, but these do not absorb the glue and paint, which can make it take slightly longer to achieve the ideal mix. Compost can also be used instead of or with the sawdust to vary the texture and, like the sawdust, it will absorb the glue and paint and become hard when dry, although the colour of the compost will darken the paint.

FlexBond and compost mix over a cut and folded heather garden screen. This was a quick way of producing a large basket of peat turf logs. When emptied from the basket they had a light, dry earthiness to them.

Monkey dung build-up. This is a coarse monkey dung that had been applied thickly and tapered from the middle to three of the outer edges. Now dry, it is absolutely solid. However, thicker applications take longer to dry and are normally used as the exception to the rule.

Bent timber-frame log, made of chicken wire, hessian and size and an apple tree bark-effect monkey dung – dry brushed for a moss and lichen effect.

Smooth bark effect created with fine dung and a wet spatula. Coarse dung was used around the opening and a weathered ring effect on the top.

Log with monkey dung in an ash wood bark effect. Note the underlayer of dung is a darker colour. This log is waiting for the paint finishing layers.

PVA-paint-Fillite monkey dung over a wire frame, chicken wire and PVA Modroc. The Fillite is being used to create a rough earthenware effect.

Polystyrene wedding cake, iced and piped with a Fillite monkey dung. The artificial flowers are fitted and glued into holes drilled in the monkey dung when it had dried.

*Macbeth* jug. Monkey dung can be used for lighter effects and to complement the textures of materials adjacent to them.

Fillite cast iron effect. The Fillite monkey dung is being used to draw disparate materials together. These stoves are made of timber and plywood frames with paper rope detail that has been dressed over with calico and PVA. The stove pipes are cardboard tubes. A graphite paste has been applied over the black Fillite monkey dung and buffed to enhance the texture effect.

# IDENDEN AND FLINTS MUD

Idenden Brushcote 30-150 and Flints Mud are very useful texture mediums and binders that are fire retardant and waterborne (they use water to help them spread, and brushes can be cleaned with soap and water), although they contain other chemicals. They can be coloured and have a variety of texture products added to them to create many different effects.

## Idenden

Idenden comes in three colours: white, grey and black. The white can be coloured with acrylic colours used for colouring and tinting. Many texture mediums can be combined with Idenden to create a wide variety of texture effects. A very good product, it is also quite expensive and comes in at about a third more than Flints Mud.

ABOVE LEFT: Flint tool. The head of this ancient tool was carved from pine and painted black. The calcified exterior is a paste made from gesso and PVA. The rest is dressing and paint.

A base layer of monkey dung being applied to coarse hessian scrim. The dung can be worked in to eliminate the texture of the scrim, building strength and smoothing at the same time.

## Flints Mud

Flints Mud is pre-coloured to a mid-brown, wet clay-like, mud colour and texture. This is actually a very useful base colour for being taken up or down with other products. The colour can be altered by adding Flints concentrated liquid pigments, or even scenic paints such as the Rosco super-saturates, but paints can alter the consistency and flexibility of the texture. Many different texture mediums can be used with this product, including sawdust (sieved or unsieved depending on the effect required), sand, foam crumbs, rubber chips, Fillite, vermiculite, glass bubbles and even garden compost, straw, hay and dried grasses. Any or all of these can be combined to create even more varied effects – just remember (as with monkey dung) not to overload the core product or you will lose adhesion. This product is also well suited to using on expanses of artificial grass to make them look more realistic by creating wear and tear, especially when given colour variation and sand, sawdust or compost is added to create distinct types of turf/soil effects.

Basically, the two products here (and they are two of many) are a modern take on monkey dung with certain advantages and disadvantages. They are both costlier and have intrinsic colours that need altering to create the required base colour (if your requirement is different from that provided) but will give a softer texture than monkey dung. They can also be used independently of any filling medium and can be applied with stiff brushes, spreaders, trowels or gloved hands. Their intrinsic flexibility makes them suitable for use with products like foam crumb and rubber chips where the flexibility of each can complement the other. They can be directly applied over a wide range of materials, from timber to polystyrene, and work particularly well on scrimmed surfaces (including poor man's fibreglass), which will provide extra durability and support.

# OTHER TEXTURE PRODUCTS

## Foamcoat

There are other products for covering polystyrene and styrofoam that produce hard, durable surfaces, which are being included here for information purposes only as the cost can be somewhat prohibitive. The majority provide a hard, plaster-like finish, but that is where the similarity ends, as these are pre-mixed products that may require vigorous mixing in the tub prior to use and are intended to be applied from the tub directly onto the product. These products have various fibre options or reinforcing products added into them, a bit like a more high-tech version of what traditional plasterers used to do by adding horse hair into the mix to prevent cracking and add resilience. These products generally have the name 'Foamcoat' in their title. Because the products themselves are very viscous, trowel application is recommended, but some provide the option to dilute and apply by brush; the manufacturer's recommendations should always be followed… but then have a play and see what you can achieve! These products, like monkey dung, can be applied and smoothed or you can create a variety of textures with them using different tools and techniques. Rosco Foamcoat is perhaps the most versatile of the Foamcoat products but is one of the costliest and generally needs a thorough remix prior to using. Ultimately it comes down to whether you need that extra versatility for the job that you are doing.

## Styro-Plast (Replacement for Hardkote)

This is a very interesting product because it is a synthetic binding medium that incorporates marble sand as its texture. You can sculpt this product into non-slumping raised detail, and it can be left coarse or made smoother, but it will always have a grit-like texture. If needed, other products could be used over Styro-Plast to smooth given areas, or the whole thing (if you were simply using it for build-up and strength, both of which it is very good for).

## Artex Textured Finish AX

This is a cheaper alternative to the pre-mixed products and has been used for decades in the building trade and interior design for the texturing of walls and ceilings. Artex comes in powder form in 25kg bags and is activated by mixing with water. Once dry, it provides a white finish that can be painted to the finish that you require. You will not get the one coat build-up that can be achieved with Styro-Plast when using Artex, but successive layers built up on top of previously dried layers will increase depth of build-up over time.

# FILLERS

Various fillers have been mentioned in passing, and now is the time to provide a little more information on some of these products. A filler is simply a product that can be used to bulk out a binding/texture medium to give it extra thickness, additional texture or both. Some fillers will influence the base colour of the binding medium, or paints/pigments added into it, whereas others won't. It is worth being aware of this before you use the products to avoid unnecessary frustration as you attempt a work-around while fighting against a deadline. As a precaution, trial the filler first.

In general, flexible binding mediums will work with most flexible, semi-rigid and rigid fillers, whereas rigid binding mediums are better suited to rigid fillers, although it is possible to use some semi-rigid fillers to favourable effect. Remember, there are always exceptions to the rule and experimentation can provide innovative solutions. Also bear in mind that although you could potentially use a binder/texture medium and one type of filler, combinations often yield more believable results.

## Rubber Chips

These look like gravel but are in fact chippings of rubber. The version that is supplied for theatre is black, but some garden centres and outdoor suppliers will sell these in primary colours (red, blue, green and yellow). Rubber chips are generally made from recycled rubber and make a very good texture medium where you require a coarse look but a soft touch, for example if it has to be walked on with bare feet or rolled around on. Rubber chips do not absorb the product and will not squish down as they have a high compressive strength, so they provide a little 'give' but return to their original shape.

## Foam Crumb

This product could be used for any number of purposes, including filling cushions and soft dummies, but it is quite expensive. It comes in three sizes – fine, medium and chunky – and has the advantage that it is very soft and lightweight as well as being flame retardant. It requires a flexible binder and subsequent paint top coats, which should also continue with the flexible theme. Being a foam, it will absorb the binder when mixed and this can allow it to be compressed to soften out, and even 'mould', the texture. This technique can take a little trial and error but works best when the binding medium is in a tacky/almost dry state. Be aware that the foam acts as an insulator and inhibiter, so it can take a while for this tackiness to work its way through thicker applications.

## Fillite

This is an inert, pale-grey, powder-like material that was initially created for use with resins to reduce the weight and volume of resin being used for castings. However, it has also proven to be a very useful product for adding into various binding mediums to add bulk and texture. A little can go a long way with this product, and effects can range from cast iron to stone. It does not absorb the product but remains suspended in it, which means the mix quantity must be just right to produce the desired texture, unless the intent is simply to bulk out the product.

# BREAKING-DOWN PROPS

'Breaking down' does not mean destroying a prop or costume, but simply giving it the impression of age and use, the patina of life and the passage of time. This can be done in a variety of ways, from traditional techniques such as paints and textures, to physically working away at certain parts of the prop, costume, piece of furniture or set with rasps and sandpaper, dyes and stains. Even an old cheese grater can be used to abrade cloth and distress wood to provide the impression of wear and tear.

This is normally something that is done to a new, or newly made item, that would otherwise stand out like a sore thumb amongst the other items on the set. If you have borrowed/hired an item it is unlikely that you will have permission to do this as borrows and hires are expected to be returned in the condition that they were supplied, unless otherwise stated. Therefore, it is important that any borrow/hire takes the desired condition for use in the production into account. For cosplay, LARP and re-enactment, breaking down can add an extra dimension, changing a nicely made prop, weapon or costume into something that breathes life into the character being portrayed. And breaking down can be as minimal as it can be exaggerated.

## Dirty Down Products

Dirty Down is a company that produces a range of products that are widely used in theatre, TV and film. This range consists of sprays, water-soluble paints and wax crayons, which can be used to create age and texture.

Theatre has come up with a multitude of effects over the centuries that will provide the look of aging and wear and tear on props and costumes and scenery to good effect, but many of them take time and effort to produce (good old craftsmanship) and, although a lot of these techniques are still valid and still in use, the addition and convenience of a range of products specifically aimed at creating the same or complementary effects in a fraction of the time is not to be ignored. The spray and paint products are water soluble, which gives the added benefit that the tonal range can be varied by using water to dilute and soften the effect of the applied products, which means there is still an element of creativity involved in that the effect will only be as convincing as the person applying it makes it.

Suitcase repair using FlexBond adhesive.

# 11
# ADHESIVES

Adhesives are an essential part of prop making – they are literally the glue that holds our props together. Throughout this book, various 'glue' products have been mentioned but here they have a chapter of their own for easy reference.

## PVA/WOOD GLUE

Polyvinyl acetate is perhaps the most essential glue that we use in prop making and carpentry. Selecting a good wood glue is paramount and sticking (no pun intended) to it will provide consistency and reliability. It is possible to buy different PVA products for different purposes but not necessary, as a good reliable product should perform the different tasks that you require of it, whether gluing and laminating wood, sticking together card constructions, creating monkey dung, layering papier mâché or scrimming fabrics. If you require a PVA for use outside then an exterior PVA needs to be chosen, as these are treated to make them frost- and waterproof, but this would be in addition to your normal PVA.

It is preferable to buy a more expensive, viscous PVA that can be diluted rather than buying a cheap, very fluid version that may not satisfy any task particularly well, resulting in wasted money. A good prop and carpentry choice is Evo-Stik Resin 168, which can be bought in economical 25kg tubs that can be dispensed into smaller pots and tubes for easier use.

Provided the lid is secured tightly, with any excess glue removed before tightening it down, PVA glue has a very long shelf life if kept away from extremes of temperature.

## SIZE

Glue size, or size, is a traditional adhesive and binding medium. In theatre it has been used for centuries to make gesso, bind powder pigments, prime and stretch canvas, and scrimming in the production of props.

Size is part of the gelatin family, and what we use in theatre is commonly referred to as 'animal size' or 'hide, hoof and bone size', as it is a by-product of the meat industry, utilizing the parts that have been deemed unsuitable for human consumption or for tanning. Once rendered down, you have a gelatin product that is dried and turned into a powder or granules ready to be mixed and heated and turned into a clean, user-friendly, non-toxic glue. There are a variety of gelatin glues available, but it is best to get size through theatrical suppliers, the granular variety being easier to mix. Fine artists like to use rabbit skin glue for priming canvases prior to painting, but from a prop-making point of view this would become very costly, as 0.5kg is about six times more expensive than 1kg of traditional glue size.

Size is a very good glue for scrimming, and it is also very cost-effective due to its mixing ratio with water (see Chapter 7). Once mixed, size should not be left lying around in its cold, gelatinous state for more than a day, as it will start to biodegrade and show signs of mould, taking on a whole new aroma. Mix what you need, adding to it as you go. Size mixes from the end of the previous day's work can be reheated the following morning. Excess glue size can be mixed with sawdust and thrown away as it is a naturally biodegradable product. Do not tip excess glue size down the sink as it could cause problems with plumbing and drainage, although washing hands and brushes with warm soapy water is fine.

# NATURAL LATEX ADHESIVES

Whether you choose Copydex, Flints...dex, F-Ball Sticcobond F1, or some other brand of latex adhesive, this is another very useful product to have available in the prop shop. Latex adhesives will glue many products – paper and card, wood, leather, even some plastics and some metals – although they work best with products that have some surface absorbency or keyed texture. Latex is another natural product and is harvested from managed sources. Being a non-vulcanized rubber, latex adhesive will biodegrade if left in direct sunlight, under UV light or when it encounters most oils or non-ferrous metals. In this book the brand name Copydex is used as a general term for latex adhesives, partly out of long habit, and partly because it is a name that you can take to another supplier to find an alternative product that does the same job. Unfortunately, Copydex is no longer available in bottles of a decent workshop size.

Copydex can be used in two ways, either as a contact adhesive on non-porous or tricky surfaces, such as foam rubber, or on porous surfaces as an application to one surface where the second surface is laid over the first and smoothed together – this may need to be done sequentially on larger surface areas. Always use sparingly to avoid excess glue bleeding through, particularly with thin fabrics and, when used as a contact adhesive, wait until it is completely dry before bonding the required pieces together. Copydex can be diluted with water for economy (do not exceed a 1:1 ratio), but drying times will increase significantly

It is best to use offcuts of foam rubber and glue spreaders to apply the Copydex to avoid damaging brushes. If you get latex adhesive onto clothing, you may be able to rinse it out with cold water if you do it quickly, but it is often simpler to let it dry and then peel it off, providing it has not been rubbed into the fabric. Always wear workshop clothing when working to avoid the inevitable.

Use vinyl gloves for latex work, and you will be able to rub your hands together to remove any excess product as you go, leaving the gloves clean as the latex balls up and peels off. Do not use latex gloves, as latex bonds to latex very well and you could find your gloved hands rapidly becoming gloved flippers as the fingers glue together.

# ROSCO FLEXBOND

Rosco FlexBond is like a cross between PVA and Copydex in that it has the durability and longevity of PVA, but with the added flexibility of Copydex. Unlike Copydex, it will not stretch but, as its name suggests, it will flex, which makes it an excellent choice for projects that require added flexibility and durability. The properties of FlexBond make it an excellent choice for flexible canes and withies (for gluing and binding), for making and repairing leather goods, for bookbinding (particularly the spines of books), as well as woods and plastics, paper and card and fabrics.

ABOVE LEFT: Rosco FlexBond adhesive – a useful addition to any workshop, complementing PVA and Copydex.

ABOVE RIGHT: Suitcase repair 1: in need of gluing and stitching. Any remnants of the old thread have been removed.

Suitcase repair 2: a Speedy Stitcher acts like a hand-held sewing machine, using a loop rather than a crossover stitch.

Suitcase repair 3: as the stitching awl needle is pushed all the way in and drawn back, it creates a loop. The end of the 'start' thread (pulled through from the Speedy Stitcher at the start) is threaded through the loop.

Suitcase repair 4: both threads are now drawn tight to complete the stitch. The process is repeated until the end of the repair is reached. A few back stitches will lock the threads in place, at which point they are snipped away.

FlexBond does rely on the absorbency of the product, and the usual approach is to apply liberally to all surfaces to be bonded, place them together and then firmly clamp them to maximize the bond. With good timing, it is possible to imitate a contact adhesive effect with FlexBond when bonding non-porous surfaces, but it does require the application of less glue and some practice.

It is a versatile adhesive that can also be added to paints and pigments to provide a flexible, durable paint finish that can be used over latex, Plastazote and Evazote products.

Suitcase repair 5: be aware that the average leather case will be a thin exterior of leather over card boards that provide the rigidity. Consequently there may not be much to stitch into, so proceed carefully.

ABOVE: Suitcase repair 7: it may not be perfect, but it will do the trick. The FlexBond dries clear and will look like the rest of the case.

LEFT: Suitcase repair 6: an application of FlexBond over this newly stitched, but very worn, edge is drawn into the leather and card and binds the fibres.

## HOT GLUE

Hot glue is a useful tacking product, but there is a tendency for those using it to get carried away and rely on it as the go-to product for all their prop making. Don't! There are certain things that it works very well with, Plastazote and Evazote being examples of this, but in most cases, it should only be used as a temporary hold prior to the main fix being applied. Once you have had to repair and remake innumerable props because someone has relied upon hot glue as their fixing medium, you will realize that it does have its limits.

## ARALDITE AND EPOXY RESIN GLUES

Araldite is an epoxy resin adhesive that is available in a variety of forms, including rapid and standard set versions, in tubes or ready-to-mix syringes. Epoxy resins are very strong and will bond to a multitude of surfaces, making this adhesive invaluable for repairs and makes. It is very useful for making jewellery pieces and gluing items that have minimal contact for the required bond.

## SUPERGLUE/CRAZY GLUE

Apart from being a sure-fire way of inadvertently gluing your fingers together, or to the prop you are making (always wear gloves), this is another glue that people see as being the be-all and end-all of adhesives. Yes, it does have its uses, but it also has its limits. Bear in mind that although the glued object may dry very quickly, it can be 24 hours before the glue has fully cured and is ready to be put through its paces.

Sauce bottle repair 1: over time, due to conditions and wear and tear, a lot of adhesives can simply 'let go'. They lose their grab, and that is what can be seen here.

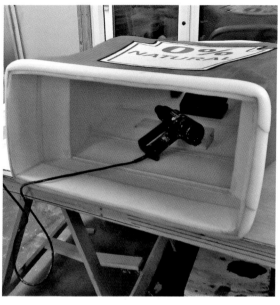

Sauce bottle repair 2: the structural supports have been tacked with hot glue and taped with masking tape to hold them in place. Masking tape grips to Plastazote very well.

Sauce bottle repair 4: a hot-air gun, set to a low heat, is being used here to speed up drying. The ambient temperature was quite cool.

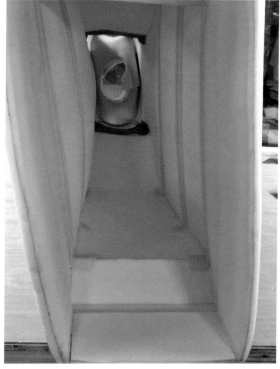

Sauce bottle repair 3: FlexBond has been used to glue in lightweight canvas strips. The glue is applied to the Plastazote, and the canvas is smoothed down over it. Rubbing over the canvas gently with an offcut will cause friction and encourage the glue to dry quicker.

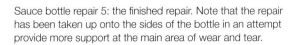

Sauce bottle repair 5: the finished repair. Note that the repair has been taken up onto the sides of the bottle in an attempt provide more support at the main area of wear and tear.

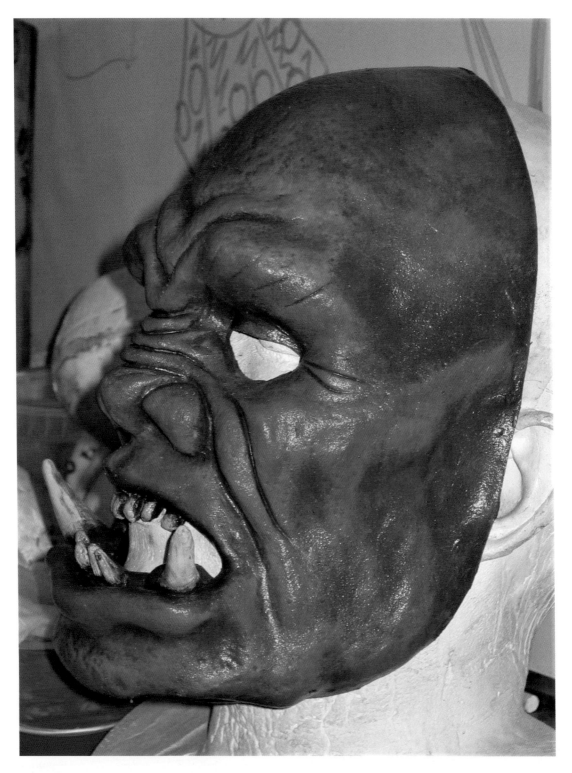

Orc mask. This epitomizes the need to apply layers of paint to bring life into any painted object. This is a slush mould latex casting from a one-part plaster mould taken from a grey clay sculpt.

# 12
# PAINT AND
# PAINTING TECHNIQUES

It can be quite bewildering deciding what paint product to use, but as a rule of thumb, the most suitable paints are going to be those used for theatre, television and film. These are products that are specially designed for decorating sets, props and costumes with the intention that they can be mixed and blended with themselves and other products to create multifarious effects and textures.

From a prop-making point of view it is easier to use pre-mixed paints, as we generally do not paint to cover the same amount of surface area as a scenic artist would, although the mixing of powder paints with a variety of binding mediums is a time-honoured tradition that goes back to the dawn of mankind.

For the purposes of this book, the assumption is that you have some understanding of the concept of colours and colour complements, and of blending and toning, highlight and shadow.

## EQUIPMENT

### Paintbrushes

These essential tools range from fine art brushes through to a variety of decorator's brushes from 12mm (½in) through to 100mm (4in), with a choice of straight and angled bristles (but you can work out what you require as you progress). It is possible to get starter packs of artist's brushes if you are not sure what you need, and trial and error will aid you in progressing to better versions if

you want to. Likewise, there are budget packs of decorator's brushes that can be purchased through various outlets; these have the advantage that they are cheap enough that you can trim and shape them for different projects and if they do get ruined, it won't break the bank. Falling into this category is a type of budget brush referred to as a 'resin brush', which is usually used as a disposable brush for GRP work but performs a respectable job as an inexpensive paintbrush. The best ones have wooden handles, which better fit with their disposable ethos.

### Paint Rollers

Rollers, although time-consuming to clean properly, are an effective way of supplying an even layer of paint to larger areas after 'cutting in' with a brush around detail, edges and corners. Rollers and roller trays come in several assorted sizes and it is useful to at least have a 4in (10cm) mini roller and a 9in (23cm) standard roller available for use. Different roller heads can be used for specific products or effects.

### Natural Sponge/Foam Rubber Offcuts

If you use foam rubber for making cod props or upholstery, you will have various offcuts that can be put to advantageous effect as paint applicators. Of course, if you are flush with funds, you can

246 PAINT AND PAINTING TECHNIQUES

always buy natural sponge. Sponge/foam offcuts work superbly as tools for applying and blending paint and providing believable texture, shadow and highlight effects for props and scenery. Applying paint with sponges can be very economical, particularly when used with colour-rich paints, as the application can be achieved in microns of thickness of paint. This also means it generally dries quicker than paint applied by brushes, and as an extension of this, brushes and sponges can both be used for an invaluable technique called 'dry brushing'.

## Dry Brushing/Sponging

This technique uses the minimal amount of paint possible on the brush or sponge, often achieved by drawing the brush over, or dabbing the sponge onto, a piece of cloth or paper towel and then lightly drawing over or sponging onto the object being painted. The aim is to highlight specific areas by raising the texture, or simply increasing the tonal range so that greater realism is brought into the prop, be it a mask, corpse, tree or wall.

Once again, if you look at the colours and tonal range on each side of your hands, or on your face, you will realize that this cannot be achieved in one coat of paint, especially when considering veins and areas where more wear and tear is evident. If you have gone to the extent of providing added detail through texturing or texture-mapping an object, it would be a pointless exercise if this effort were not complemented by a decent paint finish. With experience it is possible to cut corners in the construction process and still end up with a robust and very viable prop, but where you should not cut corners is in the paint finish, as this can make the difference between a good prop and an unsatisfactory prop.

## Paint Palette

Paint palettes are invaluable for quality of technique as well as economy of product use. The size of your pallet will need to be appropriate to

the scale of the individual piece being undertaken – bigger palettes for large pieces, smaller ones for smaller pieces. The purpose of a palette is to provide a selection of paint colours appropriate to the work at hand that will give range and tone, light and shade.

Palettes can also be used to work out mix ratios when trying to establish specific colour mixes for bulk quantities for base coats, washes and glaze effects on larger projects.

## Graining Tools

Graining tools are devices used primarily for creating wood grain effects. There is a lot of choice here, from diverse types of combs to rollers and heart grainers, which cater for many grain types from softwoods to hardwoods, long grain to short grain. Again, the choice is yours as to whether you buy manufactured products or make you own. There is an art to the process of wood graining, but a little practice can create some very convincing effects once you have got to grips with base layers and top layers and tried to simulate different cuts and finishes of wood grains that you see around you.

## Glazes

Glazes are available in emulsion and acrylic variants, and as gloss or matt/flat. Glazes can either be used as an application over a finished item to provide a protective surface, or they can be mixed with paint to provide greater spread or make the paint more translucent. Glazes can be diluted with water, but always check the manufacturer's guidelines for your specific product for guidance on mixing ratios. Gloss and matt glazes should be part of your paint stock.

## Washes and Glaze Wash

Paint can be diluted by adding water or glazes to act as finishing top coats or provide a series of intermediate coats, separating different layers of paint and creating a greater appearance of depth within the finished product. The difference between washes and glazes is that the former simply uses water to dilute the paint, and the base colour or tone will have more or less influence on the applied wash depending on the ratio of paint to water. This wash process, when dry, gives a non-shiny dry look. A glaze wash is also intended to allow the base colour or tone to influence the wash, but uses a plastic medium to suspend the paint, allowing for greater depth in the tonal range and providing a varnish-like effect, ranging from matt to gloss (depending on the type of glaze and any dilution used) when it dries.

# LIGHT AND SHADE, DEPTH AND TONE

All scenery, props and costumes require these, otherwise they can appear flat and uninteresting under stage lights. We have talked in terms of layers of paint and building up these layers. We have talked about complementary colours, top coats and dry brushing/sponging. These are all part of a whole process to create a finished look to the prop that you have taken hours to make, and that will determine how well that prop is received. Outlined here are the steps that can help you to build this tonal range.

## Base Coat Depth Detail

You can think of this as being your primer coat: it is the foundation that all other layers are built on, and it provides body to the subsequent layers. This does not need to be an all-over colour but can simply be used as a darker complementary colour to the next base coat and is applied into the deeper areas of the prop to define the lines and detail and help to exaggerate areas of shadow. It can be tempting to use black paint to provide this effect, and in certain cases this will work very well, but it is better to work with a darker version of the subsequent base coat.

## Base Coat

As the name implies, base coat coverage is about applying an overall base coat onto the prop, providing a complementary colour tone that will blend out from the depth detail base coat. Do not eliminate the depth detail, just work out from it, blending and toning so that one becomes a natural progression of the other. Base coat can be applied as a single colour in certain instances, such as when painting furniture, but will give greater 'life' to the prop if it is applied as a mix from a palette, using the same/similar colours to that used for the base detail but adding in lighter tones.

## Secondary Layers

The idea of the secondary layers, the layers beneath the top coat, is that they start to add more in the range of colour tone and depth to specific areas of the prop. Expanding upon the base coat by extending the tonal range from the depth detail, through the base coat and into these layers will develop the depth and 'feel' of the prop.

## Top Layer

The top layer ties the whole thing together, putting the flesh onto the muscle and bone of the previous layers, as it were. This is usually a complementary lighter tone to the previous layers that draws them all together and, in some cases, this can be the finish of the prop.

## Highlights

Highlights can be added at this point to exaggerate raised detail and complement points of shadow, and are best applied by dry brushing/sponging. Highlights may also be used to add detail such as grime, patina, sweat stains and blood.

## The Finish

This is the final coat, be it a protective layer or something to add the effect of water, slime, dust and so on or, for panto, a little bit of glitter.

The above is a simple breakdown of the process of painting a prop. Not all the steps need be used for every prop, and it is not necessary to execute them as separate stages, as it is absolutely possible to make them more of an organic process, working one naturally into the other, blending and toning as you progress to the end of the completed paint job. The only thing to be aware of with this more organic way of working is the effect of 'paint bleed'. Paint bleed occurs when the base layer/s of paint are not as dry as you think they are and end up darkening the layer above, sometimes completely overriding the desired effect. In this instance, it is preferable to put the painting to one side and come back to it when it is fully dry.

For certain items it is easier and more effective to use paintbrushes, while for others it is more beneficial to use sponges/foam rubber, but this is something for you to try as your painting techniques develop.

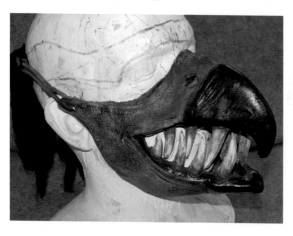

Harpy mask. The sculpt texture allows for extra depth to be given to the paint layer build-up and will also influence the way that light plays on the mask. Note the contrast of matt and semi-gloss aspects and how they are reacting to light.

ABOVE: Two Audreys. The small Audrey is a papier mâché casting, whilst the larger one is Celastic. Both are made over grey clay sculpts and covered with a pale-green jersey fabric that has been painted into.

LEFT: Another Jabberwocky head. This is a slush latex casting taken from a two-part beta plaster mould from a grey clay sculpt. The barbules are trimmed, heated and shaped Plastazote. Note that on this creature, the darker areas of the skin are the highlights.

Bear claw hand coverings made from quality faux fur glued onto grey suede. The fur has had paint teased through it to break it down.

Grimoire for *The Knight before Christmas*. It was constructed from timber frame and EPS, epoxy resin GRP with a heavy-duty canvas laminated spine and paper rope and 12mm (½in) felt decoration, and scrimmed with calico. All that work would be wasted if as much effort wasn't put into the paint technique. This book has many hidden tricks.

Grimoire – one of three turnable pages. Note the detail of foxing that makes the work believable. The pages were made from skin ply glued between layers of heavy calico.

Trout for *Wind in the Willows*. This simple 2D cut-out is brought to life by a rudimentary paint job.

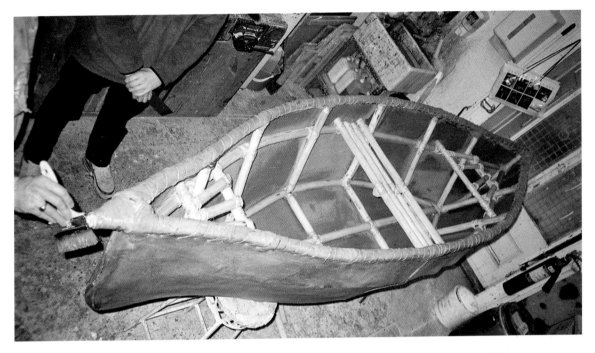

The umiak 'skin' effect is water-soluble stains and glazes. The flat bottom of the canoe was to enable it to sit flat on the stage floor.

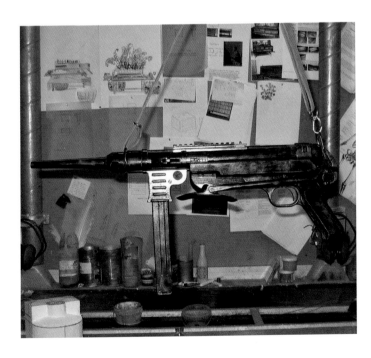

Toy machine gun, turned from a plastic-looking toy into something with a bit more gravitas with paint and a gun-metal effect.

An ostrich feather fan with ostrich egg detail (EPS), enhanced by paint providing a patina effect.

Hatolite light bulb and glass paint produces a rich blue colour. Painted on the exterior with a brush, it produces a wonderfully even coating.

Hatolite fire red gives a glossy, even effect when painted on. Hatolite paints are resistant to quite high temperatures, being designed for use with light bulbs.

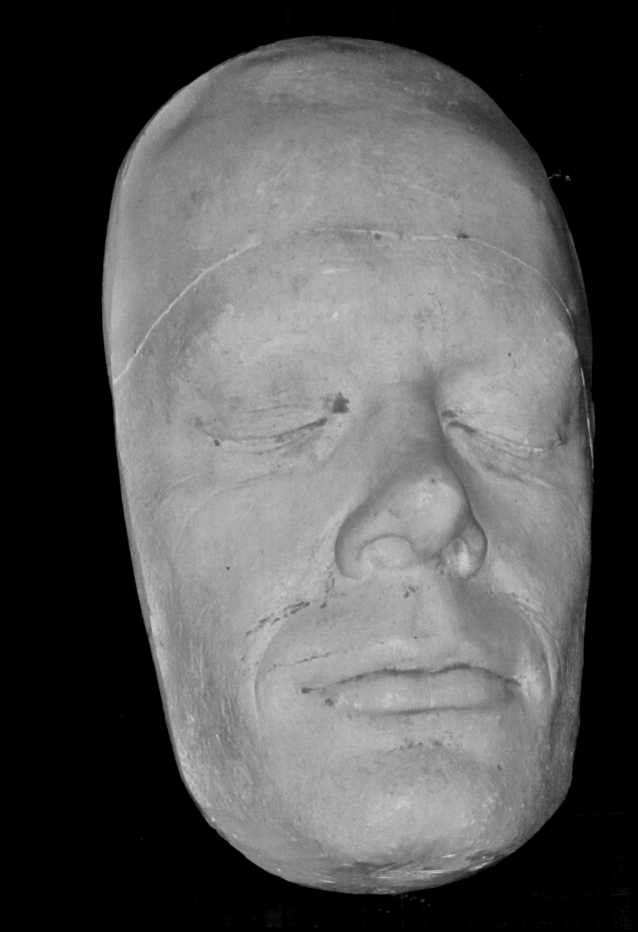

# 13

# AN INTRODUCTION TO LIFE CASTING AND STILL LIFE

First, let us explore what is meant by 'life casting'. For most people the term means taking impressions of faces and body parts, and this is certainly true, but it can also be used to refer to taking castings from other objects from life, such as fruit and veg, meat and fish – in short, foodstuffs – which could be referred to as 'still life', as the intention is to produce long-lasting replicas of otherwise perishable items.

Although it can be very tempting to want to take a facial life cast/body cast from an individual, there are certain pitfalls that you should be aware of, and it is inadvisable, for the safety of your subject and your own peace of mind, to attempt life casting in an unsupervised situation. Undertaken correctly, with appropriate materials and facilities, facial life casting and body casting is perfectly safe. Undertaken without full knowledge of the materials and processes and potential hazards, there can be a real risk to life and limb.

This chapter covers the various materials available for life casting but will not go into the processes for face and full body casting as that is something that requires practical experience with the materials and, ideally, a hands-on course to guide you through the processes. The way in which you can develop your knowledge and experience of the materials, before approaching the more complicated aspects of life casting, will be detailed, and basic life-casting principles will be examined.

## MATERIALS

### Casting Plaster

Casting plaster can be used for taking impressions from organic but inanimate objects such as foodstuffs, but should **never** be used for taking

Having a dedicated space to take and store life castings is a luxury. What is important is making space to store them safely.

OPPOSITE: A face cast. A life cast taken using the pink short-set dental alginate. With a setting time of 2–3 minutes, it would not be suitable for a full head cast.

life castings, due to the risk of severe burns and 'locking in' the body part being cast. Severe burns may sound a little implausible when dealing with a powdered rock mixed with a high volume of water, but when plaster and water are mixed an exothermic reaction commences. As the plaster changes from a fluid into a solid state, over a period of about twenty minutes, the temperature rises, reaching a peak at setting point, and it is this period in contact with the high heat inside the mould that can cause extreme discomfort, burns or even loss of fingers and toes. The more thickly the plaster is applied, the higher the temperature can get, but even for a modest thickness of mould the effect can be that of plunging the body part into scalding water.

## Plaster Bandage/Modroc

Plaster bandage does not cause the same problems of heat build-up as casting plaster because it is only used in three layers of application, resulting in a general thickness of about 3mm (⅛in), so can be used on humans. The person being cast may experience a brief feeling of mild warmth, but no more than that. Application and removal is quick but should be done with consideration because there is always the chance of a stray hair being trapped. As with all life casting, removal of the cast should be done with the assistance and co-operation of the person being cast. In the case of facial life casting with Gypsona plaster bandage, not working with your model and attempting the removal without their assistance could result in a minor bruise on the bridge of the nose.

Plaster bandage has the added advantage that as well as plaster positives, you could, after removing any oil residues, take a latex casting from it. Although it can pick up some fine detail, there is also a tendency for it to leave behind the texture of the supporting gauze bandage as well. Not a huge problem for productions taking place behind a proscenium arch, but for work that will be inspected more closely, this is a less desirable trait

that requires a reworking of the plaster positive form, resulting in a loss of finer detail.

For many years in theatre, plaster bandage was the only medium we had for 'safely' taking a facial or body cast because it was the only product readily available to us. Alginate existed, but it was expensive and could only be acquired through dental suppliers willing to sell it to non-dental buyers. Plaster bandage is still very much in use today, but you are more likely to see it being used to create supporting cases for products like alginate and Skinsil in the theatre, television and film professions, than as a directly applied life-casting medium. Theatre productions are still limited by small budgets and plaster bandage is a much quicker and cheaper way of attaining an accurate limb or body form when the need for detail is not paramount, but accuracy of shape is required. For facial life casting, it is preferable to use alginate as you cannot use plaster bandage behind areas of undercut, such as the jaw line, due to the risk of locking in the person you are casting.

Plaster bandage castings will grip readily into facial and body hair that has not been well greased with white petroleum jelly. Do not attempt to take a plaster bandage life cast on anyone who has anything more than a light beard stubble. Castings can be taken above the hair line if you fit your model with a bald cap or swimming cap.

## Alginate

The cost of alginate has come down by about a third over the past twenty-five years, largely because it now has a broader market than just the dental trade. The important thing to bear in mind is that there are several types of alginate, which will provide you with setting times varying from 2.5 to 8 minutes, depending on whether you have bought a quick-set dental alginate (usually pink or blue in colour), or a slow-set body casting alginate (white in colour). Although you can achieve a face cast with dental alginate, the setting time is too quick for a full head cast. Setting times can be extended by using chilled water; this can make it very uncomfortable for anyone being cast, but can be a useful trick when casting food. As a rule, for life casting, the temperature of the water should be the same as that of the room.

Mixing of the alginate product should be done according to the manufacturer's instructions for use, as this will produce optimum working and setting times. Tap water, allowed to acclimatize to room temperature, is used to hydrate the alginate by pouring it into a container that already contains the 'fluffed' alginate, stirring vigorously with a plastic spatula or an immersion mixer, until an even, thick creamy mix is achieved. Make sure you work fully into the corners of the bowl so that no dry product is left behind. The physical effect is like mixing a heavy cake mix, but there is no opportunity to rest when mixing the alginate because the quicker it is mixed, the longer you will have to apply it. To give you an accurate measure of your overall working time to the 'set', you can make up a small test mix of alginate and apply it to the palm of your hand and time the process from start to finish. The larger the quantity of alginate used, the longer it takes to mix, the less time you have available to you to apply it. Take a deep breath (without breathing in the alginate!), mix thoroughly and work methodically.

Once the alginate application is done, it is simply a question of applying the supporting case using Gypsona plaster bandage. In the interest of getting the case completed as quickly as possible, use the following method:

1. Put a quarter teaspoon of salt into the water used for wetting the plaster bandage.
2. Have the bandage pre-cut into appropriate lengths that, overlapped, will cover the whole of the alginate mould.
3. Cut three pieces of each length of plaster bandage strip and position them on your workbench in their stacks of three in the order that they will be applied.
4. Pick up your first triple stack, immerse it in the salted water, squeegee out the excess water between your index and forefinger as you remove it from the water.
5. Apply the wetted triple layer bandage directly to the alginate mould, starting at the perimeter, smoothing the bandage gently but snug to the alginate surface. The aim is to produce a close contact but not to distort the alginate mould by pressing too hard onto it. However, because the alginate is very flexible, it is possible, through over-working of the plaster bandage, to reshape the alginate if the bandage should set with the alginate mould being distorted, especially with a softer/more flexible form under the alginate.
6. Continue wetting and applying the triple layer Gypsona plaster bandage, completing the perimeter and working consistently inwards until the whole of the alginate mould is supported. Extra supporting layers of bandage can be applied to reinforce the edges and more vulnerable areas of the mould.
7. Adding salt to the water that the plaster bandage was wetted in should have significantly accelerated the setting time of the bandage, resulting in the plaster bandage case being removable within five minutes of the final piece of bandage being applied. How you remove the case and life cast mould will very much depend upon the object being cast. When removing a face or body cast, it is preferable to have the alginate supported by the plaster bandage case as the whole mould is eased away from the model, to avoid the risk of the alginate tearing. With an object like a chicken or joint or beef, it may be necessary to remove the plaster bandage case and gently flex out the original form, possibly making strategic cuts in the alginate, before carefully re-seating the alginate mould back into the plaster bandage case.
8. Take a positive casting. This is usually done with casting plaster (although melted wax/wax-based clay can be used, or even Jesmonite for a tougher positive), as soon as you can – preferably once you have cleaned your model up and seen them off the premises, and then tidied the workshop for this next stage.

An alginate mould can be kept in stasis for a brief time by placing damp towels into the mould, but for best results a casting should be taken from the mould within an hour of it being removed from the model. Failure to do this will result in subtle changes to the alginate as it loses moisture due to evaporation and starts to shrink and curl, reducing the chances of producing an accurate reproduction of your model or form. Over a period of a few days, the mixed alginate will shrink to about half its mixed volume once all the water has evaporated away, if left in a warm environment.

## SECOND-GENERATION MOULDS

It is from here that the real work begins. The positive casting is your 'master' and will only be used

<br>

**CASTING OPTIONS FOR ALGINATE**

Although plaster is the norm when taking a positive casting from an alginate mould, and wax, wax-based clay and Jesmonite have been mentioned, it is also possible to use some fast-cast silicones and urethane resins such as the product ranges sold by Smooth-On. Any product that you choose should be moisture tolerant, or adverse reactions could occur between the products; it is worth doing a small-scale test if you are unsure how certain products might react, after referring to the manufacturer's guidelines and the technical data sheets. It goes without saying that Smooth-On has invested a lot of time and money in developing a range of products that work in concert with each other to save the customer the hassle of chasing down compatible products.

As a rule, it is better to create a plaster or clay positive from your initial mould that can be checked for errors and cleaned up prior to making a second-generation mould, rather than risk all and attempt a resin casting in the alginate without knowing what imperfections may be present in the mould. If, however, this is what you want to do, to avoid making a second mould, the better option would be to cast the model in Smooth-On's Body Double life casting silicone (*see below*), which is intended for multiple, accurate castings.

<br>

to create the second-generation moulds (full or partial) that will be used for making second-generation casts that any future modelling will be done on. Just to clarify, any prosthetic or mask work modelling that is to be done will be done from the second-generation casts, not the master, as it is important to maintain the detail integrity of the master in case it becomes necessary to make a new second-generation mould (because the current one is starting to show signs of wear and tear, for example).

The second-generation mould is best made from silicone rubber – after sealing the plaster with a non-silicone-based release agent, such as Ambersil Formula 5 Release Agent (a spray wax release) – as this will provide you with exceptionally high detail reproduction, making subsequent castings as close to the master as possible. From the silicone rubber second-generation mould, it is possible to take castings using a broad range of materials from GRP to expanding foams, casting waxes and wax-based clays to plasters. As a rule, standard latex products will not work in silicone moulds as they need the combined processes of evaporation and absorption to fully cure, which is something that the silicone does not provide. Foam latex products will work well with silicone moulds but foam latex requires baking after the gel period has been reached.

If you create a wax or wax-based clay casting from the second-generation mould, then a third-generation mould can be made in plaster from the wax/clay cast to facilitate the use of standard latex products for casting if desired.

Partial moulds can be made from the 'master' cast by constructing a wall of clay or plasticine around the area you wish to cast, isolating it, and then pouring mixed alginate (or silicone) into the clay 'box'. Once set, the clay wall can be removed, the alginate or silicone block eased away and set up for casting (in plaster or whatever you choose) by building another clay wall, recycling the original clay wall and adding to it, around the alginate or silicone and filling with your plaster mix.

## Skinsil Smooth-On Body Double Fast Set

Skinsil is a two-part silicone product that comes in a dual-cartridge system that requires a dual-cartridge dispensing gun for application. Working time is about 90 seconds and the setting time is about 7 minutes. Upon fixing a mixing nozzle to the dual cartridge and placing it in the gun and squeezing the applicator's handles together, the correct mix of silicone and catalyst are dispensed and can be directly applied to the item being moulded. If you are working with a live model, it is necessary to apply Body Double release cream – although the product is skin safe, this is primarily aimed at sealing eyelashes, eyebrows and fine body hair. Application of Skinsil should not be done over head hair or beards and areas of longer body hair, as these require masking with bald caps or similar to prevent the hair becoming trapped in the silicone. It is possible to mould over 'well-released' short beards and body hair, working the release cream right down to the skin, but experience and caution are the key words here.

Skinsil will provide a more detailed casting than even alginate will, and it has the added advantage that it is a permanent mould that can be used for multiple castings. As with alginate, plaster bandage is used as a supporting case for the Skinsil, but there is nothing to stop you creating a more enduring case from plaster or GRP once the first successful casting has been taken, by taking a second casting (to preserve the original, just in case things go pear-shaped). Leave it in the mould, once set, then remove the plaster bandage case and set up the mould for the durable case process, which will vary depending on whether it is to be a single case, for an open mould, or a dual or multiple case for a closed mould.

In the UK, Skinsil is currently about six times more expensive than an equivalent volume of alginate, although mould thickness is thinner and therefore coverage is slightly greater. Skinsil does, however, have the benefit that moulds can be used multiple times. It is easier to use, more controllable and a less rushed application process

than alginate because of the nozzle application method and the fact that the product is not activated until it has been squeezed through the nozzle. It is essential to work consistently with the product, however, so that new silicone being applied is a continuation of silicone that has not yet set. Once a sufficient area of silicone has been applied, it is usual practice to smooth over the area with a spatula to ensure that there is a good and even coverage over the whole form.

The applicator gun is not inexpensive, but is a one-off expenditure, whereas the mixing nozzles are a one-shot usage. A nozzle is no longer viable once the silicone mix has stopped being pushed through it, as any mix left in the nozzle will cure, blocking it. Fortunately they are not expensive and should last a full cartridge if product is kept flowing through it, but always have at least one spare available. If you finish application of the product and there is still content in the cartridge, release the plunge pressure on the gun, remove the mixing nozzle from the cartridge and replace the original sealing cap, and the remaining product will be available for the next time you need it.

Skinsil is not essential for a small workshop or budding prop maker or hobbyist, as there are other products that can be used, but it does have the advantages of highly detailed reproduction of many objects and easier application for sectionalized castings. Body Double Fast Set can also be purchased in a dual tub set, like the standard set, detailed below, which opens up options for use with the other Smooth-On Body Double additives.

## Smooth-On Body Double Standard Set

This is another two-part, direct application, silicone life casting system. The standard set has a working time of about 5 minutes and can be removed after about 20 minutes. Unlike Skinsil, this system does not require an applicator gun as the product is supplied in two containers (silicone and catalyst) that you measure out in equal parts and mix together

## MOULDS AND MOULD STORAGE

It can be very tempting to keep every mould that you make, whether from life-casting projects or from sculpting projects, but moulds take up quite a lot of space. They should be stored in a dry place, preferably not in the main workshop but in a separate closed and ventilated storage area, at an even, comfortable temperature. The ventilation is to provide a through-flow of air to reduce/eliminate the chances of mould starting to grow on the moulds. Some form of racking that allows easy and safe access to each mould is ideal, with smaller moulds higher up, bigger moulds closer to waist height for easier handling, and medium-sized moulds closer to the floor, to follow the lifting and handling guidelines of the H&S executive. The main thing is that you don't have to pull down a heavy mould from overhead that could fall and seriously injure you, or lift a larger mould from the floor that could result in you straining yourself or damaging your back. Technically the stacking should run as follows:

Top: small moulds
Top middle: medium-small moulds
Middle top: medium-sized moulds
Middle: large moulds
Middle bottom: medium-sized moulds
Bottom middle: medium-small moulds
Bottom: small moulds

Small, medium and large in this context refer as much to weight as size, but it is often easier to store items of the same volume in the same area even if the weight varies substantially.

If a separate large area is not available off the workshop, then racking with doors or protective screens is worth looking at, or even under-bench storage, but ideally you want to keep dust and detritus out of your moulds.

in a separate pot prior to application. Application is achieved with tongue depressors or spatulas and is a similar process to that of alginate but, like Skinsil, produces a reusable mould. Plaster bandage is again used as a supporting case to prevent the mould from flexing and distorting once removed.

Smooth-On provide a wide range of support products that can be used to complement Body Double, including thickening and thinning products designed to provide the user with wider options for helping to achieve the best casting possible. If you add their Hyper-Folic release additive to the Body Double silicone this enables the silicone to 'self release' from hair and it is then possible to mould over short beards and longer body hair. Even so, the Body Double release cream has to be well worked into the skin and hair of the area concerned, and mould removal in these areas should be done as slowly as possible to minimize discomfort to the model.

## STILL LIFE PRACTICE

Before progressing to a life model, consider trying out casting techniques on a range of fruit, vegetable and meat or fish products. In the performing arts it is not uncommon to have to reproduce meals or food products that are never eaten but are used to set a scene, such as a banquet or a costermonger's barrow. It is possible to buy pre-made products from companies like Replica Ltd, (replica.co.uk, formerly Replica Foods), but when you are on a budget and you require multiples of an item it can be more cost-effective to make them yourself and have moulds in stock for future castings, provided you have the time. Building up a varied library of foodstuff moulds can be very useful and convenient for future work, but be aware that moulds take up space and, ideally, should be catalogued and kept somewhere safe.

# CASTING PROJECTS

## Casting Plaster for Still Life

It is not uncommon to use casting plasters for still life castings, the advantage being that you can take a slush-mould latex casting as soon as the mould has been 'rested' following removal of the form. The process is basically the same as that for setting up for any other moulding process, whether single part, multiple, box or balloon. The only difference may be an element of butchery, depending on what you are casting and what you want to achieve with the casting process. If you require a roast chicken that is to have the wings and legs removed then these will have to be moulded separately from the body; likewise if you wanted to use the chicken to act as a body form for a chicken that had recently been dispatched but not plucked. A well-trussed chicken or pheasant could be cast in a two-part mould since the wings and legs are pulled tight into the body, and strategically placed modelling clay can close up any inconvenient gaps.

An item like a pig's head could be cast with the ears on, but removal and separate casting of these makes the process more straightforward, although you now need to make three two-part moulds. As with the dissected chicken, however, you then have the option of using the individual parts for other projects, thus creating versatility in your moulds.

## Alginate for Still Life

Using alginate could not be easier for creating a simple one-part mould of various foodstuffs, particularly where that item has a relatively flat profile and is lying on a plate or board, and the other side of the casting is not seen. Simply place the item on a wipeable surface in a natural pose, mix the alginate and, using a spatula or tongue depressor, work the alginate over the surface of the object and down to the board. You are aiming for a covering of about 12mm (½in) all over, making sure to work out any air bubbles and get into the detail and undercuts of the object. Once set, apply three layers of plaster bandage over the alginate mould and leave to harden.

When the plaster bandage case has set, remove it and ease the alginate mould and object from the work surface and gently extricate the object from the mould. It may be necessary to trim some of the alginate away from where it has worked its way under the object, but this is normal procedure.

Realign the alginate mould into the plaster case and set it up for pouring a mix of casting plaster, Jesmonite or melted wax-based clay into the mould. It is highly likely that the alginate will not survive the first casting taken from it, but the emphasis should now be on the quality of the casting rather than preserving a one-off mould.

It is possible to create self-supporting single-part alginate moulds by pouring the alginate into a container and immersing an object into it, something that is quite common when taking castings of hands, but it is important that the object is wide enough at the top so that it can be drawn out through the aperture that it has made in the surface of the alginate. Ideally, the container that the alginate is poured into should have a slight taper to it, so that it is wider at the top than at the bottom. This makes it easier to remove the alginate mould from the container once the positive cast has been made, to break the alginate apart and get to the casting.

A variation is to place the object on a wipeable work surface and build a retaining wall around it as if making a box mould. The wall could be made from clay, offcuts of wood or even a section cut from an empty plastic tub/bottle that you place around the object and hot glue into place around the outside the base, or seal in place with clay… you could even use old Lego bricks to make a robust wall and seal it in place the same way. Once ready, mix your alginate and pour in at one corner or edge, letting the alginate flow over the form and using a tongue depressor to make sure it isn't creating air pockets, and fill the mould so that the object is covered to a depth of at least 12mm (½in). Once set, remove the wall, turn the mould over, gently remove the cast object and take a positive casting using your preferred method.

## Life Casting a Hand

This is one of the safest life-casting projects to do to help build confidence, providing you use the correct materials. You can even try this out on yourself if you use the container technique mentioned above – but it is always better to have an associate, who has an idea of what is going on, to help as moral support and to hold the mould still while you gently wriggle your hand free. Lubricating your hand with a little white petroleum jelly or Body Double release cream should make removal of the hand from the suction of the alginate a little easier.

The alginate can also be applied with a spatula, and/or your hands. This process has the advantage that you use a lot less alginate, but you will need to apply a plaster bandage two-part case to support the mould. The cured alginate will also require cutting up to any pinch point to allow for removal of the body part being cast. The cutting can easily be achieved by using a plastic spatula, slightly sharpened tongue depressor or plastic knife-edged clay modelling tool, kept for the purpose, or a pair of round-ended scissors. Whatever tool you use, always be aware of the safety and comfort of your life model.

To execute this moulding process, mix the alginate in the usual way and directly apply to the pregreased area of the model that you are casting. If casting a hand, foot or a limb, work the alginate over and around the body part, starting at the highest point and allowing gravity to assist in the flow of the alginate, making sure that it is worked into any undercuts and watching out for trapped air bubbles as you work the alginate over the body part. Gravity is your help and hindrance here, as it will aid in getting the alginate to where you need it but it will keep on going towards the floor if you don't keep an eye on it and sweep it back with your hands or the spatula. You are aiming for a thickness of alginate of no more than 12mm (½in); any more thickness than this can cause the fleshier parts of the model to distend by being drawn down by the weight of the alginate and the effects of gravity, something that can have a very negative effect on the casting and

the humour of your life model. A plaster bandage case will then be applied over the alginate.

## Plaster Bandage Life Casting

When using plaster bandage as your moulding medium for life casting an entire body part (remembering that a full plaster bandage life cast cannot be done on a head), or even using it to produce a supporting case for an enclosed mould of alginate or Skinsil, it will be necessary to apply the bandage in two parts. In the case of our hand mould, this means the back and palm of the hand, selecting a suitable divide line that avoids creating any 'locking points', where the fingers or wrist could get trapped. An eyeliner pencil can be used to draw a mid-point line around the hand, indicating where front and back will be separated, and as the bandage is applied for each layer, it can be folded back on itself to follow this line and reinforce the edge at the same time.

### Materials
- Water at room temperature for wetting bandage
- Pinch of salt to accelerate bandage cure time
- White petroleum jelly to work into model's skin as a release agent
- Plaster bandage/Modroc cut into appropriate-sized strips and pieces for the life-cast – three layers' worth

### Equipment
- Polythene sheet to protect worktop
- Bowl of salted water
- Scissors to cut the bandage
- Eyeliner pencil to mark divisions
- Disposable apron/overalls to protect model's clothing
- 12mm (½in) brush for applying white petroleum jelly as a release between the two halves of the mould

### Process
1. Mark the dividing line between front and back halves of the mould on the model's hand with the

eyeliner pencil. Draw another line around the wrist/ forearm to mark where the mould is to terminate.

2. Being careful not to eradicate the marked line, work the white petroleum jelly over the model's hand, between the fingers and into the cuticles.

3. Have the model rest their elbow onto a corner of the worktop or a board placed across the arms of the chair they are sitting on. The crucial points are that you can get to both sides of the hand easily, and that the model is positioned comfortably. The hand should not change position from where it has been set as this may affect the accuracy of the mould. Extra support/cushioning can be added beneath and around the elbow to increase the model's comfort and the arm's stability. Do not allow rotation of the wrist while applying the two bandage halves, as this can result in misalignment and separation of the casting from the model as the radius and ulna (the bones of the forearm) move around each other and change the shape of the wrist.

4. Apply the first layer of plaster bandage to the palm of the hand and inside of the wrist, folding the bandage back on itself as it reaches the guideline, until the whole of the palm side is complete. As a starting hand pose, it is best to attempt an open, relaxed hand with fingers and thumb lightly pressed together. It is possible to cast the hand with the fingers and thumb splayed but to do this it is best to bridge between the gaps with plaster bandage, which you smooth down thoroughly on the inside in between the fingers, and this 'web' will need to be greased with white petroleum jelly before the second half of the mould is applied.

5. The second and third layers can be applied as a dual layer, again folding back where they meet the divide line, and being careful not to press too hard into the first layer, as this could cause dents within the positive casting.

6. Grease any 'webs' created, if moulding between splayed fingers, and a 12mm (½in) strip around the leading edge of the first part of the mould by applying the white petroleum jelly with the paintbrush. This is where, as you apply plaster bandage to the back of the hand, you will create an overlap of the palm half of the mould by about

12mm (½in) so that one sits over the other, like the lip of a plastic lid on a tub, a process that will aid in correct alignment of the two mould halves.

7. Carefully apply the first layer of bandage to the back half of the hand, working it into the detail, and follow this up with the two support layers as in step 5. If moulding splayed fingers, simply work the bandage over the fingers and onto the greased 'webs' created by the first half of the mould, making sure to work the bandage tightly around the fingers themselves.

8. For increased rigidity, you can add external support by using plaster bandage to affix thin dowel or bamboo garden cane, or even rolled strips of the plaster bandage to create reinforcing ribs along and around the mould halves. This can be a useful precaution when dealing with larger mould segments.

9. Once the two halves have set, gently ease them apart by using a tongue depressor or an old clay modelling tool to tease along and between the overlapping halves – this will help separate the top half from the bottom half. With the join line separated, the two halves of the mould should come apart quite readily.

10. Once separated, set the mould aside and see to your model, thanking them for their participation and make sure they are comfortable, and show them where they can get cleaned up.

11. Having seen to your model, what you do next depends on what the cast objective is. If you are intending to create a plaster positive, simply realign the two halves and secure along the joining edge with more plaster bandage. Once this has set, place the mould in a plastic bucket or old tub of a suitable size, making sure that it is lightly packed around, to prevent the mould from moving as it is filled – this can be achieved with old carrier bags filled with screwed-up newspaper or offcuts of foam or even lumps of old clay.

12. Mix your plaster as normal and then pour the mix into the mould, aiming to achieve a steady flow that fills the mould gently and evenly. When the mould is full, tap the mould or supporting bucket/ tub about half a dozen times or so, to encourage the release of any air bubbles trapped in the plaster

or, more importantly, against the internal surface of the mould.

13. Leave the plaster to set completely, making sure the casting has cooled fully before removing the mould. This is a waste-mould process, as the mould will be destroyed either in part or in full when removing the casting. It is important, however, that the mould and casting are not permitted to dry completely, as this will make it much more difficult to remove the mould, which will become quite hard, so the risk of damage to the casting is significantly increased. After approximately an hour, the plaster should have set and the heat of the exothermic reaction dissipated. Starting at the sealed divide line, find an edge of the plaster bandage and peel it back. The bandage should still feel damp, and with a little effort should peel away from the adjoining layers. Continue in this way until the whole of the casting is revealed, taking care around the fingers to avoid snapping them off. If needed, a tongue depressor or old clay tool can be used to help with peeling back the layers.

14. Check the casting for imperfections and tidy up any seam lines by gently removing with a sharpened tongue depressor or a metal clay modelling tool with a fine flat edge. Set the casting aside to dry fully.

What you do with the plaster cast next is entirely dependent on why you have taken the casting in the first place. If it is simply to have a plaster sculpture, you are pretty much done other than sealing the plaster and painting and mounting it in whichever way you see fit. Be aware that large plaster objects, even when dry, are heavy and have little intrinsic strength. Alpha plasters are more durable, and Jesmonite even more so due to the plasticizer/resin component that is used in the place of water.

If your intention is to use the plaster casting as a master for the purpose of producing props or prosthetics, you will need to create a flexible mould from which you can produce secondary castings. Media you could use for such a mould include: casting silicones; foam latex; polyurethane resins, or rigid and flexible foams; GRP (fibreglass); and even prosthetic gelatin.

A face cast that was taken for an Ugly Sister panto joke about losing your head. This casting is latex from a plaster bandage mould (water, **not** PVA), The eyelids and eyes were modelled with milled cotton and slush latex. The head is an EPS core, skinned in 12mm (½in) foam, calico and slush latex, and the ears are foam and slush latex.

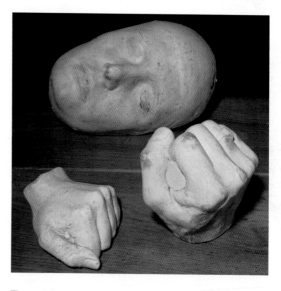

Three alginate life castings. The small fist was cast in this position on a table. The large fist was cast by immersing the hand into a bowl of alginate. The face was a standard practice face casting.

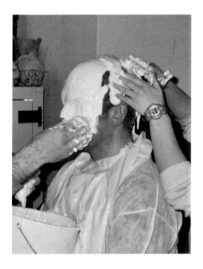 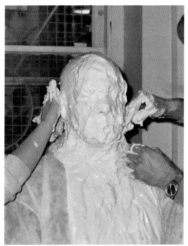 

ABOVE LEFT: Taking a full head cast. It is important that you are all set before your model enters the studio. Important: there is Vaseline-coated cotton wool in the model's ears to prevent the alginate from entering the ear canal. An extra pair of hands can make a full head cast easier.

ABOVE MIDDLE: The alginate needs to be no more than 12mm (½in) thick. Note there are no straws up the nose. With a good casting procedure, starting at the nostrils first, it is unnecessary and provides the model with better air flow.

ABOVE RIGHT: The plaster bandage case being applied, framing in the divide between front and back parts of the case and working in towards the nose from either side.

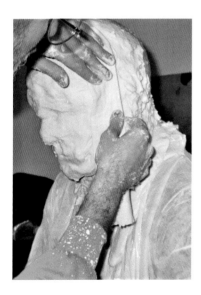  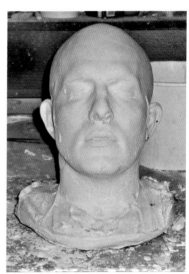

ABOVE LEFT: Once the front of the alginate is fully supported, reinforcing, double-folded strips are worked around the perimeter of the front case to provide added rigidity. White petroleum jelly is used as a release between front and back cases.

ABOVE MIDDLE: The life cast removed. The rear case is taken off first, the alginate 'cut' down the back with a wooden/plastic clay modelling tool. The model then assists in the removal, as instructed beforehand by the life caster.

ABOVE RIGHT: The plaster positive taken and ready to be cleaned.

# CONCLUSION

## CAREER PATHS

There are numerous fields and professions that use prop making without necessarily knowing that it is a career that dates to the early days of theatre.

Ironically, with cuts to arts funding in Britain over the past three decades, more and more theatres are choosing not to employ resident staff as prop makers or carpenters or scenic artists, preferring to freelance out any specialized work that needs doing. This has resulted in a rise in the number of freelance props and construction companies vying for work, who will take on the staff that they need when the workload gets busy and release them when things calm down. This being so, you could visit different companies at different times of the year and probably find craftspeople that you had seen at another company only a few weeks before.

Freelance companies and prop makers charge higher rates than those who are resident, partly due to the transient nature of the vocation and the necessity to cover living costs and overheads, and partly because it is a demand and supply industry. Because the demand is there, the cost of supply is higher, as the things being asked for cannot be acquired by popping down to your local superstore. They are made by talented people who are prepared to work long, hard hours, often at short notice, to provide magic and illusion, and as such they are expensive. Conversely, a resident prop maker is on a fixed salary, making whatever the company requires for a significantly lower hourly rate of pay, but with the added benefit of job security.

To cater for the lack of resident prop makers, theatres over the years have advertised for ASM/ prop makers. These individuals are employed as assistant stage managers but also have the creativity and skills to deal with most of the day-to-day, small-scale, props that the company requires and are able work with limited resources to do so. The more adept that they are, the more opportunities they are likely to have afforded to them. This can be a good stepping stone to entering a career as a professional prop maker, along with developing a good portfolio.

Animatronic pug dog puppet. The assembled puppet resting on its custom cushion. The control rod and trigger protrude through the cushion.

OPPOSITE: Animatronic pug dog puppet 1. This picture illustrates the moulds and casting require to make a relatively straightforward puppet.

# FREELANCING: WHAT ARE YOU WORTH?

As a freelance prop maker, you can work for yourself, creating items in your own workshops. You could also be taken on temporarily by props and construction companies, or even theatres on a project-by-project basis, trade shows, carnivals – the opportunities can be endless. Whatever the case, it is important to address the issue of what you are worth. Assuming you have all the requisite skills and experience or, at the very least, the potential, what are you worth on an hourly basis or by the job? You can charge what you like, providing someone is willing to pay you what you are asking. This is not to suggest that you try and fleece people for all they have, but rather that you make sure you charge enough to cover all your overheads and expenditures. If you are working more than forty hours a week and not getting paid enough to get by, despite your customers being happy, you are not charging enough. If you are only working a couple of hours a week and you aren't making enough to get by, you need to find more work.

Do not offer discounts, do not work for free, don't let people take advantage of you; because if you do, you are not only undervaluing yourself, but all other craftspeople. As stated before, what we do cannot be found in your everyday retail outlet, but must be crafted, and that costs money. If you undervalue yourself by working at discounted rates in the hope that the next time you will charge the full price and the client will be happy to pay, think again, because next time the client will want to pay what they paid last time and will underpay the next

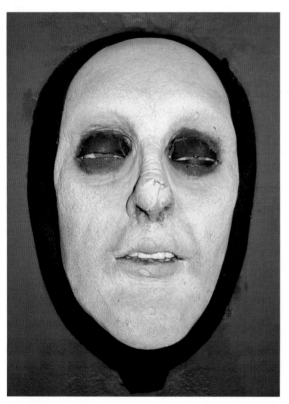

Jacob Marley cable-operated animatronic face with a foamed latex skin. The face was a clay sculpt taken from photographic reference, as this had to be smaller than his actual face size.

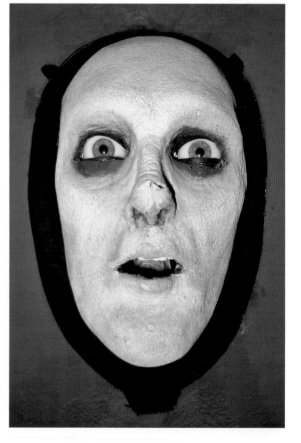

Jacob Marley with eyes and mouth open.

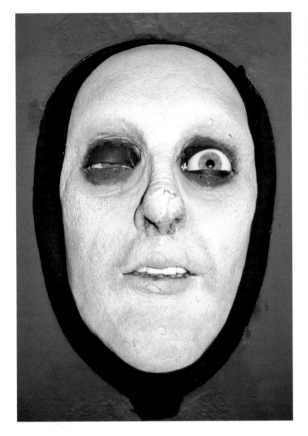 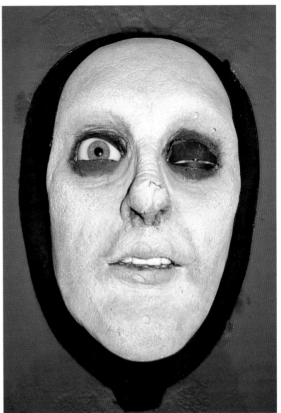

ABOVE LEFT: Jacob Marley – right eye wink.

ABOVE RIGHT: Jacob Marley – left eye wink.

'discount muggins' because they can. Not every-one will try to take advantage, but it is wise to be prepared and for both parties to fully understand the terms and conditions to be applied to the pro-ject. If the client makes last-minute changes that are going to incur extra expenditure, they should pay. If you make a mistake resulting in a reworking of the project or having to hire more help, that is a cost you will have to shoulder, but if you are charg-ing a decent hourly rate, it shouldn't leave you out of pocket. Third party liability insurance should be a consideration when working freelance, as this will afford you some level of protection should the un-foreseen happen.

## THAT'S IT!

Whether you are a hobby prop maker, making props for amateur theatre, a model railway enthu-siast, shop window dresser or a budding profes-sional with dreams of working on the latest Harry Potter spin-off, practice makes perfect. Develop and broaden your skill base or find a niche that suits you. This book is a guide to what you can achieve, a springboard into the unknown and an introduction to new methods and materials that can help you achieve time-honoured skills in the most effective and outstanding way.

# INDEX